The Princeton Review

Archaeology Smart Junior

Discovering History's
Buried Treasures

D1570337

The Princeton Review

Archaeology
Smart
Junior

**Discovering History's
Buried Treasures**

by Karen J. Laubenstein

Random House, Inc., New York 1997

ISBN 0-679-77537-4

Editor: Melanie Sponholz
Production Editor: Amy Bryant
Designer: Illeny Maaza
Production Coordinator: Matthew Reilly

Manufactured in the United States of America on recycled paper.
9 8 7 6 5 4 3 2 1
First Edition

Dedication

This book is dedicated to our daughters, Katie and Krystal. Since their deaths, everything we create is really for them. This book includes glimpses of some of the things we had hoped to share with them some day. Archaeology is as full of lessons for the future as it is investigations of the past. We'd like to think we had two little angels perched on our shoulders, giggling at the adventures of the three kids we've so come to love and Beauregard, that sophisticated cat!

Acknowledgments

Like most kids, I've always wanted to be able to recognize my friends and family in a published book. Though I'm an "old kid" now, I've finally gotten the opportunity! So please, join me in applauding these great folks, for ALL of these people helped make this book in your hands become a reality. It's with deep and sincere appreciation I now acknowledge each and every one of them. Totally awesome, huh? I think so. Roll the drums, march out the bands, imagine those fireworks, and cheer along with me to recognize these many folks who made this all possible!

Kudos go especially to the U.S. Bureau of Land Management's (BLM's) Project Archaeology team (Margaret Heath, Wayne Rice, Cindy Ramsay, Jeanne Moe, and affiliate archaeologist Richard Brook); archaeologists Robert E. King, Michael Kunz, and Victoria Atkins; Anchorage teachers Richard Kronberg and Vicki Hodge; BLM Fairbanks graphic artist Dan Gullickson and public affairs specialist Sharon Durgan Wilson; my friend and *ad hoc* editor, Deborah Apperson; and Relay Alaska communication assistants for relaying computer telephone calls between Anchorage and New York City.

On the publishing end, I would like to recognize the fantastic staff at The Princeton Review and single out Melanie Sponholz, editors Stefanie Silverman and Bronwyn Collie, production editor Amy Bryant, illustrator Jeff Moores, and Random House's Tom Russell. Technical reviewers include Danielle Newman of the American Archaeology Institute, Megg Heath of the Society of American Archaeology's Public Education Committee/BLM's Project Archaeology Team (chaps 4-6), and Robert E. King, BLM's Alaska State

Archaeologist (Chap. 11). Thanks to all the other Princeton Review staff I haven't named here. It wasn't always easy working on the manuscript long-distance between New York City and Alaska, especially with a four-hour time difference. When we would be getting up to start the day, the New York staff would be breaking for lunch. By my lunchtime, they were going home for dinner! I often wished I had my own timeship to travel when needed.

I want to thank and recognize authors whose works are cited in the bibliography. Your writings inspired and educated me. Collectively, we've helped introduce archaeology to a whole new generation.

Heartfelt hugs go to Abbie Wolff, my young niece from Georgia, Vermont. Abbie helped me overcome writer's block at times when I needed to put the "fun" back into the story. At those times, I would pretend I was writing the story just for her and trying to make her laugh! Special thanks to my family, my parents Wayne and Millie Jackson; Gail (Abbie's mom) Wolff and Dianne Giddinge; and my brother, Tom ("Brother Shakespeare"). Gotcha! (Tom's been calling me "Sister Hemingway" for years.) Rascal, our hearing guide dog, always alerted me to the overnight mail person at the door. Our mischievous Binkee Kitty helped me appreciate Beauregard more.

We wish to recognize the unwavering support of Dr. Carol Mitchell-Springer, Providence Alaska Medical Center maternity nurses, The Princeton Review staff, and Alaska Mac computer friends for pulling us together in a time of personal crisis so we could work on the book.

Lastly, I want to thank my patient husband, Ron. Living with an author is NOT always easy. He put up with my waking him up or disappearing into our home office in the middle of the night with book ideas, hauled all my heavy reference books into my hospital room, coped with my frantic rushes to the FedEx airport offices before their overnight deadlines to get stuff to New York, and read around holes in the newspaper where I'd cut out articles. He scanned illustrations and surfed the Internet, faxed and copied, assisted with research and reference materials, followed me around carrying armfuls of books at bookstores, and gave me reminders to "write that book" when he left daily for his job. Most difficult and unusual, Ron's often had to be my "ears", as I'm profoundly deaf.

To Ron, besides a huge hug, I need to scream, WE DID IT!!!

Contents

Chapter 1
Catnapped: A Find Better Left Buried

Archaeology, the science of once and future things, is one of my passions. It is in my blood. In my younger days, I actually found a buried treasure. I was burying a mouse so it would ripen perfectly to smoke for mouse jerky. However, in the process I uncovered a beautiful artifact from the past. I had the handblown glass candlestick dated at the University and learned it was made in the late 1700s or early 1800s. Wow, huh? The thick cloudy green glass candlestick, with only a few nicks and scratches, was probably buried for nearly 200 years!

That candlestick still sits on the mantle back home in South Carolina. The candlestick made me realize that our backyard has a long history of other people and other lives before that of my family and the humans who live in our homes. There is a history there. The people who left that candlestick behind probably died more than 150 years ago. What they made survived to remind me that they existed. Finding the candlestick made me want to find out more and learn more about these people. Who were they? Did they have cats? Did they live on this land or were they just passing through? How did they make such sturdy glass that could stay buried all these years without breaking? Obviously, their whole culture was different from ours. That's what archaeology does: It makes the past come alive.

Since then, I've come to realize archaeology isn't simply treasure hunting to collect antiquities or just digging up things. Someday we're going to be the people and cats of the past. In fact, science fiction may be the archaeology of the future. The things we leave behind will become the artifacts of tomorrow. Archaeology is great for anyone who enjoys biology, botany, geology, chemistry, history, psychology, art, or even solving puzzles. It is a science that requires lots of imagination to help solve the mysteries of past people and past lives. To be an archaeologist, you must become a time detective, sifting out facts and clues and putting them all together to make sense of how people once lived, obtained food and shelter, used the land, clothed themselves, worshipped, dealt with their environment, and, most of all, survived. Archaeologists learn all this by studying things people left behind. Those things may not be so glamorous by themselves, but what they can tell us makes people from the past come alive. I learned that we can use the lessons of the past to better prepare for the future.

We cats always like a good mystery. I think cats are very well suited to be archaeologists. I realized that only recently because circumstances forced me into the field of archaeology. Because I stand over four feet tall, I'm an extremely good and fast digger using my front paws. Even more importantly, I can dig very carefully and sensitively, for old things are often fragile. Many of my senses are more acute than those of humans. I can sometimes locate ancient sites by smell and sight. Many of my other attributes are legendary. In fact, it is my incredible talent for sensing trouble in the making that brought me to New York City to hang out in Barnaby's new laboratory. If it weren't for that, I might have missed all of the adventures that taught me so much about archaeology.

Oh, but forgive me, I digress! I haven't even properly introduced myself. My name is Beauregard. I am a true gentleman cat in every sense of the word, used to quality living and good manners. I have silky black fur. I can trace my family of well-bred aristocrats all the way back to their origins in Africa, though most have resided in South Carolina's quality homes since the American Revolution.

Did I mention my ability to sense trouble? Little did I know how much I was getting into with those cute young humans Bridget, Babette, and Barnaby and their latest misadventures. Bridget with her bubble gum and New York Yankees baseball cap; the French Babette with her martial arts, sophisticated black clothes, red lipstick, and language skills; and Barnaby with his unforgettable wild, bushy hair that things are always falling out of and his white lab coats. Talk about mysteries and adventure! All those discoveries and treasures; the archaeological sites around the world; the travels back in time; but also the never-ending danger! Oh, but I'm getting ahead of myself. It really all began with a catnap . . .

✎ ✎ ✎ ✎ ✎

Beauregard forgot he was curled up on a laboratory table. He stopped hearing the constant tide of New York City traffic outside the lab's windows and Barnaby muttering to himself. He no longer watched his bushy-haired human friend in the white lab coat work with test tubes, microscopes, and chemicals, or scribble notes in a notebook. The young scientist was working intently on his theory that the repulsively ripe essence from very dirty socks could be used to ward bugs off plants, eliminating the need for chemical pesticides. Previously, Barnaby had successfully separated the odor from the socks, although the smell blew up his old lab. Now he worked to refine the process to avoid further explosions and test the effects on bugs.

Beauregard catnapped. He slept so deeply that he forgot his anxiety that Barnaby might blow up his new lab, too. Purring softly, Beauregard began dreaming of exotic green cat's eyes looking at him adoringly through the layers of a sheer veil. Here he was in the palace of the last great Pharaoh of Egypt, Cleopatra VII. Before him was the most beautiful femme feline of all times, Cleocatra, or "Catra" for short, a pet of the Pharaoh herself. Beauregard sighed in sheer bliss while Catra danced to the romantic music of a flute.

Beauregard was sprawled on fluffy pillows amidst the splendor of ancient Alexandria. Colorful silk curtains surrounded them, swaying gently from warm Mediterranean breezes. He sipped milk, careful to wipe his white mustache off with a silk hand-kerchief and not dislodge his fedora. Catra smiled fondly at his exceptional manners and stopped dancing, walking gracefully to his side.

"Beauregard," she begged, "stay here with me in the past. You will be happy. We cats are sacred objects and worshipped here in Alexandria and Egypt." Her eyes stared deeply into his own.

"Yes," Beauregard nodded, mesmerized. "I know. My ancestral cousin Caesaro Ptolemy once told me that Egyptian cats are so important they are even worshipped as gods, like the cat goddess

Bast or Bastet. Bast is the Egyptian goddess of love and fertility with the body of a woman and the head of a cat. Hmm, wise to have a feline worshipped as a goddess of love and fertility, I think. Besides controlling the Nile River's rodent population, Caesaro told me cats are even trained to hunt and retrieve birds while on a leash!"

Catra cuddled up to him. "Yes," Beauregard sighed happily, "this is a good time to be a cat. Though my breed doesn't yet exist. If I recall, Egypt is the homeland of shorthaired cats traced back to African wildcats about 4,500 years before I was born. You Egyptian Caffra cats are not my breed, Catra. If my parents won't be born for almost twenty centuries, how can I even exist in this time? Oh Catra, this must be a dream and I fear I'm going to wake up some day and just disappear from your life and times! If you can imagine, this is more than 2,000 years **before the present (B.P.)** time that I have been living in! Even my ancestors haven't been born yet."

"No Beauregard, you never have to leave," Catra purred and blinked her long lashes enticingly. "None of that matters. It is a state of mind, Beauregard. Stay with me! Just think, throughout this Mediterranean world, we cats are traded along with other treasures and antiquities. Some of us are even mummified and buried in the tombs with our pharaohs and wealthy owners. Why, oh why, would you ever want to live in other times when this is not so?"

"Why, indeed?" Beauregard murmured, becoming persuaded in spite of himself. This beauty was very convincing.

"Beauregard, it's true. You're so valuable here in Egypt, you can't go back to your future time," Catra beseeched him, "you can't leave me. You would be a god for us, because of your incredible size. While we are revered and sacred to our humans, Beauregard, more than in any other place in history, you would become a national treasure. Egyptian laws even forbid the removal of cats from this country. If you leave me, you will be breaking the law!" She began to groom her sleek fur, her green eyes like jewels behind her veil.

Beauregard watched her and fell in love. His heart pounding, he knew he never wanted to leave her. He hugged Catra to him. "You're right, absolutely, my princess. I can never leave you. I will stay throughout time until eternity, if only we can be together! I will—" Suddenly, his whiskers twitched, and he was rudely jolted out of his dream.

✎　✎　✎　✎　✎

"Drats," he muttered. Instead of Catra, he found himself facing the reality of Barnaby's laboratory in New York City. His whiskers twitched even more. Beauregard smelled *mouse*.

A mouse pulled him out of his dream? Disgusted, Beauregard closed his eyes and tried to drift back to Catra and Alexandria. So much for staying throughout time and eternity, though the echo of his words was almost nauseatingly sweet now that he had a cooler head. What had come over him? Had he been bewitched?

Then he recalled his plans to cook a special mousaroni and cheese dish later for a classy feline uptown this evening. Maybe all was not lost after all? His eyes flew open. Fresh mice were hard to come by lately. He knew he shouldn't let the opportunity run away. While his date later wasn't Catra, she was real. Reluctantly, Beauregard sat up and looked for the rodent.

The mouse scent was strong. Beauregard's whiskers twitched again. His ears perked up, listening. His highly developed sense of smell zoned in on the plump mouse skittering—oh no!—right for Barnaby and his microscope. Before Beauregard could even warn him, the mouse ran up Barnaby's arm. It sniffed curiously at the glass slide on the microscope. Barnaby stiffened in shock. Then several things happened. Barnaby's bushy hair stood at attention, the lab echoed with his resounding screams, and the mouse ran for its life.

"A rat! A mouse! A rodent! *Beauregard!*" Barnaby yelled. The little creature ran in blind terror, circling in and around the many test tubes and Pyrex bottles.

Beauregard stifled his laughter and watched the scene appreciatively. "Yes, Barnaby. That's a common mouse, from the Latin mus or the Greek mys, a term that can apply to any of numerous small rodents with pointed snouts, rather small ears, elongated bodies, slender tails, and a somewhat timid personality . . ."

"Beauregard, *stop!*" Barnaby interrupted. "You're a cat . . . do something!" He hollered, standing on his lab stool while the mouse continued to panic. It dashed madly for the open window and disappeared.

"Do something," Beauregard repeated, "right." He didn't wait. Besides hoping to have a fresh mouse supply for his dinner menu, now he also wanted to impress Barnaby. He heaved himself off the windowsill and into the alley below. He landed on both hind feet with a slight "oomph." After all, he was a heavy cat. He dabbed at his forehead with his silk handkerchief and quickly followed in pursuit of the mouse, trailing it with his nose, his whiskers twitching.

Beauregard was distressed to discover the rodent's trail led into a narrow dark hole, deep between the old brick buildings and garbage cans that lined the alley. He crawled into the dark opening. Using his excellent night vision and extensive peripheral vision, he could see in the dark. The mouse scuttled away through the old, musty drainage tunnel beneath New York City's streets. The tunnel reeked with the wet scent of the river and old dirt. The air was heavy with dust. At the far end of the narrow tunnel, Beauregard saw light shimmering on the waters of the mighty Hudson. He rushed after the now-frightened mouse, lunging for its tail just as it veered into a tiny pipe . . . and escaped! "Figures," Beauregard grumbled. He sneezed. He knew there was no way he could fit into the little pipe. Looks like I'll have to resort to frozen mouse tonight, he thought.

Sensitive to every clinging piece of dirt on his usually immaculate coat, Beauregard was reminded of why he usually left mouse-chasing to less dignified cats. He couldn't wait to return to the lab and clean up. But just then, Beauregard tripped. Something stuck out of the tunnel floor. He looked down, again dabbing his forehead with the handkerchief, and found a partially buried sack closed with a heavy metal padlock.

"Hmm, intriguing," Beauregard observed, and quickly dug up the large bag. It was heavy and bulky, full of an assortment of something. He sneezed again, his eyes watering.

"Wonder what Barnaby would make of this," Beauregard said and then cringed, for his voice echoed throughout the tunnel. Quickly, he lifted the bag over his shoulder and onto his back. He retraced his steps back to the lab. He didn't notice the two dark figures entering the tunnel behind him, silhouetted against the bright light on the river.

Beauregard reached the lab. He dropped the bag next to Barnaby. First things first. His paws were filthy and his sleek black fur felt sticky. Sniffing in disgust, Beauregard jumped up onto the lab table to groom the dirt out of his coat. His nose tickled. That tunnel not only smelled, it also had been dusty.

"Ah-choo!" Beauregard sneezed loudly. "Ah-ah-ah-choo!" He sneezed again, startling the young scientist out of his research.

"Wh-what?" Barnaby looked thoroughly frightened. "What exploded?" He asked, searching the room. His hair stood on end. The mouse hadn't helped Barnaby's nerves. Barnaby's wild eyes found Beauregard. He was astonished to find the large cat perched on the table next to him.

"I beg your pardon," Beauregard apologized, "I was in a dusty tunnel." He decided not to mention the mouse again. Barnaby nodded, obviously relieved that his lab was still intact, and pushed the round glasses back up onto his nose. He turned back to his microscope, stubbing his toe on the sack at his feet. "Oof!"

"Ouch," Beauregard winced sympathetically, not stopping his grooming efforts.

"What have we here, Beauregard?" Barnaby asked. He rubbed the toe of his sneaker where his foot still hurt from whacking the bag. He pulled the heavy sack up and onto one of the few bare spots on the long table. The heavy padlock clanked loudly. Barnaby tried to open the padlock. Even his dissecting kit didn't work. And the bag was made out of a material that couldn't be cut by any of his tools. Beauregard watched the maneuvering with undisguised interest.

"I can't do it, Beauregard. I need a key," the young scientist admitted, shaking his head in his agitation. "Clank!" Metal hit the floor. Looking down, they spied a heavy-duty pair of wire cutters that had fallen out of Barnaby's hair. Triumphantly, Barnaby used the cutters to remove the padlock. He reached into the bag and pulled out a perfectly chiseled stone bust—a sculpture of a woman's head and neck.

Beauregard stared in shock. "Barnaby, I think that's Cleopatra VII, the last Pharaoh of Egypt," he said, recognizing the woman from his dream only moments ago. "But that bust is so perfect, with exquisite detail. Even her jewelry is engraved! I sense this may be an original artifact, Barnaby," Beauregard observed. "Yet how can it be in that condition when it is over 2,000 years old?"

"Really, Beauregard, I fully doubt this could be a true ancient artifact," Barnaby replied, skeptically, while he inspected the stone sculpture. "This must be a modern copy! A **replica**! How could something from 2,000 years ago end up in a bag here in New York City, anyway?"

"We cats can sense these things. Besides, I've never seen anything that exists today like it. It looks too much like a person truly looks. How many ancient sculptures have you seen that really look like people do today? This sculpture is truly magnificent! In fact, Barnaby, I've seen a picture of a similar bust of Cleopatra VII in the Greco-Roman Museum in Alexandria, Egypt. However, that bust is rough and weathered from age. This one looks new," Beauregard said, puzzled. "This is a conundrum. Why would this bust look new?"

"I think it is new, a new sculpture," Barnaby said. "However, we could try to determine its age by **chronology** or, rather, **dating**. I learned how to do some of that on an archaeological **dig** once with my parents. We **excavated** Inca ruins in Mesoamerica. Not that I think there's any chance this is actually from ancient Egypt," he hurried to tell the cat. "Dating it would prove it." Barnaby washed the surface carefully with soap and water.

"Now dating I'm familiar with," Beauregard admitted, "though this is one cold female, Barnaby. Truly stone-faced, I might add. She's probably a great listener, though."

"Not that kind of dating, Beauregard! Time-dating. Figuring out how old it is and where it fits into the history of past events. There are many methods used to date things, from **radiocarbon dating** to using x-rays, potassium-argon, thermoluminescence, geochronology, cross-dating, pollen analysis, collagen content, fluorine tests, radiometric assays, and many other methods. My parents would have to help me out, since I don't know how to do any of those tests," Barnaby said as he continued to wash the surface of the stone bust very carefully.

"Out of curiosity, Barnaby, why are you giving that stone head a bath?" Beauregard asked. Barnaby patted the carving dry, his eyes getting that far-off gleam that warned Beauregard what was coming. Sure enough, the young scientist began to pace and throw his arms around as he did in his standard lecture mode.

"On the very off-chance that this might be a genuine artifact, I'm following standard procedure here. Usually when artifacts are uncovered their **environment** changes. The material can start disintegrating quickly if the proper steps aren't taken in cleaning and **preservation**. That's why it's better to let professional archaeologists handle artifacts. Even stone can accumulate salt on the surface that flakes and breaks off if the salts aren't removed with soap and warm water, thus the bath. But really, Beauregard, I don't see any evidence of surface salts here."

"Uh, Barnaby?" Beauregard tried to interrupt. It was impossible—Barnaby didn't even pause to breathe.

"I washed the stone anyway. Again, I doubt this bust is a genuinely ancient artifact. If I'm wrong, much information about it is lost because it's out of context. It's not part of an archaeological site where I can study all the clues and surrounding data. We need information and we get a preponderance of the evidence from where the artifact was originally found. Dating is based upon that evidence."

"Evidence from doing something like **stratigraphy**?" Beauregard prompted, a bit sleepily. Barnaby's lectures always made him want to snooze. His eyelids grew heavier.

"Yes," Barnaby agreed, continuing to pace. "Archaeologists excavate to study and peel away the layers, or **strata**, of earth and materials that build up on top of an object over time, burying it. As you correctly pointed out, this process is called stratigraphy. Erosion, wind, weather, and even earthquakes or volcanos help bury things. It makes sense that things found deeper down in the earth are usually older than things found closer to the surface. But with this stone bust, I simply can't tell much by just looking at it out of context. When I can excavate or dig, I study what's around an object, under it, on top of it, or anything else about it," Barnaby mused. "Just being handed the object or artifact away from its surroundings loses all those clues."

Beauregard's soft snores filled the room.

"Beauregard," Barnaby continued, still so lost in thought that he didn't hear the snores, "maybe the other stuff in the bag will shed some light on this bust's age," Barnaby said, excitedly. He carefully tipped the bag. Several items clanked loudly against the lab table, waking the cat.

"Uh, excuse me, but can't a cat get any decent shut-eye around here?" Beauregard grumbled. Barnaby didn't hear him. He was too busy examining a funny-shaped gun from the sack, its barrel shiny and wide like the end of a trumpet.

"Ah! A blunderbuss," Beauregard remarked, "but that, too, looks new."

"A what?" Barnaby obviously had never heard of a blunderbuss before.

"Blunderbuss," Beauregard repeated. "That's a muzzle-loading gun with a short barrel. The flaring muzzle makes it easier to load. Those weapons were used around A.D. 1660, the mid-seventeenth century, in colonial times. Blunderbusses were also used in Europe and the European colonies around the world, too. Because the gun rarely shoots straight, a person today who moves unsteadily or in a confused way is sometimes called a 'blunderer' or 'blunderbuss'. Incidentally, I call such bumbling cats 'blunderpusses'."

Barnaby laughed, then looked puzzled. "I'd like to know if this is an authentic blunderbuss or a replica. I rather doubt it was made and used almost 350 years ago. It looks nearly brand new! Another thing for my parents to help me get dated."

Beauregard's eyes were becoming heavy again. However, he roused himself to make a suggestion. "Since Bridget's father is a keen historian, maybe he could also help us?"

Barnaby nodded absently, studying the blunderbuss to see if he could discover any writing on the weapon. "I'm going to search the Internet and find out what I can on blunderbusses," Barnaby announced, moving to his computer and leaving the weapon next to the bust and still-full sack on the lab table.

Beauregard slipped deeper into his catnap, visions of Cleocatra filling his head. Maybe he could even resume where he had left off earlier, those soft Mediterranean breezes, Catra cuddling next to him, the flute playing so softly, the . . .

Bang! The door to the laboratory and Beauregard's eyes flew open. Astounded, Barnaby and Beauregard watched in horror as a huge, salivating black dog rushed ferociously at them. His wet, floppy tongue bounced between monstrous, pointed teeth.

Beauregard sniffed in disdain at the terribly rancid, hot, smelly dog breath that permeated the laboratory. The beast distracted Barnaby and the cat so they didn't see the fierce man in the black cape and stovepipe black hat following the dog. The man grabbed the blunderbuss off the table and pointed it directly at Barnaby.

"Give us the bag!" The man commanded, holding out a gloved hand. Beauregard instantly wished he had never found the padlocked sack. He instinctively knew the bag was full of objects better left forgotten.

✍ ACTIVITIES ✍
Why Is the Past Important?

As an introduction to the study of our archaeological heritage, try a few of the following activities with your family or friends to help begin to discover why and how we study the past.

1. Find an object (artifact) or photograph that tells about your own or your family's past. Write down facts about your object or photograph. You can include a description of the object/photograph; the age; where it came from; and any other facts about yourself or your family's past that you can observe looking at the object/photograph. Share your photograph with a friend and have that friend tell you everything he or she can figure out about you or your family from the object or photograph. You may want to have the friend write down his or her observations to compare with your own. Then you can compare lists and share any additional information on what the object tells you about yourself or your family.

   • What things did you write down that you already knew about the object or photograph that your friend couldn't observe from it?

- Did they see or imagine things that weren't true about the object/photograph, but they thought the object showed? Where did they think the object came from? What does this exercise tell you about finding an object, photograph, or other item?

2. You may want to answer the following questions and later compare what you think now with what you think after finishing this book.

   - Is it important for you to know about your past? Why or why not? If your past is important to you, what statement can you make about the importance of the past in general?

   - Humans have lived on earth for more than 5 million years. Is it important for you to know about their lives? Why or why not?

3. Brainstorm ideas on what we can learn about the past.

Food for Thought

You may want to answer the following or write down your thoughts in your journal. There are many answers. This is to help you organize what you've just learned.

1. What have you learned about the history of cats from Beauregard's dream?

2. When archaeologists find objects from the past, do they look new? Why or why not? What have you learned about the condition of most objects when they're discovered?

3. List basic needs every human being has. What is needed in order to live? Explore a different culture or lifeway from your own and list how that culture/lifeway meets the basic human needs. Compare it to your own culture/lifeway.

Vocabulary

(Listed in glossary at back of book and covered in Quiz #1 in chapter 3)

A.D. (Anno Domini)

antiquities

archaeology

artifact

B.C. (Before Christ)

Before the Present (B.P.)

C14 (carbon) dating (see dating methods)

chronology

culture

dating methods

dig

environment

evidence/clues

excavate/excavation

lifeway

preservation

radiocarbon (carbon 14) dating

replica

stratigraphy/strata

Chapter 2
Time Thieves: A Threat from the Past

"Give me the bag!" The fierce man in the black cape demanded again, nudging Barnaby with the blunderbuss. Next to him, the black dog growled at Beauregard. The cat ignored him and began grooming his coat. Catnapping was impossible with all the commotion.

"Wh-who are y-you and that d-dog?" Barnaby stammered nervously, though he realized the blunderbuss probably wasn't loaded. These two intruders gave new meaning to the word *intimidating*!

The man grinned nastily, showing uneven, yellowed, pointed teeth. He took off his hat with his free hand, and swept it through the air with a flamboyant bow.

"Dastardly P. Looter, at your service. That mutt's named Sneakers, sneaky critter that he is," the man coughed. "And, that bag's ours. Your cat stole it from us."

Beauregard sniffed. He managed to look insulted and yet dignified. "I beg your pardon, Mr. Looter, but I did no such thing. I do not steal. The item in question was on public property, or rather, a very public tunnel," he pointed out. "Furthermore, I wasn't the only one down there. I merely rescued the bag as any decent citizen might have done. However, allow me to introduce myself. It's much more appropriate than calling me 'that cat'. My name is Beauregard."

Beauregard ignored Dastardly's surprise when he discovered the huge black cat could talk. Though Beauregard could do a good silent cat imitation when the situation required it, with Sneakers, that salivating beast, polluting the room, he wasn't about to hide his superior talents.

"Besides, Mr. Looter," Barnaby challenged the man, "where did you find these objects?"

Dastardly looked a bit uncomfortable, but covered it by shaking the blunderbuss against Barnaby's chest. "I got the bag firsthand, let me put it that way. We only put it in the tunnel temporarily to evade those nosy New York Harbor Patrols. No sense losing everything because they confiscate it, eh? We returned for the loot and saw you disappearing up the tunnel with our bag. Sneakers sniffed out the cat's . . . er . . . Beauregard's trail."

"If you were evading the Harbor Patrol, you obviously didn't come by this bag by honest means," Barnaby pointed out, pushing the bag farther away from the man and closer to Beauregard.

Dastardly nodded, his grin sinister. "True, absolutely true. Honesty takes all the fun out of things. Always has. Now, GIVE ME THE BAG!" The man was beginning to sound like an echo, the same thing over and over. Barnaby ignored the outstretched hand and shoved the bag even farther away on the table. Beauregard shuffled backwards in that general direction, determined to put more space between himself and the dog's bad breath.

"Moreover, if we were honest," Dastardly contemplated, "we never would've experienced time travel—"

"What?! How?!" Barnaby interrupted, stunned as his thoughts rushed to their friend, Dr. Tempus Fugit, and that esteemed scientist's time travel machine, *Lady Liberty*. In earlier adventures, Barnaby and his friends had used *Lady Liberty* to explore American history.

"Let's say that we came into possession—" Dastardly bragged.

"You mean *stole*," Beauregard clarified righteously, ignoring the man's irritated glance.

"Ahem!" Dastardly cleared his throat, holding his head higher. He obviously had an overdeveloped ego. "We *acquired* the plans and built our own timeship, *Money Probe*. Though," he admitted, "we did have some problems fine-tuning and couldn't always identify where we went and where it was in time. In fact, once we returned to the present, something in *Money Probe* malfunctioned. The timeship won't go back in time anymore—it only goes to places in the present. That's why you HAVE to give me the BAG!"

"This is totally blowing my mind!" Barnaby exclaimed, momentarily forgetting everything but the fact that these crooks had Dr. Tempus's time machine plans. "You actually stole the plans and then built a replica timeship? Where are the plans now?"

Dastardly grinned, enjoying the reaction he was getting. The man actually began gloating. "Stealing the plans and building the timeship were easy for intellects such as Sneakers and me. From there, we traveled through time and took the treasures in that bag. We even saw humans who were closer to apes. We brought an imprint of a footprint back from some of them, since they ran away when they saw us. Don't let anyone tell you that humans weren't close to apes. Now I believe in that **Charles Darwin** character's **theory of evolution**. We saw the facts. Not much improvement in some of us, even now," Dastardly eyed Barnaby's bushy hair critically. "We'll get Sotheby's or some other auction house to auction those objects off, and then we'll be rich! Rich! Rich! RICH!" Dastardly's harsh laugh caused Barnaby to feel goosebumps break out on his skin. He felt like throwing up.

"The plans?" Barnaby prompted.

"Er, the plans, yes," Dastardly suddenly looked sheepish. "Sneakers ate them. But not before we had *Money Probe* built," Dastardly hastily assured them. The dog, hearing his name, wagged his tail and again growled at them menacingly.

This confirmed everything Beauregard felt about the lack of intellect in canines. Dogs just didn't have it, especially the vile specimen in front of them. Eating the plans?! Good grief! He continued grooming and wished he could escape into another catnap. At least a snooze would be a better use of his time.

"Let me get this straight," Barnaby tried to clarify. "You stole Dr. Tempus's time machine plans from Liberty Island—"

"How did you know they were Dr. Tempus Fugit's plans? From Liberty Island?" Dastardly interrupted suspiciously. His eyes darted nervously around the laboratory as if suddenly afraid this might be a set-up and law enforcement officers would materialize around the rows of lab tables. When he became nervous, one of his eyes twitched and he began coughing in great hacking heaves. Sneakers growled low in his throat.

"You two did all of this, stealing these objects from the past, just for the money?" Barnaby pursued incredulously, hopping a bit as he tended to do when excited.

"That about sums it up," Dastardly agreed, looking nasty again once he realized he wasn't being set up. The dog thumped his tail on the floor, obviously in agreement.

"Unbelievable! Don't you realize what you have done?" Barnaby scolded. "Beauregard was right all along, these are genuine artifacts. I'm flabbergasted at your sheer audacity, Mr. Looter! You stole things from the past with no consideration for what that might do to the future! Don't you realize that when you get these artifacts dated, they won't be old? They'll be NEW! They will only sell as modern art or crafts or replicas of ancient artifacts. More importantly, Mr. Looter, you've lost all the value of these items as antiquities and artifacts because you took them out of their context. It sounds like you don't even have any idea where or when these things came from. You contributed nothing to modern knowledge with your time travels or your souvenirs, because you didn't care. You just let the opportunity to solve some of the past's mysteries slip through your fingers in your greed. You also played a more dangerous game by fiddling with the past than you can apparently grasp." Barnaby shook his head, appalled.

"Definitely," Dastardly acknowledged proudly. "What of it?"

Barnaby could remember almost losing Beauregard in time during their travels on *Lady Liberty* and the fear they'd had that they weren't going to get back to the present. Yes, he'd learned a great deal about the dangers of time travel. Barnaby's eyes began to glaze over, like they did when he was thinking intently about scientific data. Beauregard smiled his cheshire cat smile, recognizing that a Barnaby-lecture was coming. He hoped the lecture would put both the horrific salivating beast and the distasteful ugly human to sleep.

"Let me explain two theories of time travel, Newtonian and Quantum Mechanical Physics," Barnaby commenced his monologue, pacing and throwing his arms up and down, leaving the sack of artifacts in Beauregard's protection. Dastardly and the dog watched the young scientist in total bewilderment. Beauregard's smile grew wider: Barnaby was on a roll.

"With the Newtonian theory, anything changed in time will affect the future. Adversely, the Quantum Mechanical Physics theory of time travel states that changes in time are on a different timeline. They'll have no effect on the present one. For example, if you go back in time and keep your parents from meeting— will you exist?"

Dastardly shrugged, speechless at this turn in the conversation. The dog's tail banged methodically on the floor in time to the young scientist's pacing. Barnaby continued, "The classic Newtonian time theory, used in the movie *Back to the Future*, predicts that if you keep your parents from meeting, you will fade from the future. The Quantum view, however, is that time travel is possible along distortions of space-time called 'closed timeline curves.' This is more like time travel used in the various *Star Trek* television shows and movies and the *Terminator* movies. Reality exists as infinite possibilities. Thus, if you travel back in time and prevent your parents from meeting, there's no paradox because your parents will still meet and conceive you in the timeline you traveled from."

Dastardly looked stupefied, overwhelmed with the information. Barnaby paused to take a deep breath, but concluded before anyone else could say anything: "Dr. Tempus told us that though these are both theories, there is danger in taking things or changing the past during time travel because we don't know what effect, if any, it does have on the future. It's dangerous. It's just not done. There's too much risk."

"So what?" Dastardly shrugged. "I DON'T CARE. The past already happened, it's gone. It's only now and the future I care about. We'll get rich from all this, especially when we explain about the time machine so the world will know these items are originals from the past, even if they test as new. That will confirm the validity." The man stared over Barnaby's head, lost in his narrative.

"Just think, we'll be able to build a Looter Tower in New York City or buy a professional sports team. We can own a tropical island hideaway or a cruise ship. We'll have Hollywood producers at our feet. No concerts or movies will ever be sold out for us! We'll be guests on late-night talk shows and we'll—" Dastardly rasped out, coughing uncontrollably.

"You know, you really should cut back on the smoking," Barnaby advised, seeing a fat brown cigar sticking out of Dastardly's black coat pocket. The man just glared at him.

"Okay, okay, I get the message," Barnaby added sadly, staring into the man's eyes to keep his attention. He and Beauregard exchanged a quick look, knowing they would do anything to keep Dr. Tempus's time machine plans secret. That would mean not ever returning the artifacts in the bag to this man. If Dastardly had the bag of artifacts, he had proof of the time travel, unless no one believed him. Of course, the man was holding the blunderbuss.

It was now or never. Barnaby began to slowly back up, putting distance between himself and the blunderbuss.

Everything happened very fast. Dastardly lunged for the bag at the same time Sneakers hurled toward Beauregard. In the commotion, Barnaby grabbed one of the test tubes from the table next to him and quickly pulled out the cork stopper. He hurtled the contents over the man and his dog, ignoring their howling as the odiferous, overwhelming, concentrated, all-encompassing essence of very, very dirty socks stunned the man's and dog's olfactory systems, wiped out their chemosenses that involved taste and smell and touch, and then sent mind-numbing impulses into their brains that even affected their balance and sent them sprawling onto the floor. It was like getting a concentrated whiff of pure ammonia. Barnaby exulted in the moment, realizing that his theory that the essence would keep bugs (and every other living creature) away from plants was going to work after all! In other circumstances, Barnaby would've danced around the lab in absolute joy. However, now was not the time.

Barnaby quickly covered his face with a gas mask to keep the powerful fumes from overwhelming him, too. Finally, both the man and dog succumbed to the fumes and fainted into unconsciousness. The blunderbuss clattered to the floor.

Jerking backwards to keep the essence in front of him and the bag out of the thief's grasp, Barnaby's sudden movement dislodged several items from his hair. Beauregard, overcome by the sock fumes, fainted in a slow, graceful motion across the lab table. As he fell, his front paws stretched out before him. He inadvertently caught a pepper shaker that fell from Barnaby's hair. It landed upside down, its fine and hot red pepper powder pouring through Beauregard's claws and down into Dastardly's and Sneakers' faces. The red pepper blinded the two, in addition to everything else that had happened to them. Beauregard's faint across the lab table also caused him to knock another test tube of the dirty sock essence onto the floor. The glass broke and compounded the original dose. A double whammy!

At first, Barnaby didn't notice the unconscious cat. "Hurry, Beauregard, let's get out of here!" Barnaby yelled as he gathered up the bag of artifacts. He knew the dog wouldn't be smelling any trails for a while.

"Hey, Beauregard?" Barnaby looked in dismay at Beauregard sprawled in a dead faint across the lab table, an empty pepper shaker dangling at the edge of one paw. Barnaby filled a glass beaker with water. He tossed the liquid onto the cat. Spluttering, Beauregard came to instantly. He hated getting wet! Without waiting for Barnaby, he jumped off the table and ran out of the lab. Chuckling, Barnaby hurried in pursuit, taking the bag of artifacts and his backpack as he followed Beauregard out the door.

"Barnaby! Beauregard! What a surprise!" Bridget opened the door to her home, astonished to find her friend and the large cat, both reeking suspiciously of very dirty socks. She pulled her New York Yankees baseball cap down further on her head. "Phew! You two stink!" She announced, as always, not afraid to say what she doesn't like. She didn't hug them or pet Beauregard like she normally did.

"It's a long story," Barnaby said tiredly, dropping the heavy bag onto the floor at Bridget's feet.

"You didn't blow up your lab again did you? I mean, the smell?" Bridget asked Barnaby worriedly. "Or sabotage an engine like your dirty socks once did to the *Lady Liberty*'s, did you?"

"Oh, no, no, nothing like that," Barnaby hastened to reassure her. "Just knocked out a couple of criminals."

"What's that . . . um . . . essence?" Bridget's mother came to the door, holding a tissue to her nose. She didn't seem surprised to find Barnaby and Beauregard there. Instead, she smiled in welcome. "I assume you've come to borrow our shower?"

Barnaby nodded gratefully. Beauregard grimaced, realizing that as much as he hated water, he would probably have to take the first shower of his life to get rid of the essence of dirty socks. Would today's torture never end? He sighed, knowing his usual grooming wouldn't work this time. He'd even lost his sense of taste and smell from the odor exposure and would be unable to tell when his fur was fully groomed!

Bridget's mother led them directly to the family's large bathroom, and even provided sweats to wear while she laundered their clothes to get rid of the nasty odor.

Later, they filled Bridget in on the whole story of the two thieves. The two friends worked at Bridget's computer and prepared an e-mail message to Dr. Tempus Fugit. Worn out from all of the stress of the past few hours and his dreaded shower, Beauregard catnapped on Bridget's bed.

Dr. Tempus responded almost immediately. His e-mail message read as follows:

>Thank you for news of the theft. I'm concerned for the danger Barnaby and Beauregard experienced. Made many modifications to show you. Please come to Liberty Island tomorrow morning. I will have everything ready. Looks like you must return all artifacts to their origins. Will assist you in this quest. Warmest regards, tempus fugit, ph.d.<

"Cool! We might be in for more time travel!" Bridget said excitedly, chewing and snapping her bubble gum.

"Do you think there's enough time for Babette to join us?" Barnaby wondered.

"Frenchie? Of course!" Bridget agreed. "Let's e-mail Babette in Paris and see if she can fly here tonight. It's about an eight-hour flight or shorter on the supersonic Concorde. If she can sleep on the plane, she'll be all set to join us tomorrow morning on Liberty Island."

Barnaby quickly prepared the message, sending it over the Internet and hoping Babette would check her e-mail in time. With the high long distance phone bills to Babette in Paris over the years, Bridget had agreed to pay for any long distance calls she made from her allowance or babysitting money. Since Bridget had just stocked up on bubble gum from the food warehouse, she didn't have any funds just now to afford a call to Paris. She was too proud to ask Barnaby for money.

"Hey, kiddo, let's hit the sack!" Bridget yawned after the mail was sent and she logged off the Internet. Nodding, Barnaby left the room to crash on the sleeper couch that Bridget's mom had made up in the living room. Bridget realized she was going to have to squish around Beauregard. The cat looked like nothing could rouse him.

Little did they realize that copies of the e-mail messages were going to Barnaby's laboratory computer. Back at the lab, Dastardly and Sneakers had regained consciousness and rinsed their red and swollen eyes with water. They grumbled or growled and suffered from headaches and stuffy noses that amplified their bad moods. In fact, they felt like it might be days before all of their senses returned.

"More than curiosity can kill a cat," Dastardly muttered at one point as he winced in pain when he stepped on the glass from the broken test tube. In the time since they had come out of their faints, they had searched the lab in vain for clues on where the young scientist and the large cat might have run. Just as they were about to despair, the computer's alert message beeped and flashed, telling them everything they wanted to know.

The chase was on!

✍ ACTIVITIES ✍
How Old Is Old?

1. What did you learn about time travel? Make a list of the dangers of time travel. You can refer to the two theories Barnaby explains to Dastardly Looter, the Newtonian and Quantum Mechanical Physics theories.

2. **Classification** of **data** or information is an important part of any scientific study, including archaeology. Scientists must categorize data based on various **attributes** such as age, shape, color, function, type of material, or other schemes. This makes the data less complex and helps archaeologists examine the relationships between different types of data. For example, it isn't possible to compare each individual house cat with every other member of the cat family. All house cats are not identical, but all have similarities and fall within a range of variation. The category "house cat" can be compared with the category "tiger," or "lion," or "panther," or "lynx."

   Take objects you may have on your bureau or a shelf on your bookcase at home and try to categorize them by organizing them into one or more classification schemes. When you are finished, write out an explanation of your scheme. Which attributes did you use to place an object in a certain category (shape, color, function, type of material, other)? How else could you have separated the objects? Do you think one type of classification system is better than another? Why or why not? What colors are present? How many different shapes are there (name them)? How might these objects be used? You may need to regroup your objects based on the questions asked.

   Using a classification system often depends on what the archaeologist wants to know. Before beginning fieldwork and bringing found artifacts back to the laboratory, archaeologists first decide what they want to know and how they are going to organize their data.

3. Archaeologists follow a procedure of **scientific inquiry** when they explore the past. To learn how this process works, try this activity. Look around your desk or that of a classmate, friend, or family member. Archaeologists want to answer questions about past human behavior and must use material remains to do so.

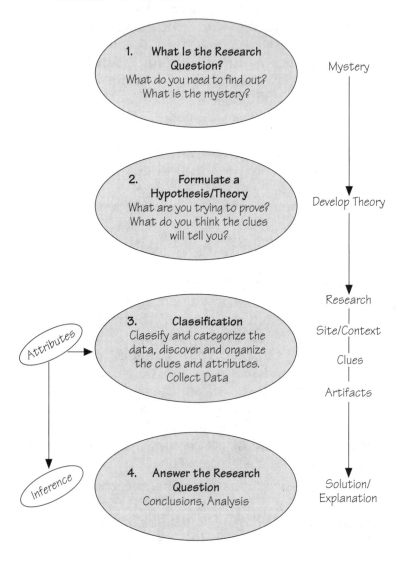

Scientific Process

The inquiry process begins with a question.

Consider the following question: "Is the person who uses this desk a saver or a thrower-awayer?"

Formulate a hypothesis.

If there are many items not required for schoolwork, then the person is a saver.

Classify the data.

Only two categories are essential—items required for schoolwork and items not required for schoolwork. If you are doing this exercise with friends, family, or classmates, discuss how you have different opinions on what is required for schoolwork and what isn't.

Answer the research question.

Which category contains the larger number of objects? If there are more items that are not required, then we **accept the hypothesis**. The owner of the desk is a saver. You have made an **inference** (hypothesis) about the behavior of the desk's owner and have tested your inference using classification methods to organize the data.

Vocabulary

(Listed in glossary at back of book and covered in Quiz #1 in chapter 3)

attributes

Charles Darwin

classification of data

hypothesis

inference

scientific inquiry

Theory of Evolution

Chapter 3
Time Detectives: The Quest Begins

"Hey, I'm doing the best I can!" Bridget tried to let more air out of the bubble she blew to transport them to Liberty Island.

"We must all hang together, or, most assuredly, we shall hang separately,'" Babette quoted. "Your American Benjamin Franklin said that."

"More air, Bridget, let out more air! We'll miss the island entirely!" Barnaby urged, watching the Statue of Liberty still way too far below them. "The aerodynamics are against us. In fact, air is flowing faster over the top of the bubble, causing lower pressure. The slower-moving air below us is higher-pressure, buoying us along and making it more difficult for us to descend. This difference in air pressure is creating a lift. We're also dealing with a breaking force caused by the air pushing against us, the drag. All aircraft are affected by this lift and drag—"

"Ah, pardon me? If I may make an observation?" Beauregard interrupted Barnaby's monologue. "At this rate we will most likely be dumped far out into New York Harbor or even the Atlantic Ocean somewhere, miles from land. Maybe the Coast Guard's patrolling in the area? Quite frankly, I got wet enough yesterday to last me for awhile." Beauregard grimaced, remembering the only shower he had ever taken in his life. At least it removed that vile odor of dirty socks.

Bridget sighed heavily, and as she did, air rushed out of her bubble and caused them to descend so fast that they all immediately became dizzy. They grabbed her legs even harder, hanging on for dear life.

"Whoa!" Babette gasped, the four of them watching the cold waters of the bay becoming closer and closer directly below them.

"Cool! This must be like skydiving from an airplane, only without a parachute," Barnaby exclaimed, exhilarated by the free fall.

"Not the water, not the water, puh-leeze, not the water!" Beauregard cried loudly.

"You Americans. We don't want to skydive, Barnaby, but you can let go if you want to test your drag and drop theory. That water looks freezing! Do something, Bridget!" Babette begged.

"Drag and lift," Barnaby corrected her.

Beauregard curled his long tail around Bridget as high as he could, afraid that at any minute they'd be submerged. He closed his eyes shut and plugged his nose, thinking it could be all over.

Bridget frantically blew more air into the bubble, ignoring the ache that was spreading from her jaw, down her neck, and through her shoulder blades. Whoosh! Immediately, their free fall ended and they jerked upwards, stopping only yards from the choppy, cold waves. Some spray from the surf blew against them, giving them a sense of how bitterly cold the water was. Straight ahead was Liberty Island and the Statue of Liberty.

"Now that was a dive!" Barnaby laughed.

"Luckily, it was not," Beauregard said, shivering. "Now, if only we can land . . . on land."

"Good job, Bridget," Babette acknowledged, relieved. They were moving slowly several feet over the waves and in the direction of Liberty Island.

Barnaby cleared his throat. "A person free-falling at a speed of fifty yards per second will gradually slow to a five-yards-per-second fall wearing a parachute. By blowing the bubble larger, Bridget provided a sort of parachute that caught the air current, causing us to rise upwards. Luckily we are heading into the wind and it will be easier to land. This way, the speed of the wind is not increasing our speed. This reminds me of the words of Charles Lindbergh," Barnaby observed, his legs dangling in the air as if he were pacing. "Lindbergh said, 'I owned the world that hour as I rode over it . . . free of the earth, free of the mountains, free of the clouds, but how inseparably I was bound to them.' Free we were!"

"Hey guys, hold on! We're landing!" Bridget warned, her words causing the air to rush out of the bubble. It burst. They tumbled onto the lawn of Liberty Island, only a few feet from a rock wall and the chilly water.

"Remind me to wear a crash helmet and parachute next time," Beauregard grumbled.

They found Dr. Tempus Fugit waiting for them in his lab within the pedestal of the Statue of Liberty. He stood in the long hall full of computers and telemetry equipment, obviously expecting them. As usual, Dr. Tempus looked like a mad scientist. His snow white hair stuck out all over his head and, like Barnaby, he wore a white lab coat. His pockets bulged full of papers covered with mathematical formulas. Behind his wire-rimmed glasses, his eyes twinkled at them. To the kids, he was their Einstein, their genius. They were glad to see him again.

"Come, be my guests. I've been waiting to show you my latest invention," Dr. Tempus greeted them, his white handlebar mustache quivering. He led them towards the darkened corner of the huge room where he kept *Lady Liberty*. As usual, the timeship was draped with a large tie-dyed drop cloth.

"What's that?" Barnaby asked, pointing to the second drop cloth covering something as bulky and tall as *Lady Liberty*.

"Take a look, Barnaby," Dr. Tempus urged. He handed Barnaby the remote control that released the drop cloth. One press of the button and the second cloth was quickly whisked away.

"Unbelievable. In fact, I don't believe it," Barnaby murmured. They all stared at the huge gray boulder.

"How did you get that humongous rock in here?" Babette asked, obviously dismayed to find that the "modifications" Dr. Tempus mentioned in his e-mail involved a large stone.

"A rock, Dr. Tempus? That's, um, solid, anyway," Bridget pointed out, reserving judgment.

"You invented this? It's just a . . . rock." Barnaby said doubtfully. They watched Dr. Tempus furiously push more buttons on the remote. Bright lights shimmered down onto the boulder, causing them to squint against the glare. The lights were like those at Cape Canaveral before a space shuttle launch. Dr. Tempus continued to fool around with the remote and mutter to himself.

Without warning, a piece of the rock slid open the same way an elevator door opens. The kids and cat watched in amazement. There wasn't a seam or any clues to show this was anything more than a colossal boulder. Until now.

"Ha! I do believe we have a new timeship!" Barnaby declared, hurrying for the door before any of the others overcame their astonishment.

Beauregard sniffed the air for a minute. "Food?" He asked. "I do believe I smell sustenance, and of the most flavorful variety!"

"Yes, Beauregard, there's a galley built into the timeship, a stocked kitchen," Dr. Tempus confirmed. "I hope you'll advise me if there are any deficiencies, nutritional or otherwise. Keep your dirty socks out of the engine this time, Barnaby," he suggested. The young scientist managed to look abashed, his face reddening.

"Superb! Absolutely, superb!" In a flash, Beauregard enthusiastically disappeared through the rock's door, already reviewing menus in his head. He'd probably have to make human food for his young friends, but that was a challenge in itself!

"Hey! Wait for us!" Bridget and Babette yelled in unison, jolted out of their momentary stupor to run after their friends. Dr. Tempus followed, chuckling, his hair waving wildly.

Inside the spacious cabin, several one-way windows looked out into the laboratory. One of the two doors along the back wall led into the galley. Beauregard could be heard banging pots and pans and opening and closing cupboard doors. The other door was labeled "Rest Room." These were two luxuries that they had missed on *Lady Liberty*. Four pull-down bunk beds snapped flat into the wall between the galley and rest room doors. Barnaby was busy examining the controls and computerized equipment along the walls.

"Why make it look like a stone, Dr. Tempus?" Babette asked curiously, as she and Bridget flopped into the comfortable seats, outfitted completely with arm rests and seatbelts.

"A stone won't draw much attention," Dr. Tempus explained. "When you go back in time or to anywhere in the world, it would blend in better than a statue or something. I've made major adjustments, yes, adjustments to this timeship." He walked over to the computer consoles and controls in front of Barnaby.

"Like *Lady Liberty* there's also a transporter. The transporter has the ability to transport you from any location back here to the cabin. The timeship can move anywhere on Earth in the present time," Dr. Tempus focused on the equipment, as he appeared to get stage fright when lecturing. "It also can move backwards to any point in the past by setting the tempometer, like *Lady Liberty*. However, this has been adjusted to allow travel to millions of years ago and in different dimensions of time."

Barnaby studied the digitized tempometer and saw how time could be adjusted to indicate years either B.C. or A.D., by B.P. for years before present, or by using solar or lunar years and even the Egyptian and other calendars. Months, days, and times could be digitally entered on the computer. Most intriguing, there were **geologic time periods** on the menu. Barnaby knew of the Jurassic and Cretaceous periods, but many others were new to him, like the Pleistocene, the geologic time of the last great Ice Age. There was also an adjustment for travel in the present, adjusting to international time zones and longitude/latitude for places around the world with respect to the standard time kept in Greenwich, England, on the prime meridian.

Era	Period	Epoch	Millions of Years
CENOZOIC	Quaternary	Holocene	0.01
		Pleistocene	2
	Tertiary	Pliocene	5
		Miocene	25
		Oligocene	38
		Eocene	55
		Paleocene	65
MESOZOIC	Cretaceous		145
	Jurassic		215
	Triassic		250
PALEOZOIC	Permian		285
	Carboniferous		360
	Devonian		410
	Silurian		440
	Ordovician		500
	Cambrian		600
PRECAMBRIAN	Proterozoic		1,000
	Archaeozoic		3,000
	Azoic		4,600

Prehistoric Time

"Absolutely beyond awesome!" Barnaby whispered happily, overcome by the possibilities.

"No periscope on this baby," Bridget laughed, pleased with the visibility provided by the windows. "And there's a full instruction manual, something we could've used before on *Lady Liberty*."

"Who needs a manual," Barnaby retorted. He always preferred to figure things out on his own to reading someone else's instructions. He was a scientist, after all, wasn't he?

"Adventurers, I promised to help you in your quest and I am," Dr. Tempus declared. "This timeship is specially designed for research and travel. I made even more modifications for archaeological expeditions after learning of your quest to return those artifacts."

"Archaeology?" Babette echoed, puzzled. "Why archaeology?"

"Why archaeology indeed! You need to accurately identify and return those artifacts to save our secret of time travel, of course," Dr. Tempus said with a frown, surprised they hadn't yet figured it out for themselves. "Otherwise, those thieves could prove time travel can be done. Not to mention the fact that their thefts from history may effect the future. Archaeology is the key to discovering all of the information you need. We can't go to a museum curator and explain how we got those artifacts, can we. You'll have to become amateur archaeologists and research the items to figure out where and when to return them. Only when all of the things are returned to the past and are out of the reach of those thieves will the danger be over. Are you ready for more adventures?"

"Ha! He asks if we're ready for more adventures?" Bridget giggled, rolling her eyes at Babette. "When aren't we, Dr. Tempus? I'm ready to surf the timewaves or timeframes or whatever you call it. This is sooo cool! Like, when can we leave here?" Bridget discovered the chairs swivelled easily and began spinning on one, around and around and around, the cabin's interior passing in a blur.

Babette looked thoughtful. "But Dr. Tempus, why can't we just research the stuff in the sack using the computer or by going to an archaeologist or a curator at a museum? Wouldn't history books and atlases provide the information we need?"

"No, no, no, no!" Dr. Tempus shook his head and his white hair jerked in agitation. "That's almost impossible given the situation. Books won't have the answers you need. As you go, you'll understand this better with experience. Whatever you think archaeology is, I guarantee that by the time that bag is empty and you're all ready to return home, you'll have a different concept and view of the world. You'll also be better prepared for the future. Many believe if you don't understand the mistakes of the past, you're fated to repeat them in the future."

"Makes sense," Bridget agreed dizzily. She pulled her baseball cap lower on her forehead. "Do I make a great Indiana Jones or what?"

Dr. Tempus smiled, then looked serious again. "You'll find that Indiana Jones is more of a treasure hunter than an archaeologist. You won't be hunting treasures, but returning artifacts to their time and context."

He frowned. "However, I'm obligated to warn you that I do feel there is some danger involved. Those thieves were crafty enough to steal my time machine secrets, build a replica timeship, steal all of those objects, and bring them here to the present. Um, I wouldn't underestimate them by any means," Dr. Tempus cautioned them. "And then there are all the risks that come with time travel and different cultures and people and environments. You must remain safe. There's too much at stake." Bridget and Babette looked at each other worriedly. Dr. Tempus's warning was not going unheeded. They glanced at Barnaby to make sure he had heard the scientist. He was obviously lost in his own world, muttering as he continued to explore the timeship's computerized controls.

"Hmm, we can adjust time as one of the fundamental quantities of the physical world, being similar to length and mass in this respect," they heard him muttering. "Of course, there are three methods of measuring time in use at the present. The first two are based on the daily rotation of the earth on its axis and are determined by the apparent motion of the sun or stars in the sky, solar or sidereal time. Then of course, there's the third method of measuring time, based on the revolution of the earth around the sun or emphereris time . . . ."

Bang! Clank! Bang! Rattle! The sounds behind them from the galley increased. It sounded like Beauregard was rearranging the kitchen. Barnaby's mumbling became indecipherable with all the noise.

"Hey, Dr. Tempus," Bridget said, "I still don't get this archaeology stuff. Isn't archaeology just history?" She popped more bubble gum into her mouth to replace all of the gum she'd used to transport them to Liberty Island.

Dr. Tempus nodded. "In some ways, archaeology complements human history, often filling in missing pieces that written records may not cover. In the strict sense, 'history' means an account of the past recovered by written records. Even with written records, the history isn't always accurate. There are too many perspectives and biases, since everyone writes about how the events affected them personally or how they saw them. They may miss what was happening to others. They may also embellish, dramatize, exaggerate, or under-report facts depending on who they think their audience is.

"Like rumors and hearsay?" Bridget asked, " Or how stories change every time they're repeated?"

"Yes," Dr. Tempus agreed. "By studying things people used and made, archaeology helps to fill in the missing blanks and history. Besides, written histories are limited to thousands of years, yet humans have been on earth for *millions* of years. That's why you need to learn about archaeology to understand what isn't written down and available. Most archaeologists call the time before written records exist **prehistory**. However, there are also historical archaeologists that research peoples and cultures up to present-day, modern history. Some also separate prehistory and history in the Americas as precontact and after-contact or post-contact. This distinguishes the time before Europeans and Russians first came to America and wrote about it."

"So in conclusion?" Bridget prompted impatiently. She wanted to be off on adventures and not listening to endless lectures. Let them learn archaeology hands-on, she thought. The banging in the galley had stopped, but Barnaby still muttered, absorbed with the computer console. Babette closed her eyes, probably experiencing some jet lag. Bridget could understand her friend's fatigue. After all, the time difference between Paris and New York City is five hours. It would take a little time for the girl to adjust.

"In conclusion, one definition of archaeology is the study of things made and used by past people to learn about their behaviors and culture, how they went about their daily business and interacted with each other. The information comes from what the people made or used and left behind. I like to equate the study of archaeology to science fiction, the study of once and future things. In fact, many archaeologists are sci-fi fans," Dr. Tempus winked at them.

"Great! I love all of the *Star Trek* TV shows and *Star Wars* movies," Bridget admitted. "But I don't see how sci-fi relates to studying the past."

"Science fiction attempts to figure out the mystery of the future based on what we know today, right? Archaeology does the same thing, except it figures out the mysteries of the past, based on the present. In fact, I think archaeology can be more thrilling because it's real. It deals with real battles, real conquests, real civilizations, and in your case, real objects. More important than the facts you learn about the past, will be the way you'll learn to get those facts. Some think archaeology is all digging or, rather, excavating."

"The word 'excavate' comes from the Latin *ex* (out) and *cavare* (to make hollow)," Babette announced importantly, obviously listening with her eyes closed.

"Frenchie and her languages!" Bridget grinned.

"True, Babette," Dr. Tempus agreed. "Excavating is an important research tool, but any excavation destroys the site that is excavated. That's why you will be joining professionals who have been trained to get as much information as humanly possible rather than doing any digging on your own. There are many laws and regulations worldwide about where, what, and how you can excavate. Often a permit or official paperwork is required," Dr. Tempus sighed. "So much information has been destroyed by people just taking things and not working scientifically to uncover clues."

"Really, Dr. Tempus, can we get on with it? This seems to be taking a long time," Bridget said testily. She didn't like having to sit still so long and listen to so much.

"Yes, yes, of course, Bridget. Now, you're hereby all given an assignment as time detectives, and I hope you won't take your investigations lightly. Most importantly, you're going to need your imagination to help you work your way to the right places and peoples in the past. With all of your skills—and you will need them—you should be prepared for some incredible adventures," Dr. Tempus concluded dramatically.

"What about dinosaurs? Will we see dinosaurs? I like the American author Michael Crichton and his novels *Jurassic Park* and *The Lost World*," Babette said. "Raptors and Tyrannosaurus rex and—"

"Babette, you're thinking of **paleontology** now," Dr. Tempus shook his head, his hair flying every which way. "That's the science that deals with the study of **fossil** remains and prehistoric life forms. Dinosaurs lived roughly 228 million to 65 million years ago. The oldest fossil plants are around 3 billion years old."

"Billions?" Bridget echoed.

"Yes, that's billions or more years old. The oldest known upright-walking humans existed about 3.5 million to 4 million years ago.

There are still heated debates on when these early **hominids** actually became what we consider to be human," Dr. Tempus said.

"*Paleo* means 'old' in Latin," Babette informed them. "*Archaeo* comes from the Greek *archaio-* meaning ancient or the French *arche* meaning 'beginning'."

"Yes, and archaeologists study the types of foods people ate, the shelters they built, the clothes or tools they made, and the lives they led. They study past people's culture, customs, and beliefs. They're not interested in the prehistory of the earth before the time of humans. However, sometimes an archaeologist searching for artifacts may find dinosaur bones or other fossils. They will work together with paleontologists or other scientists and specialists to help solve the past's mysteries. Also, excavations are the primary research tool for archaeologists, although some geologists and paleontologists also do some excavating."

"Yeah, my mom and dad brought me on an Incan dig once in Mesoamerica," Barnaby announced, swinging his chair away from the control panels to join in their discussion. "I learned that archaeologists may work with anthropologists, who study human behavior and cultures, often that of modern societies. They may also work with paleontologists, who study fossils; biologists or zoologists, who study animals and marine life; geologists, who study the earth and its formations; historians, who study histories and records; botanists, who study plants; forensic specialists, to help with dating of artifacts and bones; astronomers, who study the solar system and how humans have viewed it throughout time; meteorologists, to learn about climate and weather changes; philosophers, to understand spiritual thought; surveyors and statisticians, to—"

"Whoa, Barnaby, enough! That's quite a list," Dr. Tempus interrupted, roaring his words out so they actually stopped Barnaby in midstream. Beauregard pokes his head with its oversized white chef hat out of the galley to see what was going on. Satisfied that there was no crisis, he disappeared into the galley again. Babette yawned sleepily.

"A very long list, yes," Bridget agreed, fidgeting in her seat.

"Okay, let me show you how to get one of your first clues," Dr. Tempus said, beckoning the three of them over to the control panels and computer console. He pointed at what looked like a microwave oven built over one of the computers.

The scientist explained, "Archaeologists have never had this research tool I've invented for you, of course, but you don't have a lifetime to find all your clues. I call it an 'archyfactor.' It's specially designed and linked to an archaeological database stored right on this timeship. You place the artifact in the archyfactor," he swung open the door, demonstrating, holding out his hand toward Barnaby. The young scientist was so intently studying the control buttons on the device that he didn't notice.

Bridget nudged him, none too gently.

"Er, huh? Wh-what?" Barnaby looked around, bewildered. "Clue me in!"

"Give Dr. Tempus an artifact, hey?" Bridget told him. Barnaby reached into the bulky bag and pulled out what looked like a clay imprint of a human footprint.

"This is actually more of a fossil, I believe, but it still should work," Dr. Tempus placed the object into the open box of the archyfactor and pushed the "start" button. Immediately, words starting scrolling down the computer screen below until the following appeared:

```
>Possible   location:   Laetoli,   Tanzania,
Africa<
```

"There!" Dr. Tempus smiled, satisfied. All was in working order. "Somehow this footprint relates to that location. It is probably an archaeological site where similar footprints have been found or are being excavated. That will be your first stop. Now, let me caution you that one of your most crucial tasks will be recording every possible clue and keeping accurate written information. You'll all have notebooks that you can use for your records. You may also need to use the database to research what other archaeologists have discovered. This equipment here is a color laser printer so you can print out what you find. Investigate what is known about a people or item, and confirm you've found some answers."

"No problem," Barnaby said. "Then we just take the artifact back to where it came from, right?"

Dr. Tempus shook his head warningly. "Learn all you can BEFORE returning the artifact to its place in time. Those backpacks strapped along that shelf are all archaeological kits with materials you may need to use at an established dig. Why don't you open those now?" Dr. Tempus directed them. "There's even one for Beauregard."

They took their backpacks down and opened them. Each pack contained the following:

- an archaeology field guide and manual
- assorted sized paint brushes, several toothbrushes
- a camera and extra film, batteries
- a compass and a map of the world showing latitude/longitude
- disposable gloves, pair of heavy-duty work gloves
- a dust mask
- a flashlight with extra batteries
- heavy string
- matches and a headlamp
- measuring tape and a calculator
- plastic trash bags, a box of plastic sandwich bags, and empty plastic containers
- a scraper, a trowel, a pocket knife, pruning shears, tweezers, a small hammer
- a sheet of wire mesh/screen
- two notebooks with pencils, pens, and sheets of metric graph paper

"Dr. Tempus?" After examining the contents of their packs, all three shouted the scientist's name, trying to get his attention. He held his hands up, warding them off.

"Whoa, wait, I can see you all have questions. First, however, I am sending you to Southwest Colorado for a one-day archaeology field school. I called Bridget's mother just before you arrived and she is making sure none of your parents worry about you while you are gone. The school can prepare you better than I can lecturing to you here. Following the school, you'll be ready to head to Africa and begin investigating this first object," he pointed at the archyfactor where the footprint still rested. "I will be here in my lab so you can teleconference me, hopefully at any time, if you have questions or need help." Dr. Tempus began moving toward the door.

"Wait! What do you call this timeship?" Barnaby asked, putting his backpack back on its shelf and strapping it in.

"It's *Archy Stone*," Dr. Tempus chuckled. "Appropriate, eh?"

"*Archy Stone*? I like it," Bridget grinned, giving the name her approval.

"Pizza's ready!" Beauregard made his appearance at last, still wearing his oversized white chef's hat and apron. Scrumptious odors wafted from the pan in his paws. "I've also got fries and sodas. Best of all, there's even a dishwasher in the galley."

Dr. Tempus laughed, his hair flying in every direction. "Okay, food first. Then you're off to the Montezuma Valley and Southwest Colorado," Dr. Tempus promised, helping himself to a piece of Beauregard's pizza. Dr. Tempus pulled at a handle in the floor and it rose to make a sturdy table. The kids didn't wait. They suddenly realized they were famished!

None of them heard the commotion outside of the Statue of Liberty when a boat docked on the island and was tied up by a tall dark figure accompanied by what appeared to be his dog. In the boat was what looked like a metal rocket with a huge dollar sign painted on it. Tourists and park rangers stared.

Dastardly and Sneakers had arrived.

✍ ACTIVITIES ✍

QUIZ #1
Discovering the Past

Match the definitions with the vocabulary words listed below.

_____ 1. Method for studying past human cultures and analyzing material evidence, artifacts, and sites.

_____ 2. Study of dinosaurs and fossils.

_____ 3. Any object made or used by humans.

_____ 4. Characteristics or properties of an object such as size, color, or shape.

_____ 5. Conclusions based on objects.

_____ 6. An arrangement of events in the order in which they occurred.

_____ 7. Systematic arrangement in groups or categories according to established criteria.

_____ 8. A set of learned beliefs, values, and behaviors generally shared by members of a society.

_____ 9. Information, especially information organized for analysis.

_____ 10. A proposed explanation accounting for a set of facts that can be tested by further investigation.

_____ 11. The study of layers of earth and materials.

_____ 12. Before written records.

a. stratigraphy
b. archaeology
c. prehistory
d. hypothesis
i. paleontology
f. artifact
g. attribute

h. culture
i. inference
j. classification
k. data or evidence
l. chronology

Food for Thought

Artifacts in context are the basis for all understanding about prehistoric people. Archaeology is a science of context, or the relationship that artifacts have to each other and the situation in which they are found. Imagine that an archaeologist finds your classroom a thousand years from now. Make a statement about how artifacts in the context of your classroom will help the archaeologist learn about you and your class.

Vocabulary

(Listed in glossary at back of book)

fossil

geologic time

hominids

Chapter 4
Eagle Mesa: The Field School

"Wow! It worked! There are mesa cliffs, sagebrush, desert!" Barnaby said excitedly. "The soil even looks reddish, like rust!" The *Archy Stone* travelers looked out of the windows onto a different world.

"We're in Cortez, Southwest Colorado. It's 82 degrees Fahrenheit outside and we're about a mile higher than sea level. The time is two hours behind New York time—Eastern Standard Time, that is. This is Rocky Mountain Time. In fact, we've gone back in time almost two hours between New York and Colorado!" Bridget announced, reading the data off the computer screen.

"The higher elevation means we may have more trouble getting oxygen and may pant until we get used to it," Barnaby informed them. "I'm going to try teleconferencing Dr. Tempus as he suggested, so he knows *Archy Stone* worked and we got here okay." Barnaby moved to the computer and began typing on the keyboard, pulling a miniature camcorder from its compartment next to the archyfactor and pointing it at himself.

"But where's this field where we have school?" Babette wondered, applying fresh red lipstick and adjusting her sunglasses in the wall mirror inside *Archy Stone*'s cabin. Her black pants and shirt were unwrinkled and looked brand new. Bridget compared her wrinkled jeans and tee shirt and wondered how Babette always managed to look so sophisticated and cool.

"Frenchie! A field school doesn't necessarily mean the school's in the middle of a field," Bridget attempted to explain, joining Babette by the windows. Outside, the sun appeared very bright. The sky shone a deep, deep blue. "It means the classes are hands-on lessons with some kind of work 'in the field,' though usually only for a short time—a day, a week. It's not like going to classes all year."

"Maybe I should be going to field schools instead of regular school? I like the short time approach," Babette pointed out. Bridget and Barnaby laughed. Beauregard was busy studying the contents of his archaeology backpack.

"Hmmm, that's exceedingly strange." Barnaby puzzled, frowning.

"What's wrong?" Bridget asked quickly.

"I'm getting his computer, but Dr. Tempus doesn't answer the teleconferencing call. I can see his lab and it looks like there's no one there. Even worse, it looks ransacked or something. Look! Papers are everywhere, things are knocked over. Remember when we left Dr. Tempus he said he was going to remain at his computer until he heard from us?" Barnaby pointed at the screen. They all looked at it, worriedly.

"Maybe Dr. Tempus was looking for something and had to go to the bathroom or went somewhere?" Bridget reasoned.

Barnaby shrugged. "I hope so, though this bothers me. I'll try again if the field school bus hasn't yet arrived for us."

"Truly excellent!" Beauregard muttered, bringing their attention back to the scene outdoors. "As a connoisseur of the cuisine arts, this place is a chef's heaven! In fact, I can probably find fresh pine nuts from the pinyon pine while we're here. They add a special touch to many a dish. Ah! I also believe Dove Creek is within these environs. The town's well known for Anasazi and pinto beans. And let's not forget those famous southwestern green chili peppers and fresh cilantro for seasoning," he mused. "Not to mention the great chuckwagon and western range cuisines. All that grazing beef, and I recall that llamas too are now being raised in the area! In season, there's also game such as elk, mule deer, jackrabbits, and, for us cats, prairie dogs, gophers, voles, field mice, and so many bird species!"

"Prairie dogs, Beauregard?" Bridget echoed.

"Yes," Beauregard agreed. "In fact, it's a prairie dog metropolis. There are so many prairie dog colonies that the fields have become pockmarked with the holes leading down into their burrows and tunnels. Hmm . . . I will have to find some wholesale deals if I can. Too bad we don't have better cold food storage in the *Archy Stone*; that refrigerator's too tiny."

"This is a timeship, Beauregard," Barnaby reminded him. "Building a restaurant-sized walk-in refrigerator just wouldn't be practical."

"So it is, so it is," he agreed. "I also believe there's more than the normal population of cats in the area, helping to control rodent populations around homes and farms to prevent the spread of hantavirus from field mice and rats and bubonic plague from prairie dogs." He smiled slyly, mumbling softly so the young humans couldn't hear him, "I'd like to check out some of the local felines. As a rule, they're pretty self-sufficient, sleek, and superb hunters!"

Out loud, Beauregard announced, "In fact, I haven't made any fresh prairie dog stew for a date since . . . .."

"Food, Beauregard?!" Bridget scolded. "We just ate pizza! We're only here tonight and tomorrow for the field school, then we're off on our travels. We've got stuff to learn, things to do."

"Yes, things to do. I believe our field camp is in the shadow of the Sleeping Ute," Beauregard said, and pointed at a huge mountain on their left. "There is the Ute Mountain Ute Reservation around that mountain."

"How do you know all this stuff, Beauregard?" Babette asked curiously.

"Sleeping Ute? What's that?" Barnaby asked, to Beauregard's relief. The cat was glad of the change in subject. He didn't want to get into a discussion of his social life.

"The bus should be near here soon, and remember, we just look like a gigantic stone, so the bus driver won't stop. We've gotta be outside, waiting in plain sight. Let's get our backpacks and pack our overnight bags," Bridget suggested, as Beauregard explained the mountain's name.

"There's a legend that the mountain is actually a sleeping Ute chief, a Native American, who will one day awake and save his people. Over there, toward the south, those cliffs are Mesa Verde National Park. We're in the Montezuma Valley. The city of Cortez lies just to the east of us. We're not far from what's called the Four Corners, where the Colorado, Utah, Arizona, and New Mexico borders all come together. Also, this is Navajo country, home of the Navajo Nation, the largest Native American reservation in the United States," Beauregard informed them, looking pleased that he remembered so much from having toured the area before.

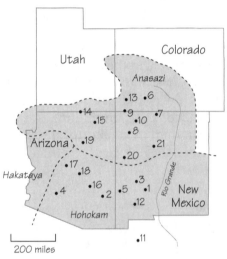

Southwestern Sites

1	Bat Cave	12	Mimbres
2	Cienega Creek	13	Mesa Verde
3	Tularosa Cave	14	Kiet Siel
4	Snaketown	15	Betatekin
5	SU Site	16	Point of Pines
6	Talus Village	17	Grasshopper
7	Navajo Reservoir	18	Kinishba
8	Chaco Canyon	19	Hopi Mesas
9	Aztec	20	Zuni Pueblo
10	Salmon	21	Rio Grande
11	Casa Grandes		

"Ah, our Beauregard is a regular tour guide. Are the Ute also Navajo?" Babette asked the cat.

Beauregard shook his head. "No, separate peoples. There are several other Native American groups in this area. The Ute have three different tribes—the Northern Ute, the Southern Ute, and the Mountain Ute. There are also many different Pueblo and Apache tribes, and many others in nearby New Mexico and Arizona. See how those cliffs and rock formations look almost sculpted? That's because this whole area is part of the Colorado plateau and once was a huge inland saltwater sea in prehistoric times. Now most of it is desert, but it's spectacular, huh?"

The three friends and the cat walked out into the soft, dry air outside of the *Archy Stone*, carrying their backpacks and overnight bags. It was amazing how different the environment was from what they'd just left in New York City. They still felt a bit lightheaded from their speedy travel.

"Beauregard! What about those snow-covered rocky mountains far off to the east?" Barnaby asked, pointing.

Beauregard shaded his eyes and looked off towards the mountains. "Those mountains are part of the Rocky Mountains, the western slope, called La Platas. Cross them and you come to the famous old western town of Durango. There's a scenic highway that makes a large loop from Cortez to Durango to Gunniston and Telluride, then back, with incredible views, old ghost towns and gold mines, off-road jeeping trails, large herds of elk and mule deer, and—."

"Hey, what's that? Oh, here comes an old bus," Bridget said, chewing her bubble gum nervously. "Do you think that's part of our field school? Yes! It says Eagle Mesa Archaeological Center on the side!"

They hurried out to the rambling bus. Behind them, the *Archy Stone* blended in perfectly with the dark shadows of the pinyon pines, juniper, and colored rock formations. No one could guess a timeship was parked there.

"Welcome!" The bus driver greeted them. "I'm Larry. We were told to pick you kids up way out here and . . . er . . . " The man stared at Beauregard, speechless at the sight of the large black cat. They quickly climbed onto the bus, dropping their packs and bags on empty seats.

"I'm Bridget, and this is Babette, Barnaby, and . . . ," she concluded, pointing at the cat, "Beauregard."

Beauregard bowed slightly. "How do you do?"

"He t-t-t-t . . . " the man stuttered.

Beauregard studied his manicured paws. "Talks? Hmm, yes, I do. Are we far from the field school? We've had quite a day," Beauregard sat.

"Field school. Okay, yes, we'll hurry," the man agreed, still flustered. The bus creaked and rolled over the bumpy terrain. Larry shouted to be heard above the noises. "The school is just beyond this small canyon. You're here for the short program? From New York? How did you end up waiting for me on this old road?"

"We had a ride from the airport," Barnaby improvised, "after we landed from New York. Sure is beautiful country here!" Babette decided not to mention Paris. It was possible this school was only for Americans, and she didn't want to complicate anything. The man seemed to accept their explanation.

"Are you an archaeologist?" Bridget asked the driver. He nodded, but had to concentrate on the road ahead. The rattling and other noises increased. Several times the bus lurched so sharply it felt like it was going to roll over . . . or break apart. They drove up to several adobe buildings built along the foothills of Ute Mountain. After registering at a table set up in the mess hall, Larry led them to several round adobe cabins in the back.

"These are the student and staff cabins. There's room for eight in each cabin. That trail leads to the latrines. Rocks line the trails to help keep you from wandering off. Ladies are assigned to these cabins. I'll show you where the guys are, and, er . . . .." Larry paused and stared at Beauregard uncertainly.

"I'll stay with Barnaby," Beauregard announced. The man smiled, leading Barnaby and the cat away up the trail.

Bridget and Babette found comfortable bunks and furniture with Navajo blankets, rugs, and crafts in their cabin. For washing, there was a large basin and pitcher of water on one of four bureaus. Six of the bunks were already taken, with suitcases, gym bags, and other stuff, though their owners were nowhere in sight.

After leaving their things in the room, they walked outside into the warm, dry air. "Wow!" Bridget and Babette said in awe, staring at the scenery all around them. Brilliant colors streaked across the sky behind them towards Utah and Arizona in a breathtaking sunset. In front, the Mesa Verde cliffs and snow-covered La Platas peaks shone like pure gold, reflecting the brilliant sunset's hues.

"Hey, Bridget—Look at that huge bird up there! Could it be an eagle?" Babette pointed at the sky where a black silhouette circled above them, rising higher and higher.

"Hmm, he looks like a very big bird," Bridget responded. "Probably even too big for Beauregard to catch." They laughed, both of them watching the bird soar far above them, and then dive and disappear into the canyon near the *Archy Stone*. Over the La Platas, the moon began to rise, large and full. The sky turned from red to purple to black. Stars began to twinkle overhead, appearing closer and brighter than any they had ever seen before.

Babette yawned. "Yikes! I'm exhausted. We've got a big day tomorrow. Though I want to meet our cabin mates, I think I'd rather get some sleep," she suggested, heading back into the cabin. Babette agreed. They hit the bunks.

The next day, after Beauregard convinced the cook to let him make an incredible breakfast of huevos rancheros—Mexican eggs—they sat outside on bleachers arranged in a large circle at an open theater. Larry stood in the center with a microphone and several other adults wearing khaki safari-type clothing or cut-off jeans and heavy boots. All wore cowboy hats and belts with large buckles on them. The adults stood waiting for all of the students to arrive, as many had returned to their cabins after eating to get their notebooks.

"Babette, can you believe our Beauregard?" Bridget laughed, shaking her head.

"He sure is a magnificent chef! *Oo lá lá*, as they say in my country," Babette giggled back, still amazed at how the cat had taken over the kitchen to feed over thirty people. Now, Beauregard was nowhere in sight.

Slowly, the bleachers filled. Barnaby joined them, looking worried.

"Barnaby, is something wrong?" Babette asked as he sat down next to her.

"Definitely. I don't know how much more wrong it could be. I talked Larry into driving me back towards the *Archy Stone* early this morning before any of you were up, giving him a story about my wanting to go jogging on that old road. He let me go alone and I tried teleconferencing again. Dr. Tempus was not there and nothing looked changed from yesterday. Something is definitely wrong." The bleachers had filled up fast.

"Welcome to Eagle Mesa Archaeology School and Southwest Colorado," Larry bellowed out over a public address system, his microphone ringing from feedback. He sounded like he was at a pep rally. "Most of you know by now I'm Larry. I also have four other archaeologists with me. Let's give them a big hand!" He pointed and introduced each of the four adults with him, to the roar of applause from the bleachers. "Suzanne! Chico! Vic! And lastly, this is Eddie!" The students clapped and hollered, many stamping their feet to contribute to the noise.

"Eddie's from the Ute Mountain Ute Reservation. He's great at chipping projectile points from flint and stone, what some of you still call arrowheads. He'll be giving demonstrations to you before lunchtime today. Anyway, a big, big welcome!" The students cheered. Larry waved to get their attention again. "We'll be dividing you up into four groups for the day, each of you assigned to one of us archaeologists, except for Eddie. You know what he'll be doing. Now, one of the questions that has faced humankind throughout our history. Why, oh why, are you here?" He grinned.

The thirty or so kids raised their hands, hoping to be called on.

"Tonto! We're not in Kentucky anymore," Babette whispered to Bridget, studying the man's clothes. She'd never seen anyone dress like that in Paris or New York City, but out here in the midst of the pinyon pines, it looked perfect. A girl next to them chuckled, having apparently overheard Babette.

"It's Toto, the dog, and Kansas, not Kentucky," Bridget pointed out, laughing. She chewed her bubble gum rapidly, adding, "But you're right! This certainly isn't New York City! Oh no, Larry's picking Barnaby! He doesn't realize his tendency to lect—" She stopped and then turned to the girl next to them. "Oh, hi! Sorry to be rude on the intro's. I'm Bridget and this is Babette," she told the redheaded girl.

"And I'm Becca from Chicago," the girl whispered back before Barnaby took center stage. The young scientist stood up, his lab coat flapping in the mild breeze, obviously beginning his lecture-mode.

"Hi, I'm Barnaby from New York City. We're here . . . to learn about archaeology," Barnaby began, as Larry nodded, the poor man not yet realizing what he was in for. Barnaby continued, "Field techniques and methods, researching, recording data, and," he began throwing his hands around wildly, pacing along the bleachers as the students and staff watched with growing fascination, "I believe we're to learn how to reconstruct lifeways, or rather, cultures, of past ages through the study of objects created by humans and known as artifacts."

"Yes, very good," Larry responded, mistakenly assuming Barnaby was finished. Both Bridget and Babette knew better. Barnaby was on a roll. While the class watched him with stupefaction, he moved next to Larry and the other archaeology educators, continuing his monologue that sounded suspiciously like a textbook. Bridget and Babette were amused to see some of the students scribbling his words down furiously.

Barnaby continued, of course. "Though a relatively young science that is still developing, archaeology has come into its own. It has been popularized in such things as Indiana Jones adventure movies and Agatha Christie novels. The reality of archaeology is much more than the discovery of treasures and things from the past. It is also using imagination and interpretation to figure out what past people's lives were like. It's partly anthropology, the study of humanity and culture. Anthropology is so broad that it is usually broken down into three major areas: physical or biological anthropology that studies the evolution of human physical characteristics through physical remains such as skeletons; cultural or social anthropology that analyzes human culture and society including ethnography and ethnology; and lastly archaeology, where archaeologists study past societies and cultures mostly through their material remains—the buildings, tools, trash, cooking areas, and other artifacts people left behind."

"True, thank you—" Larry tried to interrupt, still not realizing it was almost impossible to interrupt Barnaby when he was in his lecture mode.

Typically, Barnaby didn't pause or even seem to notice Larry's words. "Archaeology's a way to preserve humanity's cultural heritage. Archaeology is a part of and contributes to history, too. By history we mean the whole history of humankind from its beginnings possibly over 5 million years ago through today. It differs from written history, though many archaeologists use written history as a tool to help teach about more modern cultures and peoples. Written history only begins about 3,000 years ago in Asia, and much later in most other parts of the world. In fact, written history in Australia didn't begin until about A.D. 1788 or about 200 years B.P., before present. Archaeologists can learn about people and their lifeways before anything was written about them. They study human prehistory and history, using the development of written records as the dividing line between prehistorical and historical archaeology."

"Um, are you through?" Larry attempted again, almost angry now. He had a field school to run. The students laughed, never having seen this happen before—except for Bridget and Babette, of course. Becca kept rolling her eyes at the two girls, obviously wondering if Barnaby would ever finish.

Barnaby didn't seem to hear and continued his lecturing. "Archaeology's also a science. When artifacts are found, we have to keep careful records about their locations and any other information about where they were found. We have to analyze them and compare them to other artifacts. These records and analyses are the beginning data. Using the methods of scientific inquiry, the scientist collects data and evidence, conducts experiments, develops a hypothesis or proposition to account for the data, and then in conclusion develops a description or model that best seems to summarize what the data contains. That's what archaeologists do. In fact—"

"Enough, Barnaby! Enough!" Babette cried, finally getting his attention when she and Bridget stood up and waved their arms frantically. Though Barnaby still looked entranced by his subject, he let his friends lead him to his seat. Becca, like the other students, was laughing so hard that tears were actually flowing down her face.

Larry cleared his throat, his relief all too visible on his face. "Very good, Barnaby. Okay, in summary, archaeology is part of anthropology, history, and science. Now, before we begin, I want to point out that none of you should leave today thinking you can go out on your own and start digging," Larry said, as the students looked disappointed. "You'll understand better why I'm saying this as we go. Most important, every archaeological site that is excavated is gone forever. We can't recreate it. If it is done with poor or improper planning and documentation, the information is lost forever to everyone. It's better to assist professional archaeologists and do it right. Only by understanding the how's and why's of excavation can all of the information be gathered and contributed to science. We can only understand the past by what's been left behind. If that's taken away, then there's nothing. Any questions?"

The students all shook their heads, although Barnaby raised his hand. Larry had obviously learned his lesson about Barnaby earlier and didn't want to risk another takeover. He pretended to not see Barnaby's hand.

"Good! Now, we've got an exciting day ahead of us, full of discoveries and learning new ways of doing things. This morning will be mostly a mock sandbox dig to learn about excavating. This afternoon we'll go on field trips visiting Cliff Palace and other ruins at Mesa Verde National Park. Finally we'll be visiting the Anasazi Heritage Center to learn more about the Anasazi and archaeology in this area," Larry announced, sensing the excitement that spread through the bleachers. Let's break up into groups of seven or eight. This will be your work group for the day. Bridget and Babette were in the same group, along with their new friend Becca, and Vic as their archaeologist. Barnaby was in a different group under Chico. Beauregard was still missing. They went to the classrooms in the administration building.

Vic grouped them around a large sandbox. "We're going to discuss the past and why it is important. When I call on you, please introduce yourself first so the group can learn who you are. Okay now, when your parents or grandparents or adult friends tell you about their childhood, although it's very real to them, don't you feel like you're listening to a fairy tale or story instead of something you've personally experienced?" Vic asked them. She pointed at a boy with long black hair and thick glasses next to Bridget.

"Hi, I'm Bruce. I'm fourteen, and I'm a Navajo. I live on Navajo Nation, just outside of Gallup, New Mexico," he told them. "To my parents, their childhood is a very real past to them. It is something they lived and experienced. It is memories they have and experiences they went through to help them become who they are today. They share those experiences to explain to me and my sister why they act the way they do. Though very real to them, their pasts are stories to us. I think who you are very much depends on what you learn and experience through your childhood and what you inherit from your parents, grandparents, great-grandparents, and other family."

"I agree, Bruce," Vic said. Bridget raised her hand and Vic selected her next.

"Today will be your past when tomorrow comes, right?" Bridget said, liking the sound of it. Almost like a line for a poem or a song lyric. Becca nudged her in the ribs, laughing again. "Oh yeah, I'm Bridget from New York City. Anyone want some gum?" She offered her bubble gum and most of the students took it.

"Thanks, Bridget," Vic said with a smile, obviously relieved that the Barnaby-lecture-syndrome didn't extend to his friends. "I'm trying to help you view even the far distant past as a continuation of a process that you are going through every day, as time passes. I'd like each of you to make a timeline showing the major events in your past up until today. A chronology of your life. Draw a line with a ruler, make dots and write in what you feel is important. When you can make your own past real, then make that of your parents real, and finally even relate to tools made by a Stone Age man as your ancestor. Then you're ready to begin learning how to become an archaeologist. Don't write your names on the papers, though. Hey, kids, what are you waiting for? Begin!" Vic said.

When the students finished, Vic collected the timelines and passed them out again. Each person had someone else's timeline. She called on a tall boy in the back row.

"Read that timeline out loud," Vic suggested.

"Okay. I'm Jesse from Frogmore, South Carolina," the boy drawled. "That's on St. Helena's Island in the low country. This timeline begins in 1984, birth. 1985, begin walking. 1988, get Sparky, my dog. 1989, begin school. 1990, meet best friend Juanita. 1994, trip to Anaheim, California, to Disneyland and Knott's Berry Farm. 1996, begin middle school," Jesse read.

"Good job, Jesse. What if that's all anyone in the future ever knew about that person? That timeline?" Vic asked them. Everyone looked at the timeline in their hands.

"This really says very little about the person," Babette pointed out.

Vic nodded. "True. Now, what if someone grabs the timeline out of a time capsule we plan to leave for future generations. They destroy it. What happens?"

"I'd be lost," a girl in the front row responded softly, "Future generations finding the time capsule wouldn't know I existed."

"Yes, you're probably right," Vic agreed, somberly. "And who are you?"

"I'm Felicité from a little town outside of Tucson," the girl replied. "Um, Arizona. Juanita is my best friend. She couldn't come with me, she has to babysit all of her little brothers and sisters." Felicité explained. "That's my timeline Jesse read, so I'm the one who would disappear if it was removed from the capsule."

Vic turned to the rest of them. "Archaeologists always try to figure out the age of the sites, artifacts, or events they're studying so they can place them in chronological order, into a timeline of sorts. They record this all very carefully. In fact, writing down everything and keeping accurate records is as important as finding anything. Otherwise, no one else knows and the information can be lost forever. We can use chronologies or timelines to study those people who probably never wanted to be forgotten, either. Let's make lists of why we might want to study the past, okay?" They began writing.

Meanwhile, on the other side of the classroom, Chico stood before his group with a portable flipchart. He drew several objects, then lines making layers.

"The clues about past lives are often buried," he told them. "They become buried over time by weather, erosion, gravity, and other factors. Archaeologists not only dig or rather peel the layers of accumulated dirt and materials to find artifacts, but they also record the location of everything they find. They not only write it down, but often take pictures of it and otherwise create records. This helps establish the chronological order of things. Objects discovered at the bottom of sites are usually oldest, while those near the surface are usually the youngest."

"Stratigraphy," Barnaby mumbled, absentmindedly, causing Chico to momentarily panic as he thought that Barnaby would begin another lecture. To his relief, the young scientist seemed lost in thought.

Barnaby couldn't stop worrying about Dr. Tempus and found it hard to concentrate on the field school. Across the classroom, he could see Bridget and Babette writing furiously. He wondered if he should sneak away and try to reach Dr. Tempus again or do something else. It was a dilemma. And where in the world had Beauregard disappeared to?

Little did he know that they had good reason to be worried. Quite a bit had happened after they left New York City for this field school. In fact, Dr. Tempus wasn't in his laboratory or even in New York City anymore. He was trying to fix a timeship called *Money Probe* so it would work again. He wasn't doing this willingly. In fact, a tall dark man stood at his back, holding a blunderbuss. By his feet, a threatening dog watched his every move. Dr. Tempus continued his work, worrying what would happen if the adventurers tried to call him in his lab and didn't get any answer.

He had no answers to give them.

✍ACTIVITIES ✍
Questions to Ponder

1. Why does excavating an archaeological site destroy it forever?

2. Make your own timeline showing important parts of your life from birth until today. Do you feel this timeline shows who you are? Why or why not?

3. Why is it important to leave artifacts in place at archaeological sites until all the information about their surroundings is recorded?

Food for Thought

Science is based on observation and inference. Any phenomenon being studied must first be observed. An inference is a reason proposed to explain an observation. The hypothesis is a chosen inference that the scientist will attempt to confirm or disprove through testing. Archaeologists use observation and inference to learn the story of past people.

By making observations about artifacts and sites (objects), archaeologists infer the behavior of the people who use the objects. When archaeologists find the remains of a large village (observation), they could infer that the people were farmers. To test that inference (hypothesis), they would look for evidence of farming such as farming implements like rakes, hoes, seed storage items, etc., and food remains from crops such as corn cobs or squash seeds. If they find these things, their hypothesis is verified. Archaeologists construct careful hypotheses by making inferences from archaeological data.

What do you observe about where you are right now? Write down your observations and then decide from your list what you can infer about your location. What proves your inference? What might disprove it?

Vocabulary

(Listed in glossary at back of book)

observation

projectile point

Chapter 5
Anasazi and Artifacts: The Sandbox Dig

"So this is sandbox digging?" Babette asked, as the seven of them surrounded one of four large plywood boxes filled with sand on the floor of the classroom.

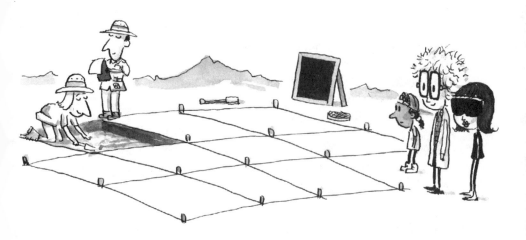

"It reminds me of when I was a little girl," Bridget said. I always loved playing in a sandbox at the playground! I used tractors, dump trucks, and construction toys, pretending to build highways and gravel pits. Sometimes I used plastic dinosaurs. All the other little kids would join me as I ordered them around our projects. I only used dolls when playing Doctor," Bridget admitted, laughing, "and my mom stopped buying me dolls when I cut all their hair and conducted brain surgery on them."

Babette and the other students laughed. "Remind me not to let you cut my hair," Babette joked good-naturedly. They knelt next to their sandbox, having plenty of room since it was eight feet long and four feet wide. It stood about twenty-four inches high, filled with gravelly sand. The other three groups, including Barnaby's, clustered around the other sandboxes.

Vic cleared her throat, getting their attention. "Archaeologists never just start digging. The excavation is a tool used to get information that can't be found in other ways. Remember, a dig destroys the site, so archaeologists have to have a good reason to start an excavation. Archaeology sites are nonrenewable resources. Does everyone understand what nonrenewable means?" Vic asked them.

"Nonrenewable means that once it's destroyed, you can't replace it," Jesse responded.

"True, Jesse thanks. Okay, archaeological sites cannot be replaced by natural ecological cycles or sound management practices," Vic informed them, "like forests. I can't emphasize enough that, once you dig a site, it's gone forever. Before we begin to dig, we need to know what we're trying to find out. We need to think carefully about what information we can only obtain by excavating the site, and then decide if that justifies disturbing the site and destroying it. Again, that's why record keeping is so important. Here's a form we'd like you to use to write down your observations, inference, and hypothesis. When the dig is finished, write down your conclusion at the bottom of the form. I call this doing the 'O.I.H.', though some students remember it by thinking, 'Oh, I hurt!' for short." Vic said with a laugh.

```
┌─────────────────────────────────────────────────────┐
│                                                       │
│        ARCHAEOLOGICAL SITE RECORDING FORM             │
│     Site Name:                                        │
│                                                       │
│     Setting: (Describe the surrounding land and plants.) │
│                                                       │
│                                                       │
│     Archaeological Remains: (Describe what you find, including │
│     permanent features such as buildings, fire hearths, or rock │
│     piles. Measuring features and counting artifacts may be useful.) │
│                                                       │
│                                                       │
│                                                       │
│     Artifacts:                                        │
│                                                       │
│     Other:                                            │
│                                                       │
│                                                       │
│     Site Size: (Measure the length and width of the site.) │
│                                                       │
│     Site Description: (Briefly describe the entire site.) │
│                                                       │
│                                                       │
│     Your Name(s):                                     │
│                                                       │
│     Today's Date:                                     │
│                                                       │
└─────────────────────────────────────────────────────┘
```

Vic passed out papers to all of the groups showing standard symbols and signs used on archaeological maps and drawings. Bridget took extra copies for Beauregard to put in his archaeology backpack. She knew they might need them later.

Becca raised her hand. "Observation, inference, hypothesis. Gotcha."

"Okay, I'm writing that down," said Jesse, with his slow southern accent. "Now, you asked what we-all want to find out from our dig, right? Well," he drawled, "I want to find out who lived here and when. What were their lives like? What did they do with their time? What did they make? What did they eat?" Jesse said. "Bet they didn't have huevos rancheros like we did this morning," he said with a grin.. "That's some cat you guys have! He can come home and cook for me anytime."

"Yeah, Beauregard is one in a zillion," Babette agreed, wondering where the cat had run off to and figuring he was probably searching out all those foodstuffs he'd been talking about last night. Babette peered closer into their sandbox, her voice rising excitedly. "Oh, look everybody! Little pieces of black and white things are mixed in with the sand! And rough orange-colored pieces sort of like sand rocks," Babette pointed out, causing everyone to examine the surface of their sandboxes.

"Babette noticed **sherds**, or pieces of broken pottery, and pieces of sandstone on the surface," Vic explained. "Write the information under "observations" on your form. You'll also need to record every artifact you find—and those are artifacts. You're beginning the 'observation' phase of the dig. What do those pottery sherds and sandstone tell you?"

Seeing the perplexed faces of the students, Vic said, "Black and white pottery is probably made by the **Anasazi**, who lived in this area about 1,200 to 700 years ago. The Anasazi also shaped sandstone and built apartment-style dwellings in cliffs." She continued, "Pottery sherds and pottery are one of the more common types of artifacts that archaeologists find in both prehistoric and historic sites. Fired clay is very durable, and pieces of vessels may last for thousands of years even if on the ground surface. Pottery styles are distinctive to particular groups of people and changed over time, so pottery helps archaeologists figure out how old a site is and which group of people lived there. Many clues can be gained by studying a pot's volume, size, and shape. Small-necked vessels probably stored liquids or very small seeds. Larger open vessels like bowls probably weren't used for storage because they're hard to seal," Vic concluded, satisfied to see most of the students scribbling the information on pottery in their notebooks.

"There are also some thin pieces of stone," Becca pointed out.

"Those are called **flakes** and are removed from a piece of rock small enough to hold by striking it with another object, probably one made of bone, antler, or other stone. Be careful, flakes sometimes have sharp edges and may have been used as cutting implements or tools. Sometimes flakes are left behind as waste products from **flintknapping**." Vic informed them.

"Now Bridget, what's your inference about this site?" Vic asked her.

"Oh, that's easy," Bridget responded. "I'm going to guess that the Anasazi lived at this site about 1,000 years ago. That's my inference."

"I think another inference might be that because there are pottery sherds, a pot may have broken here," Becca pointed out. "And the flakes show that tools or possibly weapons might have been made here."

"Good, kids. Write it down, okay? Write it down," Vic encouraged them. "Remember, your reports are as important as or may even be more important than what you find at the time. Your data may help fill in some information for someone else and other sites some day. You'll have reports to write and more research to do after your dig, so keeping great records is extremely important. Also, think of it as transporting information from the site to paper form. It's either record it or lose it. Record, record, record. Okay? Now, everyone repeat after me—"

"Record, record, record," they recited, anticipating what Vic was going to say.

"Good! Now for your hypothesis? Anyone? Let's see a show of hands for who has a hypothesis for this site. Good, Felicité?" Vic pointed at her.

"I think my hypothesis would come from Bridget's inference that the Anasazi lived here." Felicité said. "If most of the pottery we find is black and white or corrugated greyware, then yes, I think the Anasazi did live at this site about 1,000 years ago. The

Anasazi made black and white pottery for about 700 years I believe. If we find other stuff buried here not related to that time period, then it might have been some other group of people. My goal is to prove it or disprove the inference."

"Good Felicité, you've put together what you know about dating Anasazi sites to make a hypothesis," Vic praised her. "Anyone else?"

"I think if some of the pottery sherds fit together and have some similarities like painted designs or shapes, we can accept the hypothesis that a vessel broke in this location," Becca added.

"Okay, next we have to **plot** out the site. "Vic was obviously enjoying this. "You've got to use the string and plot out square sections. We've divided the sandbox into eight sections."

Barnaby raised his hand, and so did Bridget. Larry chose Bridget. "Two feet square," she pointed out.

"Four squares long by two squares wide, to make eight sections. Now, the first step in the excavation process is establishing the grid, by stretching string between the nails. You'll need to copy your sandbox grid onto your metric graph paper to create a mini-grid and **map**. We use a rectangular grid, like the Cartesian Coordinate System you learned in school. This sounds more complicated than it is," Vic assured them. "Each square will have its own map. You'll find the graph paper in your materials. You'll be writing down every artifact that you find and where you find it on your map, your O.I.H. form, and in your notes. Remember, it's extremely important to note any features and the precise location of the artifacts. Record, record, record."

"Okay, everyone, we've got lots to do today," the archaeologist named Suzanne pointed out. "Too much, actually. So maybe do the rap stuff later, okay?" Jesse nodded, returning to his sandbox, though many of the students kept absently tapping out the rap beat on the wooden walls of their sandboxes. The rhythm seemed to stick in everyone's heads.

"Okay, here's the string," Babette tossed an end of the white string out to Becca on the other side of their box. "Record, record, record," she sang softly. The sandboxes were already measured, and nails in the wood marked its division into squares. Becca stretched the string across from stake to stake until the sandbox was divided into two rows of four equal squares.

Bridget pointed to the nail in the southwest corner of the box. "That's our **datum point**, the point where our grid and dig starts. It's the point from which the entire site is measured and recorded," she explained. Jesse agreed to make the map, taking a clipboard and metric graph paper. They were making a good start. Bridget couldn't help herself and glanced slyly around. She was happy to see that they were ahead of the other three groups, and they only had seven instead of eight kids!

"Um, Bridget, what do I do with the graph paper?" Jesse asked, holding a pencil and ruler, as Babette, Felicité, and the others looked just as confused.

"Um, let's use two centimeters on the graph to represent ten centimeters in our section of the sandbox grid," Bridget answered.

Larry came over to help, pointing things out for them. "Now, attach these labels to the nails using the Cartesian Coordinate System. The datum point is A0, and each nail is numbered. This first row is Row A, the second row is Row B, and if we had a larger site, each row would continue through the alphabet. Got it, everybody? Good. Okay, this first section and nail next to the datum point is A0, the second nail is A1, the third A2, the fourth A3, and the fifth nail, but fourth section, is A4. These labels would also continue if we had a bigger site and can go indefinitely. The second row is the same except for B's instead of A's. Great! Grid done. Use those labels on your maps and notes to help record exactly where objects are found, okay? I think you're ready to begin excavating!"

Jesse studied his map on the graph paper with pride. It did look pretty great.

Bridget had her own notebook out and was checking her notes. "Okay, now we've made a rough sketch. Oh! Did you put a distance scale on the map? We're using 2 cm on our map for each 10 cm on the grid, right?"

"Right," Becca said.

"There, we've done the first step," Bridget said. "We surveyed the site and found the surface to be sandy gravel with a few artifacts of sandstone scattered over it. We've completed the second step and mapped the site, right?"

"Unbelievable," Babette mumbled, surprised at how much was involved. She wasn't sure how Bridget was figuring out all of this so fast.

Their map of their grid square looked something like this:

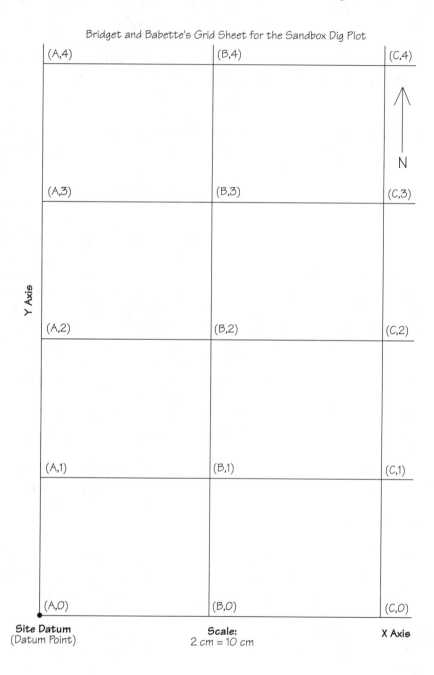

Bridget and Babette's Grid Sheet for the Sandbox Dig Plot

"Why do we have to spend so much time measuring, plotting, and drawing? I thought we were supposed to dig!" Babette complained.

"There is a lot of preparation that goes into an excavation before you dig! But where almost there," Bridget said. "Okay, let's see. We've got the grid laid out and lines strung to all the nails. The map is drawn to scale on paper and is ready to plot. There are no natural features like rocks or tree stumps or trees to mark on our map before we begin digging," Bridget pointed out. Babette smiled. Now that sounded good, something they wouldn't have to do.

Bridget continued leading their group. "Now, let's put on gloves. We have to record what we can see on the surface, then make notes on each layer. Remember, context is important. Then map the floor, including artifacts and where we found them. We need to write down any attributes like shapes and colors. Hey! I just had a great idea. Let's split up into pairs and each take two squares. We'll finish quicker than if all of us do one square on at a time. Um . . . What's your name?" Bridget pointed at one of the two kids she didn't know yet.

"Who, me?" The girl had a nice smile. "Hi, I'm Laurie Chan from Monterey, California. I'll help Becca," Laurie volunteered.

"Thanks, Laurie. And you?" Bridget asked the tall kid who looked more like a basketball player than an amateur archaeologist. He seemed to always be moving, having a hard time sitting still.

"I'm called Wheels, but my name's Wheeler," Wheels informed them. "Wheeler Thomas. I'm from Tacoma, Washington. I'd like to work with Felicité."

"Oooh," Jesse teased, poking Wheels, who ignored him and moved next to Felicité.

"Good idea, Wheels. Glad to meet you two. Let's see . . . why don't Becca and Laurie take B1 and B2. You and Felicité work together on the B3 and B4 sections. Jesse can work with Babette and me on A1 through A4 on this side. Then everything's covered. We can begin recording observations and then move to clear off the first layer." Bridget had organized them.

"This just seems SO technical somehow," Felicité pointed out. "How does it teach us about the people?"

"We're not just looking at pottery sherds and other artifacts, Felicité," Bridget explained. "People made them. Because they are here, we can assume people were here in the past. We look at the context of how we find the artifacts. We keep track of how artifacts from floors and other surfaces the people used are related. That way, we can figure out how the people used the places and the artifacts. It's the most important part of all! Does that make more sense to you? That's where our imagination and interpretation skills come in, to go beyond the data and facts and figure out what they tell us." The girl nodded.

"Okay, but like, we gotta write everything down that we find, as it's all bits and pieces of a puzzle, right?" Jesse said. "We can't figure out the puzzle until we have as many pieces as possible. The surface is just the beginning, right? We gotta carefully record where each artifact was found, then put it in a plastic bag," Jesse reminded them. He obviously played the drums, for he banged out his rap beat again on the side of the dig. "Record, record, record!" He sang as they laughed.

The seven students sat around their sandbox dig, carefully examining the sand for any objects, then showing them to Babette and Jesse to record the detailed information. They pointed out little details, like colors and shapes of paint on the sherds or sandstone pieces. They even found a couple broken projectile points in squares A3 and B4 and stone flakes on the surface of all of their squares. They also found a rawhide boot string, a piece of broken glass like that from the bottom of a bottle, and part of what turned out to be a can the size of a soup can. Two bottle caps were in the sand. They used a small whisk broom, paint brushes, and an old toothbrush to carefully brush the sand off the pottery sherds, sandstone, and other objects they found before removing them and placing them in plastic bags, carefully labeled. Each team within the group wrote the measurements of each surface artifact in their notebooks and drew in where they were found on the map of the site.

"When do we dig?" Babette wanted to know.

None of them had ever realized how much was involved in an excavation, and they knew they were only getting a sample of it. Actual sites could be huge. A few even required backhoes to move the soil.

"Now what?" Wheeler said impatiently, looking to Bridget for answers.

Bridget grabbed the pail that they were supposed to use for gravel and material they removed that was not artifacts. She then dumped her archaeology kit from her backpack onto a newspaper next to her.

"Okay, stratigraphy. **Stratification** is a process by which an area becomes layered due to human activity or actions by nature. We're need to study each layer. This surface layer is done. We've carefully scraped away the surface and put the stuff in the pail to take to the dump site.

Bridget picked up a small, narrow, pointed trowel. The other kids in the group copied her. She began carefully scraping away the first layer of sand, using the trowel. She dumped the sand in the pail. Soon, the pail was full and about three inches of sand had been removed. Babette emptied the pail for her, taking it to the huge box serving as their "dump" and pouring it through a screen. She returned with small pottery sherds that they missed because the pieces were hidden in the soft sand.

"Lucky there's a screen or we would've dumped these artifacts," Babette pointed out.

"Hey! Look! I found something!" Bridget said excitedly, her trowel hitting a rounded piece of pottery.

"Careful!" Vic cautioned, peering over Babette's shoulder as Bridget put the trowel down and picked up a large paintbrush, carefully sweeping the dirt away from the ceramic edges.

"It's a pot or something!" Babette said, watching in surprise as the small piece became a larger, undamaged vase or ceramic vessel. It had an intricate black and white design painted around it. It was beautiful!

Becca said, "I think we're supposed to make note of any large artifact and leave it where it is, so we can figure out the context before we try to take it out."

"True. Wheels, can you draw a picture of this pot in the notes," Bridget suggested.

"To help you date some of your artifacts, you can use **cross-dating**. That helps you indirectly establish a date for artifacts and sites. Remember I told you pottery and also stone projectile points were made in distinctive styles through time by different peoples? If we know that the Anasazi used specific designs on their pottery at only certain times, then we can assume that other similar pottery comes from the same time period. If the designs on the pot and the other pottery are similar to each other, then we know they are from the same time period. We can look at other site reports with dates to find similar designs. This will help us date our site! That's cross-dating. Often cross-dating is the only method archaeologists have to determine the age of sites. You can also make those assumptions for other pots found in the other sites that are similar in shape and design," Vic told them.

Within an hour, their group had carefully worked through most of their squares and uncovered several larger artifacts, from weapons and tools, to pottery sherds and even plant fragments found in a layer of clay near the bottom of the site. Wheeler even discovered the sole of an old boot near the surface.

"Probably the bootstring on the surface goes to this ol' boot," Wheeler pointed out.

"It's not rare to have a site show more than a single occupation or settlement of a group of people. It looks like you found a few newer artifacts mixed in with the Anasazi period stuff," Vic observed. "Make sure you've recorded all of that."

Wheels, Babette, and Felicité thoroughly recorded where they had found everything, mapped it, described it, and noted any other information they could think of. In addition to human-made items, they found one bone fragment. They also discovered ashes, blackened stones in a circle, and burnt charcoal, indicating that the area may have been a fire pit. Each item was carefully brushed with a toothbrush or fine paintbrush to remove all bits of sand and soil.

They had carefully tagged and labeled each item with where it was found. It had taken all morning to excavate the site. Measuring, analyzing, and studying artifacts found on a dig usually happen in the lab later, including looking at some things under a microscope or magnifying glass. None of the other groups had completed as much as theirs. They often heard Barnaby lecturing, slowing down his group beyond belief by overwhelming them with information. Most of the archaeologists seemed to hover around Barnaby's sandbox, trying to keep the progress going despite the young scientist's monologues filled with more information than the kids, and even the archaeologists, wanted to know!

"What do ya think?" Wheeler asked, as they all sat back and looked at everything.

"Looks to me like some stuff was left more recently, but the pottery, including the sherds and the sandstone pieces, the firepit, and other clues all seem to prove that the Anasazi were in this area and help prove our hypothesis," Bridget said.

"I agree," Becca said. "I think the boot, can, and glass may be from the old West or were left here recently, but most of the artifacts prove the Anasazi were once here. I don't think they lived here, for we didn't find any signs of any structures in our site, but they might have camped here or lived nearby."

"Well, let's write up our reports on what we think we found," Bridget suggested. Her new friends agreed. They got busy preparing their reports.

"Barnaby! Babette! Bridget!" The kids looked up to find Beauregard walking into the classroom. He looked disturbed.

"Beauregard!" His three friends left their sandbox digs to run up and pet the large cat happily. They had missed him. Beauregard tolerated their affection, but couldn't hide his impatience.

"What is it?" Bridget demanded.

Beauregard looked at his friends worriedly. "It's Dr. Tempus, he's been kidnapped!"

⚗ ACTIVITIES ⚗
Quiz #2
Finding the Clues

Match the definitions with the vocabulary words listed below.

_____ 1. Principle that an artifact found at one archaeological site will be the same approximate age as a similar one found at another site.

_____ 2. Theory or question to prove or disprove.

_____ 3. Conclusion based on observations.

_____ 4. An established point from which the entire site is measured and recorded.

_____ 5. Mapping a site.

_____ 6. Information, especially information organized for analysis.

_____ 7. A characteristic or property of an object, such as size, color, or shape.

_____ 8. Systematic arrangement in groups or categories according to established criteria.

_____ 9. Recognizing or noting a fact or occurrence.

_____ 10. Piece of broken pottery.

Vocabulary Words:

a. attribute
b. Classification
c. cross-dating
d. data
e. datum point
f. grid

g. hypothesis
h. inference
i. observation
j. sherd
k. strata

Questions to Ponder

1. Summarize how archaeologists use stratigraphy and cross-dating to study archaeological sites.

2. Make two lists of what you feel are renewable and nonrenewable resources. Explain why you classified the resources the way you did.

3. If the strata of a site have been mixed up by someone digging, farming, or otherwise disturbing the site, can the site still be studied using stratigraphy? If someone took a projectile point or dug out the large ceramic vessel from Bridget and Babette's site, how would it affect the information and context?

Food for Thought

From what was found in Bridget's group's sandbox dig, how would you write the report of their findings? What would you conclude? Was the hypothesis confirmed or not?

Vocabulary

(Listed in glossary at back of book)

Anasazi

cross-dating

flakes

flintknapping

map

plot

pottery sherds

stratification

survey

Chapter 6
Palaces and Cliff Dwellings

"Kidnapped?!" Bridget and Babette echoed Beauregard's words.

"Yes, Dr. Tempus has definitely been kidnapped!" Beauregard repeated worriedly, leading the other kids outdoors. "I tried to call him from the *Archy Stone*, but there was no answer. Then

I remembered to check Barnaby's Internet mailbox and found a this e-mail note:

>Hope all *Archy Stone* travelers arrived in Colorado safely? Can it be? Dastardly and Sneakers have arrived. I find it difficult to attribute their actions. They appear to be ransacking my laboratory. I hope this won't bode ill for your quest. Whatever happens, you must continue and not get sidetracked. Your quest is too important. I must go, Mr. Looter is demanding I accompany them, I w—<

"He didn't even sign it, but he was somehow able to send it before those thieves took him away,"

Beauregard said indignantly. "I believe our two perpetrators arrived at Liberty Island shortly after we departed for Colorado. I wonder if they still smell of dirty socks?"

"I think they stink even worse than that!" Bridget glowered, outraged that the duo would dare to accost their scientist.

"Poor Dr. Tempus kidnapped," Babette said, shaking her head. "Do you think they'll hurt him?"

"No. I bet they needed him to fix their timeship, the *Money Probe*. Remember? They said it wasn't working and they had lots of problems. Only, if Dr. Tempus fixes it, it means they might be able to find us," Beauregard worried.

"Oh no!" Bridget, Babette, and Barnaby exclaimed together. Barnaby added, "That's the last thing we need." The rest of the students were joining them outside now.

Larry interrupted, "We've got box lunches packed on the bus and we're already late. Everyone ready to go to Mesa Verde?" Larry noticed the cat. "Ah! The fourth member of your party has put in an appearance, I see," he observed.

Beauregard looked humble and apologized profusely, his usual good manners taking over despite their crisis. "Extremely sorry to miss the sandbox digs. I took the opportunity to do some research as I've done a few excavations before and dropped in on some archaeology classes at various colleges," he explained. He didn't bother to mention exactly what he was researching.

"Grrrr," the eerie grunt-like noise caused everyone to look skyward. It appeared to be the same huge black bird with silver gray flight feathers and a wingspan of about six feet that Bridget and Babette had noticed the night before. It was swooping so closely over them, they could see the reddish color of its head and its sharply hooked white beak. Its legs and feet were orange.

"Turkey vulture," Beauregard mumbled, staring in awe. "It's got a smaller head and slimmer tail than an eagle. It doesn't flap its wings very much, instead it tilts and glides, taking advantage of rising currents of warm air to gain altitude. It only makes noise when it's disturbed or senses danger." Like an eagle, it soared.

"It's not a buzzard?" Babette asked.

"No, no, it's not, though sometimes people mistakenly call it that," Beauregard said.

To their surprise, Babette groaned, sounding eerily like the huge bird. The bird retorted with more groans and a hissing sound.

"He's warning us of some danger, but I'm not sure what," she interpreted softly, so only her three friends could hear. They stared at her, goose bumps rising on the back of their necks. They knew about Babette's gift of languages, but to be able to talk to a type of bird she'd probably never seen before in her life? Babette was amazing!

His message given, the bird began spiraling and soaring upwards, its wings held upward in a shallow 'V', rocking side to side in flight. It only flapped its wings once, rising until it was just a dot against the bright afternoon sunshine.

"The bus is waiting," Larry said, rounding up the students.

"I'm returning to the *Archy Stone*," Beauregard told them abruptly, hurrying away before they could stop him. "Enjoy your field trip."

"I hope the danger isn't the bus ride," Barnaby commented as they climbed aboard. However, the ride to Mesa Verde National Park was spectacular! They ate their box lunches en route to the park, which was about twenty miles from their field school. From the main gate, the bus teetered up a very steep and curving road leading up through the cliffs and into the park. They could look out in all directions for hundreds of miles. They could see the huge haunting rock formation called Ship Rock in New Mexico. Larry informed them that the "ship" was actually a black volcanic plug, an old volcano core from its neck. It looked like a ghostly pirate ship in the midst of an ocean of sand.

They could see other desert formations to the south with the highway winding through them and the Navajo Nation. To the west was Ute Mountain, and even the Bear's Ears bordering Lake Powell in Utah could be seen 125 miles away! To the north was the was the Abaje or Blue Mountains in Utah and to the east were the white peaks of the La Platas.

They entered Mesa Verde National Park, following the winding road up the steep mesas and into the park. "This is one of the most visited archaeological sites in the entire United States," Larry informed them, as the bus continued its creaky climb. "The park is about 80 square miles with about 4,000 prehistoric sites, mostly Anasazi clans, ranging from the early basketmaker period with their pit houses built partially underground, to the large **pueblos** or villages the Anasazi built later. It was largely because of looting of the archaeological sites in A.D. 1906, that Mesa Verde became the first national park in America dedicated to archaeological conservation."

They were amazed to see the yellow sandstone hand-shaped brick ruins of what were once buildings along the cliffs, their golden rock walls still visible. After zigzagging up the steep sides of the mesa, the road winded through fields and forested areas. They passed a camping area bustling with people around their tents, campers, and R.V.'s. They went through a rock tunnel and resumed climbing higher upwards on the huge mesa. They passed several grazing deer herds; spied a soaring bald eagle and a hawk; laughed at a black and white magpie that hopped comically alongside the bus briefly; pointed at skittering rabbits and squirrels; paused for a waddling porcupine to cross the road; and continued to search for other wildlife. The bus rumbled and teetered through the freshly scented juniper, pinyon pine, and oak forests.

"Many small villages of Anasazi **clans** were built on the top of this mesa as early as A.D. 600," Larry told them.

"Doesn't Anasazi mean *ancient ones* or *enemy ancestors* in Navajo?" Babette asked. "And Mesa Verde means *the green table* in Spanish."

"Good, Babette!" Larry praised her. "You're pretty good with languages, I see! The culture archaeologists have identified as Anasazi covered several groups or clans of people who were first

identified by about 200 B.C. At that time, the Olmec culture was flourishing in Central America. Incan ancestors were also developing their cities, cultures, and technologies in South America. The Hohokam and Mogollon peoples lived in areas of Arizona and New Mexico and began forming clay inside baskets to create **pottery**. Hohokam engineers built irrigation canals and created the first etchings to etch designs on Pacific seashells."

"How were the Anasazi different? Bridget wondered.

Larry smiled. "The Anasazi lived in more permanent dwellings than the people who lived here before them. They grew crops instead of surviving by hunting and gathering. Corn was grown by 185 B.C. in Arizona. The Anasazi population continued to grow, making agriculture even more important. The people learned more about **cultivation** and preserved vegetables by sun drying. Seeds were ground into meal to make bread and cereals. Large pits were used for food storage. Pottery protected food from moisture, insects, and rodents. The small groups of people who lived at Mesa Verde from about A.D. 100 to 450 made brown pottery mostly with black and white designs and, along with the Mogollon with their redware and Hohokam buffware, traded their pottery as far away as the city of Teotihuacán in the Yucatan Peninsula."

"These people sound pretty advanced, not at all like I thought the people were like back then," Bridget pointed out.

"True, Bridget. I'm still amazed at their skills and lifeways myself at times," Larry admitted. "The growth of the Anasazi populations caused them to spread out from Arizona and New Mexico and come into Colorado and Utah. Trade routes were established. Traders brought goods throughout the Southwest. Some were exotic goods like the Pacific sea shells, live turkeys, or Mesoamerican parrots and macaws. The Anasazi lived here at Mesa Verde and nearby Hovenweep for about 700 years—from about A.D. 600 until they suddenly migrated elsewhere around A.D. 1300."

"Did they just build a huge city or what?" Becca asked.

"No. The size of their villages and settlements changed, from the first smaller single pit house dwellings built within the caves or partially underground, to above-ground clay or wood pueblo-style structures and farming settlements by their fields. As farming methods improved and the populations grew, big pit house pueblos and multiple-storied cliff dwellings were built and village live began. This cycle continued with smaller farm settlements, and then the larger cliff dwellings reaching their peak and highest populations between A. D. 1100 and 1300. We think there were over 35,000 people living in this area at it's peak, more than there are today. We're still not clear why the people appeared to just leave everything and migrate somewhere else. That would make a good research questions to investigate, wouldn't it?" The kids nodded, agreeing.

"These people lived here long before Christopher Columbus even sailed to the Americas, didn't they?" Laurie asked.

"Oh yes, Columbus's voyage was in A.D. 1492, almost 200 years after the mysterious migrations of the Anasazi people," Larry quickly assured them. He pulled over to the side of the road to let some of the cars pass them.

Bruce cleared his throat. "We think the story of somebody named Columbus discovering this land is ridiculous. Among native peoples, we know that Caribbean people were the ones who discovered him fooling around, lost in the ocean. He was sure he had landed in India, so he kept calling everyone Indians. We're not from that country. We lived on this land. We were here."

"Thanks Bruce, you're helping us to relearn the history of the Americas," Larry said somberly. "Few stories of human migrations have been as fascinating or raised as many questions as do those of the ancient peoples of the American Southwest. Archaeologists are still searching for clues through the study of ancient legends; artifacts such as pottery, baskets, and textiles; and studying ancient trails to help retrace the ancient people's footsteps. They're also studying impacts of other things, including the Sunset Crater volcano eruption in A.D. 1064, Haley's Comet in A.D. 1066, a full solar eclipse in A.D. 1076, and a huge drought affecting the entire Southwest in A.D. 1300. They know a construction boom following the astronomical events occurred, and there were bursts of creativity that ended with the devastating drought. People's lives had to change to survive, and many moved on in search of a better life, bringing this cultural period to a close," Larry concluded, pulling the bus back out onto the road.

"What were the Anasazi like, Larry?" Becca asked.

"Mostly farmers, growing corn, beans, and squashes. Their lifeways were exceptionally well-documented because of the dry desert soils. Even plant remains like corn cobs survived, along with clothing, sandals made from yucca plants, feathers, fiber rope, and even human burials that became mummified by the dry temperatures. Over time, these people developed more sophisticated pottery, architecture, and agricultural techniques. From A.D. 800 to 900, people built above-ground pueblo-style homes out of clay and sticks. By A.D. 950, most of the people had moved from the canyons and their small settlements, to the top of the mesas. From A.D. 1050 to about A.D. 1260, most of the villages were built within large cave-like alcoves, using stonewall masonry, the yellow sandstone and sometimes plaster on the upper walls of the deep canyons and gulches that cut through this mesa," Larry finished.

"You mentioned clans, how do you know they were of different clans?" Wheels asked.

"We know there were clans because of several carved and painted clan symbols on the sandstone mesa walls. Today, we believe most of their descendants live in pueblos throughout Arizona and New Mexico," Larry told them, at least, we think they are. "While visiting these ruins, we're asking you to walk softly, act respectfully, recognize history came before Columbus, and remember these people who were here before."

"What are alcoves? I thought they were cave-dwellings?" Wheeler asked.

"Alcoves aren't true caves and are the result of erosion from the surface winds and water seepage. Rangers here at Mesa Verde are careful to make the distinction between alcoves and caves. The buildings were made with walls of stone, then often covered with plaster." Larry told them.

"Why'd they build high up on the canyons and cliffs? Why not lower down where it would be easier to get to?" Felicité wondered.

"We think the Anasazi moved into the alcove villages because of better security against attack," Larry said. "We know they built round towers that we think were lookouts for raiders. They also had trained runners to cover the 150 or 200 miles to the Acoma Pueblo and Hopi villages. There was direct communication. By A.D. 1200, an elaborate system of roads and trade routes existed. As many as 1,000 **cliff dwellings** or houses built in overhangs or alcoves are from this period in Mesa Verde National Park."

"One thousand?" Barnaby echoed, as the bus lurched to a stop in a large parking lot. "Whoowee," he whistled. "That's a LOT!"

"Yup, sure is! And there are hundreds of medium-sized pueblos on top of the mesa. There may have been up to 7,000 people living up here at some times. Cliff Palace is the largest pueblo in the area and has 200 living rooms and twenty-three **kivas**. Spruce Tree House has 120 rooms and eight kivas. Long House has 150 rooms. There are also many mounds, the ruins of pueblos that may have each held hundreds of people, but we don't think they were lived in at the same time as the cliff dwellings."

"What's a kiva, Larry?" Bridget wanted to know.

"Ah yes, I haven't explained that, have I? You will see a kiva here at Cliff Palace. A kiva was usually a round room used as a ceremonial chamber and a meeting place," Larry explained.

"New research shows they also may have been living areas." He led them off the bus and along a concrete path with an observation point over a heavily wooded and deep canyon.

"Wow!" Barnaby gasped, pointing downwards to their left. The other students hurried to look over the railing of the observation deck and they all stared, amazed. Below them was the Cliff Palace, a dramatic stone village and apartment-like buildings built right into the cliff. They had never seen anything like it before. The reality was overwhelming. It looked like a toy village, except very real and alive with tiny people walking around the buildings.

"Hey, kids, are you coming?" Larry asked impatiently, leading them down steep stone-cut stairs and onto a narrow trail to where a park ranger waited to lead them down the steep sides of the canyon. "Cliff Palace was discovered in December of 1888, when cowboy Richard Wetherill was searching for stray cattle with his brother-in-law, Charlie Mason. The two men climbed steadily up the canyon on horseback, in the midst of snow flurries and failing light. They reached the top of the mesa and saw this astonishing sight. Clinging to those canyon cliffs was the entire mass of houses and towers of fine masonry, stacked on top of each other in terraces. It looked like a city that had been abandoned only the day before," the Ranger told them.

"Cool!" Bridget said, thinking how great it would be to be riding a horse and come upon such a fantastic find.

"When they entered Cliff Palace, timbers hung from the caved-in roofs, plaster still clung to the walls, and bones lay on the floors amid corn cobs and scraps of pottery. Wetherill wrote that it appeared 'as though the inhabitants had left everything they possessed right where they had used it last.' Their find gained international attention after Wetherill sold about $3,000 worth of 'Cliff Dweller' artifacts to the Denver Historical Society. Today, archaeologists have recovered not only those sold artifacts, but also clothing, sandals made from yucca plants, feathers, fiber rope, and even mummified human burials."

The group was surprised when the trail ended before sturdy timber ladders they had to climb to reach the trail edging the cliff and leading to the alcove village. Carefully, they moved along until they came to Cliff Palace itself. A wide walkway led along the excavated kivas, which the park ranger told them used to have roofs on them with a square hole in the center so the people could climb down into the large room by a ladder.

Though the buildings looked tiny from a distance, they were actually about 6-by-6-foot or 8-by-8-foot rooms. Some were two to three stories high, like apartments, built into the alcove. A few had plaster covering the large sandstone masonry.

"This is truly awesome!" Bridget announced. "I wonder how mothers kept their toddlers from falling off the edges of the cliff and into the canyon below?"

"Probably everyone watched out for them, and they might have used hemp rope as a halter to keep them from wandering off," the Ranger suggested. "We also suspect the canyons were probably not as densely wooded back then as they are today. We think wood was a greatly depleted resource. The type of sandstone in the overhang of these cliffs filters rain water and it would have been collected for drinking and washing," he pointed out. "Many of these buildings in Cliff Palace, such as the kiva, were excavated about a hundred years ago, with very little excavation taking place since then. Most of the artifacts found were sent to museums back east. However, many Anasazi things found in the park are at the museum at the Mesa Verde Visitor's Center."

"Will we get to see them?" Becca asked.

"Yes, come everybody, we've got to get to the visitor's center and then to the Anasazi Heritage Center, across the valley, for the day's going by too fast!"

They used the path at the other end of Cliff Palace, and had to climb another steep ladder against the cliff to reach the parking lot.

A large black cat was waiting for them by the bus.

"Beauregard!" Barnaby, Bridget, and Babette chorused, running up to pet their friend, obviously glad to see him. "How did you get here?"

"I transported from our timeship. We've got to get back to the *Archy Stone* immediately," Beauregard said anxiously. "I rounded up your overnight bags. If Bridget could do her little bubble conveyance, we can get back now," the cat suggested. He glanced at his watch and then up at the sky. The sun was no longer overhead and heavy shadows stretched from the surrounding trees onto the parking lot.

"There's no time to waste! Come on, Bridget! Blow!" Beauregard urged again, as Bridget quickly scribbled a note to explain their departure and sneaked it to Becca to give to Larry. It wouldn't do to have the archaeologist begin a park-wide search for them.

They walked around to the back of the bus to avoid the curious stares of the other students. Larry and their new friends didn't seem to notice they hadn't climbed onto the bus.

Bridget soon had a bubble so large that she was having a hard time staying on the ground. Her three friends grabbed onto her legs and waist and were soon soaring above the forests of the mesa, the view even more incredible from the air. The turkey vulture appeared, soaring next to them, as if watching over them as they floated along in the direction of the *Archy Stone*. They were amazed at how large the bird was.

"West, Bridget, go west!" Beauregard urged. They floated across the rest of the Mesa, noticing large strips of darkened land where wildfires had burned, and then downwards and across the valley towards the northern edge of Ute Mountain. They passed the Cortez airport and several farms. They could see more deep canyons and scattered farmlands towards Utah.

"There's the *Archy Stone*," Barnaby pointed. Bridget let air out of her bubble, bringing them down almost too fast. The turkey vulture left them. Bridget wished there were a way to perfect her landings.

They landed with a crash on the dirt road not far from where the *Archy Stone* waited.

"What's the rush?" Barnaby demanded, wiping the dust off that had covered them. "I'd wanted to check out the Anasazi Heritage Center, at least. And get my certificate for completing the program."

"I believe Dr. Tempus's kidnappers have already taken him to our first location, Laetoli in Tanzania, East Africa," Beauregard announced solemnly. "Dr. Tempus sent one word over the computer, 'Africa.' He must have sent it from the *Money Probe*."

Barnaby said, "What are we standing around here for? Let's go!"

"Go! Go! Go!" Babette echoed, hurriedly, buckling into her seat.

"Oh, by the way, here are your certificates of completion,"

Beauregard smiled, handing them the papers as Barnaby prepared the timeship for takeoff.

"Huh?" The three stared in amazement at their Certificates of Completion for the Eagle Mesa Archaeology Field School. "How did you—?"

"Another time," Beauregard promised, as Barnaby pulled the sculptured footprint out of the sack full of artifacts and placed it into the archyfactor so 'Laetoli, Tanzania, East Africa' showed up on the computer screen. He pushed the green button on the computer console and then—whoosh! The dizziness, the weightless feeling, the strangeness overwhelmed them, and Southwest Colorado became a blur of colors, and then only streaks of light and darkness were visible outside the wide windows. They were off.

✐ ACTIVITIES ✐
Learning about Cultures

1. What are some characteristics of the lifeways of the Anasazi?

2. Create a story about life in a cliff dwelling based on what you learned in this chapter, or imagine you were Richard Wetherill and came upon the cliff dwellings. Write down what you find, what you notice, and your feelings about your find.

3. Describe the environment (land, vegetation, and climate) the Anasazi lived in.

Food for Thought

You may want to research the Anasazi, using Internet and the library. How does the information you find help make more sense of the sandbox dig and field trip to Mesa Verde National Park?

Discover how objects and artifacts can help us learn about the lifeways and past of others. Find an old photograph taken at least fifty years ago from a magazine, or copy one from a book at a library (history book, periodical, etc.), or ask an older relative to give you one from their childhood. Make a list of all of the objects (artifacts) in the photograph and identify the items humans used to perform the activities in the picture. From the artifact list, identify which items are still in use today and which are not. What do the items that are no longer in use tell us about the past?

Try this same exercise using advertisements and list all of the artifacts shown in the advertisement. Explain what each artifact tells you about humans and their lifeways today.

A Bulletin Board Project for the Rest of the Book

You may want to start a bulletin board about archae-ology, posting a map and labeling where the kids and Beauregard travel, starting with this first field trip to Mesa Verde. Make and post notes about the people they learn about. Draw or obtain a large map to show where these people are located and estimated dates they lived there, and draw arrows to show migrations. Label landforms, bodies of water, cities, trails, or any other relevant geographical features referred to in the text.

Vocabulary

(Listed in glossary at back of book)

clans

cliff dwellings

Kiva

migrations

pottery

pueblos

Chapter 7
Footprints Out of Time: Africa

"Wh-where are we?" Bridget asked. They stared out of the windows of *Archy Stone* at the unfamiliar landscape. Gone was the desert and mesa environment of the American Southwest. Outside were wide patches of bare ground, bordered by flat-topped acacia trees, lava boulders, and tall grasses cut by sandstone gullies against the base of several mountains.

"Are we truly in Africa?" Babette whispered.

Barnaby checked the computer screen. "Definitely, we've arrived, though it looks like we just went back a few years to 1978. It's definitely Tanzania, though. Laetoli, here we come!"

"But it looks like there's nothing here. Just those funny-shaped trees—" Bridget shrugged.

"Acacia trees, in fact," Beauregard identified. "There may also be a few very wide-trunked trees called baobab. People use its bark to make paper, cloth, and rope. We're at the edge of the Serengeti Plain on an ancient plateau. Those rugged mountains are the Lemagrut, Sadiman, and Oldeani volcanos. Erosion, earthquakes, rivers, and volcanic eruptions destroyed much of the vegetation here, that's why it's so bare and there are so many gullies. There's also claystone, sandstone, and thick deposits of volcanic ash."

Barnaby nodded. "These conditions are ideal for preserving artifacts and fossils."

"And I thought it was going to be jungle!" Bridget sounded disappointed, but cheered up considerably when she noticed something in the distance. "Oh look! What's that?"

Something was moving along the rolling hills, coming their way. Mystified, they watched. Gradually, a very skinny man came into view. He used a thick stick to prod a water buffalo ahead of him along the trail. Occasionally, he poked the high grasses on each side. They could clearly see his misshapen and swollen knuckles, wrinkled face, and cloudy blue eyes squinting at their timeship.

"Oh, no!" Beauregard exclaimed. "That poor guy probably walks by here all the time and never saw a huge boulder here before. Looks like a bad case of rheumatism or cataracts is making his eyes like that. Wonder why he keeps swatting the grass? Our timeship probably appears blurry to him, or maybe he's blind?"

As the man and beast came closer, the kids could see large flies buzzing around them, especially around the water buffalo's nose. Its tail switched the flies off its back side. Before anyone could stop her, Babette rushed out to greet the man. They were soon conversing in earnest.

"I wish I could read their lips! But I doubt he speaks English," Bridget said, watching how easily Babette was talking with the man, both of them making broad gestures in the hot air.

"You'd have to read lips in Swahili, methinks," Beauregard observed. "Furthermore, I do believe the water buffalo's language is somewhat more limited." He sniffed disdainfully. "I, for one, am not in any hurry to converse with that huge, disgusting beast . . . nor its flies." He cracked them up. The inside of the *Archy Stone* rang with their laughter.

Babette returned, looking very pleased with herself. "Guess what?! This man, Taca, is a local Masai tribesman. He's been hired to work on excavations here at Laetoli with The Great Woman-Digger, he says. I suspect that's **Mary Leakey**. She's a famous archaeologist and paleoanthropologist. He says the ancient footprints are at this site. Let's check it out and see if they match our footprint. It's only a short hike up the trail beyond that hill to the camp. He said that archaeological digs are also in progress at **Olduvai Gorge**, about thirty miles away."

Bridget, Beauregard, and Barnaby grabbed their packs and headed out the door.

"No, no, wait!" Bridget yelled from the doorway, halting them. "Taca also warned me to be careful of puff adder snakes and ticks. Ugh!"

"No, no, no, no, no, no, no . . ." Beauregard moaned, running back inside the timeship, Bridget and Barnaby at his heels. Bridget hurriedly slammed the door, peering out fearfully. Beauregard was babbling, almost incoherently. "Tell me it's not s-s-s-snakes? P-p-puff adders are extremely poisonous vipers with thick bodies. They're also called hognose snakes. Even worse, they love c-c-c-cats! Oh no-no-no-no-no!" Beauregard rambled, incoherently. He no longer was in any hurry to leave the *Archy Stone*. "Pardon my absence on this great African adventure, but I'll stay here in case you need me to activate the transporter."

"Snakes are usually as frightened of people as we are of them. That's why Taca keeps hitting the grasses with that stick, to scare them away," Babette explained. "We're super lucky Dr. Tempus packed strong mosquito and tick repellent, huh? We'd better bathe in it."

"I'm definitely staying here," Beauregard mumbled again, sitting down at the computer and strapping himself in as if afraid the kids would force him to accompany them. "I'll watch everything on the monitor."

"Babette, anything else we should know?" Barnaby asked, wanting to get up to the camp. Bridget sprayed him with the disgusting mosquito and tick repellent.

"That stuff doesn't work on snakes," Beauregard warned.

Babette nodded. "We can hit the grasses, too. We'll be okay," she reassured them. Taca did mention something weird . . . some tale about a strange, big, shiny thing with green symbols. It didn't all make sense to me. He said this boulder appearing and that shiny thing are signs from his god for him to interpret. Taca's frustrated. He can't figure out any message, if there is one."

"What's he doing now?" Beauregard asked, pointing at the man outside the window. Taca looked around fearfully, then raised his thick wooden stick towards the sky and dramatically fell to his knees. He started bowing, his forehead to the ground, muttering something and holding his stick in front of him. He repeated it again and again. Finally, he stopped and glanced apprehensively again at their boulder, then stood up and prodded the water buffalo into a panicked gallop. Man and beast ran down the trail, disappearing from sight.

"Whew! Talk about stress," Bridget complained. "That Taca is obviously greatly disturbed and agitated. Babette, maybe it was your sudden disappearance? He doesn't know you're inside this boulder." She popped more bubble gum in her mouth and made sure she had a good supply for their field trip.

"True, poor Taca," Babette sympathized. "Maybe I should've taught him some special breathing or yoga exercises to help with stress. Oh well, too late now."

"You can teach me!" Beauregard offered, smiling.

"Not now, Beauregard. Let's check out this camp." Barnaby grabbed a broom, a mop, and a rake. He handed the mop and rake to Babette and Bridget. "To whack the grass and scare any snakes," he explained. They took the things gratefully and said goodbye to the cat, heading off up the trail and on their newest adventure.

"Who's Mary Leakey?" Bridget asked, intrigued, as they came up the hill to look out on the camp of tents set up near the shade of acacia trees about a half-mile or so below them. Bridget always liked to hear about women scientists.

"Oh, Mary Leakey may be one of the most famous archaeologists in the world," Barnaby told her, his voice deepening into his lecture-mode. They kept beating the grasses on the side of the trail, walking as he talked. The air was extremely hot and dry.

Barnaby continued. "Mary first became committed to anthropology when she was near our age, about eleven, when she visited a Cro-Magnon cave in southern France. Later, she took courses in anthropology and geology at University College in London and became an expert in stone tools. She married Louis Leakey, another famous paleoanthropologist. Because she was really a stone tool and Stone Age expert, she always felt she was more an archaeologist than a paleoanthropologist. The difference is that she dug more to find tools than to uncover human remains, but she still found several that changed the world's view of the origins of humankind."

"Whew! That's really something!" Bridget said admiringly when Barnaby finally paused a moment to take a deep breath. She'd love to do something that made such a big impact.

"Yes," Barnaby agreed. They reached the bottom of the hill and could spread out on the wider trail. "Mary's spent most of her adult life excavating sites here in Eastern Africa with her husband. Since he died, she's continued overseeing excavations, and her son Richard has continued the family tradition and also has made world-class finds at Lake Turkana sites here in Tanzania."

"Tell me about the finds!" Bridget prompted, pausing for breath.

Barnaby was glad to oblige. "At Olduvai Gorge in 1959, Mary Leakey found the 1.75 million-year-old skull of *Zinjanthropus*. The Zinj guy was later reclassified as *Australopithecus boisei*. This date first showed early **hominids** lived in Africa much earlier than was previously known. In 1975 at Laetoli, Mary discovered the 3.7 million-year-old jaws and teeth of a ***Homo*** species, and then of course, the trail of footprints. Trails of footprints were discovered in 1976, 1977, and 1978 and hopefully match our footprint cast. These Laetoli footprints are thought to be of the early hominid species *Australopithecus afarensis* and their estimated age is 3.75 million years old."

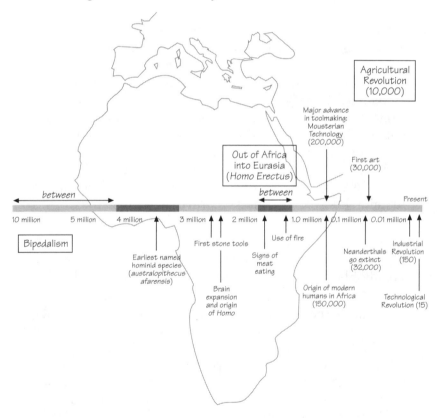

"Okay, I'm going to write this stuff down," Babette said. "Hmm . . . Hominids. *Australopithecus boisei* or *Zinjanthropus*

1.75 million years ago; then *Australopithecus afarensis* 3.75 million years ago. So the afarensis species is older and thought to possibly have made our footprint cast. Got it."

"Wow! Now *that* is a long, *long* time ago!" Bridget whistled, astounded. "We're talking *millions* of years, Barnaby? That blows my mind! Remember when we studied American History and we thought that Christopher Columbus coming to America in A.D. 1492 was a long time ago!" Bridget marveled. "I can't imagine people living millions of years ago and all of the peoples and histories that have happened between then and now," Bridget said, still awed.

"DON'T MOVE!" Babette paused only a few yards from the closest tent, holding her mop in the air, threatening something.

"What? What is it?" Barnaby said, both he and Bridget suddenly feeling the hairs on the back of their necks standing up. They, too, raised their broom and rake, holding them like baseball bats and prepared for battle.

"A snake. I don't know if it's a puff adder, but look there! It's HUGE!" Babette said, pointing at a thick black snake coiled on a rock only a few feet away. Its glassy eyes stared right at them. Without thinking, Bridget quickly blew a bubble and sealed it closed, pulled it out of her mouth, and threw it at the snake.

"Bridget! Wait! What are you doing?!" Babette yelled, shocked. She'd never read about bubble gum being a snake deterrent. However, the gum did its stuff. It stuck all over the snake's head, totally covering it, and causing it to fall and writhe on the ground, making hissing noises and seeming furious at this foreign stuff almost smothering him.

"Quick, RUN! RUN!" Bridget hollered, taking her own advice and rushing toward the nearest tent, Barnaby and Babette right on her heels.

"Well, hello!" A woman with several dalmatian dogs greeted them calmly. "Welcome! I hope you weren't being chased by an elephant. They've been pests these past few days, trying to trample on my field team."

"It was a s-s-snake," Babette gasped, trying to get her

breath. "Did you say elephants?" The woman nodded, unperturbed.

"Yes, the snakes have also been pesky this summer, especially those poisonous puff adders, for some inexplicable reason. Glad you got away. I'm Mary Leakey," she said with a strong British accent. Behind them something screamed 'go-waar, go-waar.' They jumped, their nerves still on end from the brush with the snake. "Those are bush birds, though we call them 'go-away' birds for obvious reasons. Something over there seems to have startled them. May I ask who you are and how you came to be at our digs?"

"You're Mary Leakey?!" Bridget smiled, thrilled to meet the woman scientist. "Want some gum?" She offered, handing out a piece. The woman shook her head, politely declining. "The bubbles work great on distracting snakes," Bridget added enticingly. The woman looked confused, obviously thinking she must have misunderstood.

Barnaby stepped forward, holding out his right hand. Mary Leakey shook hands with him. "I'm Barnaby and this is Bridget and Babette. We heard about your footprints and wanted to see them for ourselves, just to learn about our early ancestors," Barnaby quickly improvised, not answering her "how" question.

Babette nodded. "I've heard you've made some fantastic finds! From the Zinj human to the hominid footprints."

"I can certainly understand your wanting to see the footprints," Mary. Leakey agreed, patting her dalmatians. "This year we found the magnificent hominid footprints in a dual trail twenty-three meters (that's seventy-five feet) long. It's a most important find and settles a dispute about whether or not our earliest ancestors walked erect," she led them towards a grass-roofed shelter where many artifacts were strewn out and labeled on several portable tables in the midst of microscopes and many other items. A man was working intently at a table, painstakingly drawing artifacts into the tablet in front of him. "This is Nguli, one of my summer assistants. He's a fellow in Archaeology. His home Masai village isn't far from here," Mary Leakey informed them. "These youngsters are here to learn about the hominid footprints," she told Nguli.

"I can give them the background while you get ready for your interview," Nguli suggested. Mary looked relieved and left them to go to a desk in the corner of the tent. "Splendid!" Nguli beamed at them, his teeth dazzling white against his dark face. "Good to see young people interested in our finds! What a find it is! There are a total of forty-seven hominid prints, twenty made by a larger individual and twenty-seven by a smaller, possibly female, creature. It's too hot right now—the best time to view the footprints is in the early morning or late evening, but come see Mary's photographs. Mary's not working so much in the field this summer because she broke her ankle last summer and it's still very painful. Also, the BBC is making a television documentary about the footprints and interviewing her this afternoon. We have much to share about our earliest hominids."

"Excuse my ignorance, but what's a hominid?" Bridget asked, since the word kept cropping up but she'd never heard it before.

"Hominid is a term from the family *Hominidae*. We're a subspecies, *Homo sapiens sapiens*, of the *Homo sapiens* species. Our genus is *Homo* and that's part of the *Hominidae* family, under the order of **primates**. Primates share similar features, including: (1) enlarged brains; (2) big and forward-facing eyes; (3) distinctive middle ear structures; (4) collar bone; (5) reduced muzzle including nose, mouth, and chin; (6) thumbs made more for grasping; (5) distinctive heel bones; (6) a flat nail on the big toe; (7) usually nails instead of claws on other digits; (8) five flexible digits per limb; (9) separate tibia and fibula bones in the legs; and (10) a separate radius and ulna. Female primates usually have only one offspring at a time that sucks milk from two glands on the mother's chest. The young stay dependent on their mothers. Primates benefit from life in groups where individuals communicate food finds, combine for mutual defense, and pass on learned behavior," Nguli said, chuckling as he saw Babette struggling to write all of this down.

"Let me draw you a diagram, come." Nguli beckoned them into chairs at the tables and quickly drew a diagram that showed all the primates, including monkeys and other mammals. "Recent biomolecular evidence such as DNA and protein analysis points to the great apes of Africa as our closest living relatives. Based on the same evidence and by measuring degrees of difference in how the molecules are structured or how the immune system responds, some scientists believe humans, chimpanzees, and gorillas may have shared a common ancestor about 6 million to 8 million years ago. Again, this is all still considered theories or educated guesses. Some think the different species verged off as long ago as 40 million years ago. We continue to test, research, and look for more clues," Nguli told them.

Barnaby seemed to understand all of this the most. Nguli pointed at the tables covered with artifacts and continued, "While we've had many skulls and pieces of skeletons that have helped identify other early hominid species, there is still no fully accepted chronology of human beginnings. The proof of **bipedal** walking, increased intelligence, and **omnivorous**—both vegetation and meat—diet is proven in several early human species. We know that about 4 million years ago, bipedalism began in several species that were sort of 'human-apes'. Walking on two legs left their hands free and helped develop skills unique to humankind. We think some of these changes happened as a result of climatic change caused by the events of the Ice Ages "

"How could the Ice Ages make such a difference?" Bridget wondered. Although some of this was confusing, she found it fascinating all the same. This made much more sense to her than what she'd known earlier about **Charles Darwin** and his **Theory of Evolution**. Especially when she could actually see some of the skulls and bones of these early ancestors on the tables around her and in photographs in front of her. They were truly real!

"Well, by 3.5 million years ago, the Ice Age cold was locking up so much water that rainfall lessened worldwide. Tropical grasslands took over the shrinking forests. Here in Africa, savannah animals multiplied. Some of the ape-like creatures adapted from the forest life to the savannah also, these were **australopiths**, and the first 'true human' was likely their descendent. This is where our find of the footprints comes in. These footprints dated to 3.8 million years ago prove there was a creature with a footprint similar to modern humans that walked on two legs, bipedal. By freeing up the hands that used to be needed for climbing, grasping, and getting around, now they could be used for tools and building or carrying things. Making and using tools helped lead to intelligent thought, at least we think so. That idea, too, is controversial."

The contours of the Hominid footprint (left) are surprisingly similar to the modern human footprint (right). The contours show that weight and shape distribution are also similar.

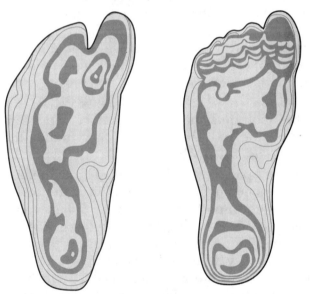

Then Nguli showed them some enlarged black and white photos of the trail of footprints. "This is the largest trail we found. Some 3.8 million years ago, the volcano Sadiman began a series of light-ash eruptions. The ashfalls occurred for several weeks as the dry season gave way to the wet. We found animal prints or hominid prints wherever a particular layer of volcanic ash, or **tuff**, was exposed. Eventually we identified eighteen sites with tracks worth recording, though our long hominid footprint trail wasn't found and excavated until this summer, our third season here. The ash in these locations is about six inches thick, gray and fine-grained. It looks and feels something like ancient slabs of cement, as you can see." The photo Nguli showed them looked like their footprint cast. The kids could hardly contain their excitement. It looked like they had lucked out! They'd identified the origins of the footprint cast.

"How did you find the trail?" Bridget asked.

Nguli smiled, beckoning for them to follow him. "Let's go see the real thing. We found four prints two summers ago, interestingly when one of the guest scientists was teasing the others by throwing elephant dung at them. In the process, he stumbled onto the first print. When we discovered more, scientists argued whether they were hominid or animal prints. We wanted to find hominid prints and kept at it until we did," Nguli said happily. "This was after months and months of work. This is not easy work. Finds don't happen without more work than most people are willing to do."

"Are the footprints more important in understanding human evolution and early humans than finding human skeletons would be?" Babette asked curiously.

Nguli smiled patiently as they walked through the camp towards the hominid footprint trail. "In many ways, the prints are more important than bones. When you have bones—and scientists have gathered *australopith* leg, knee, and foot bones found at sites as far apart as South Africa and Ethiopia—they were still unable to agree about the early hominid's posture and gait. Bones could be interpreted in many ways, but the footprint trail is graphically clear," he said proudly. "Those early hominids stood upright and walked on two legs as easily as any **Homo Sapiens** do today," Nguli told them. "Interestingly, at one point on the second trail, the smaller, possibly female, person even stopped and turned momentarily to the left, then continued on her way. It looks as if she saw or heard something and turned to have a closer look. It gives the whole thing a very human aspect."

"It does, doesn't it?" Bridget agreed, studying the picture he had given them.

"At one point, we thought we even had a romance on our hands," the man laughed, enjoying the kids' obvious interest.

"A romance? How so?" Babette asked.

"Well, we thought the tracks might have been left by a male and female, whom we nicknamed Adam and Eve." He chuckled. "That might explain the size difference, though the larger prints were blurred as if the male had shuffled or dragged his feet. But then again, maybe the ground was simply loose and dusty. Another intriguing fact about the footprints is that some of the prints seemed way too large, like eleven to twelve inches, or twenty-eight to thirty centimeters. The australopiths were small, the largest only about 5'2", or 157 centimeters."

"This doesn't sound like romance, just because some prints were big and the people were small!" Bridget pointed out.

"True, forgive me for rambling," Nguli said. "Anyway, to explain the romance theory. We thought the two individuals were keeping step and walking very close together, occasionally stepping in each other's footprints. When we tried it, we realized they had to be almost too close together, walking arm-in-arm. At that point, Mary thought we should name the trail "Lover's Lane." Most of the summer, we discussed this: How did the trail happen? What were the hominids doing? It was a great mystery."

"And?" Bridget prompted, wanting to hear the outcome.

"And, we didn't think it was possible to walk that close together. We thought this behavior in the Pliocene—"

"Huh?" Bridget interrupted.

"Pliocene. That's the **Geologic Period of Time** from about 2 million to 5 million years ago," Nguli answered.

Barnaby perked up. He knew geologic time! "Yes, the Pliocene was followed by the period of the last great Ice Age, the **Pleistocene**, from about 2 million to 10,000 years ago. The period of time since then, from about 10,000 years ago through the present, has been named the **Holocene**. So we're living in the Holocene. If you really want to be wowed . . . the Pleistocene and Holocene are part of the Quaternary Epic in the Cenozoic Period. The Pliocene is one of five epics in the Tertiary Period of time dating from 65 million years ago. What you've undoubtedly heard about was the Jurassic period of the Mesozoic, because of the dinosaur movie *Jurassic Park* . . ."

"Barnaby! I don't want to be wowed. We were having a discussion here. That's quite enough on geologic time," Bridget said. "Let's get back to the great footprint trail mystery. Did anyone discover what was going on? Why they were so close together? Why were some prints so large? Do you want some bubble gum?"

"Yeah, I'll have some gum. If you can believe it, only today was the mystery solved!" Nguli informed them.

"Today? How?" Bridget asked, intrigued.

"By the BBC cinematographer filming Mary's interview today. He said the footprint puzzle was easy, for there were actually three hominids walking together when the volcano erupted. One had deliberately walked in the footsteps of the other, following the leader. As he reminded us, chimpanzees often do this for fun or when they're nervous, with the one behind holding onto the hips of the one in front."

"I've done that in deep snow before in upstate New York," Bridget said, remembering. "I followed in my dad's footsteps and held onto his waist to keep from falling in the deep snowdrifts. That's amazing. I'm glad the mystery is solved."

Babette cleared her throat. "Nguli, how did you come to pick this site to excavate in the first place? I've been wondering about that ever since I learned about digs and archaeology. How do you know where to dig?" They were following a rocky trail through the bush. The kids all kept a wary eye out for snakes or stampeding elephants, swatting the brush with their house tools—the broom, mop, and rake—to Nguli's amusement. Bridget kept chewing her gum, adding pieces, in case she would need it.

Nguli nodded, remembering when he had once wondered the same thing. "Clues to the past often are found by chance. Natural forces, such as the wind, rain, erosion, or even burrowing animals, may uncover remains. Many accidental discoveries have been made by people hiking, plowing, fishing, or involved in construction work. Some remains are obvious, like ancient temples, stone statues, mounds of earth, or pieces of broken pottery. Aerial photographs can show crop marks, shadow marks, and soil marks, and infrared photographs can help archaeologists identify sites. Written evidence, sonar waves or echoes from the deep, magnetic clues due to the changed strength of the earth's magnetic field, and electrical clues by measuring the resistance to an electric current passed through the ground are all other ways archaeologists identify potential sites. Underwater remains can also be found using sonar equipment."

"Or you can use Beauregard to find sites," Barnaby added.

"And I thought they found sites based on legends and myths," Babette said.

"True, legends can also help archaeologists because they're sometimes based on facts and have sometimes helped find spectacular discoveries. Archaeologists searching for Noah's Ark, for example, have uncovered countless artifacts in their search. The Greek legend about a Minotaur—half bull and half man—living in a labyrinth in Knossos on the island of Crete led one archaeologist, Arthur Evans, to uncover a vast palace at Knossos with a layout as complex as any labyrinth. Knossos had many earthquakes, which can sound like an angry bull," Nguli told them.

"Why did you excavate here, at Laetoli?" Bridget wondered.

"Oh, Mary Leakey actually visited the site with her late husband, Louis, twice before setting up a camp and excavations here. In 1935, a Masai tribesman showed them fossils he found in this area, including fragments of extinct elephants, antelopes, rhinos, and giraffe. On their first journey, Louis even found a hominid's tooth, but at the time he thought it was a monkey's. **Potassium-Argon dating** hadn't been developed back then. In 1939, another explorer and scientist, the German Dr. Ludwig Kohl-Larsen, discovered a fossilized hominid tooth and very primitive elephant specimens. These finds intrigued Mary. By 1974, when her friend and neighbor George Dove showed her a handful of fossilized zebra and antelope teeth from Laetoli, she became more than interested. She decided to conduct excavations of her own. Louis had died by then. I came to help, as the earlier finds were discovered by a friend of my father's. I got my bachelor's degree in anthropology, then went on to complete my master's in archaeology. Now I'm working on my doctorate. I always wanted to become an archaeologist," Nguli told them.

"That explains a lot," Bridget agreed. "What makes a creature human, then? Standing on two feet?"

"No, Mary thinks it's the way hominids began using tools," Nguli said. "Though walking on two feet definitely plays a significant and possibly the primary role. We don't know exactly why these hominids stopped using all four limbs to get around and began walking on two feet."

"But today many primates, birds, and other species use tools," Barnaby pointed out.

"They don't make them, though," Nguli explained.

"We may still find irrevocable facts," Barnaby pointed out. "After all, it was very recently that scientists finally found proof that an asteroid hit the earth by the Yucatan peninsula, wiping out the last of the dinosaurs on Earth and opening the possibilities of potential dangers to the human race. My point is what this discovery has done to modern scientific theory and thought . . .."

"Asteroid? What discovery is this?" Nguli demanded, obviously surprised by the news. "When? Where?"

"Barnaby, it's 1978," Bridget said hurriedly, reminding him. Barnaby grew red. Suddenly, a local man came rushing up to them on the trail, yelling indecipherably in his local language, then continuing on toward the camp.

"LET'S GO!" Nguli called back to them as he began running up the trail. The three kids followed. The extremely hot, dry winds rushed against them like heat from a furnace. They came to the trail of footprints, two rows in the hard cement-like material, exactly like the one they had back in the *Archy Stone*.

"We're here. It's the footprints!" Barnaby said happily, recognizing the footprints, leaning over to try to get more oxygen.

"Yikes! What are we going to do?" Babette gasped, not looking down, but staring straight ahead.

"Do?" Bridget and Barnaby echoed together, looking at Babette like she was out of her mind.

"Yeah! Now that Dastardly has found us," Babette pointed at the silver *Money Probe*, its green dollar sign prominent on the side of the timeship. It was parked at the end of the footprint trail, across a gully.

"Maybe we'd better get outta here," Bridget suggested, "and return the footprint to its own time." She was too late. Dastardly appeared, pointing his blunderbuss at the crowd of about thirty people gathering in front of him. Many of the Kamba and Masai workers gestured and talked excitedly in their own languages, obviously never having seen a blunderbuss before, let alone knowing what the timeship was.

"Big shiny thing with a green symbol. It was Dastardly Looter!" Babette said, snapping her fingers as she realized what Taca the Masai tribesman had been talking about.

"I want the kids!" Dastardly yelled threateningly, screaming to be heard over the commotion. "And I want my property! NOW, no arguments accepted!" Sneakers and Dr. Tempus were nowhere in sight.

"You can't have them!" Mary Leakey proclaimed defiantly, saying something in Swahili. Instantly, several of her workers surrounded the three of them. "Property?" Nguli whispered, bewildered.

Dastardly crossed the footprint trail, ignoring the prints at his feet. He scowled at them and the three kids huddled closer together behind the barrier of the local workers. As Dastardly approached, he pulled an object from his pocket. Barnaby recognized the red pepper shaker from his laboratory.

"Oh no! Duck!" He yelled, just as Dastardly shook the contents onto the tribesmen. They screamed and began rolling on the ground, rubbing at their eyes. Dastardly came closer, reaching out triumphantly towards the kids.

"I wouldn't do that if I were you . . ." Barnaby warned, moving to give Babette more room. She crouched into her martial arts position, ready to defend them. Dastardly moved towards her, appearing as if in slow motion. Bridget, hiding behind Barnaby, began blowing a bubble as fast as she could, hoping to provide them with an escape. It was lifting her already. Barnaby caught her feet, yelling for Babette to grab on.

"Hee-yahhhh-" Babette screamed, using a karate kick to knock the blunderbuss out of the man's hand. She twirled so fast she was just a blur as she again crouched into position. Dastardly reached upward, trying to grab Barnaby before Bridget's bubble caused them to rise in the hot air, but he missed. Babette landed a half-kick against the man's soft stomach, careful to only knock the wind out of him to give them time to escape.

"Oof!" Dastardly groaned, doubling over and actually growling. The workers were getting up from the ground, still moaning in pain and rubbing their stinging eyes, but they caused Dastardly to stagger and trip.

Babette swirled again, getting ready to push the man over onto the dirt. Her foot came up and—

"Owww! Ouch!" Babette cried as her foot struck the inside wall of their timeship instead of Dastardly's shoulder.

"Transporter," Beauregard announced happily. "Welcome back. I saw your progress to the footprints using the binocular camcorder device and was able to zoom in on all the action. Thought you'd probably want to get out of that hot air," he snickered, pointing to an infuriated Dastardly tearing at his hair and shaking his fists in the air on the computer monitor. "Now to retrieve those floating friends of ours. Bridget and Barnaby rose so fast they're heading directly for the volcanic peaks! I fear a collision."

With a flick of a switch, Bridget and Barnaby materialized inside the timeship, quickly rising to the ceiling under Bridget's bubble. Bridget opened her mouth and they came flying downward, landing on the floor in a heap.

"As always, a very graceful landing," Beauregard observed. "Welcome back."

Babette helped Barnaby up and pushed him toward the computer console. "Quickly! Let's put in the data about the footprints and get out of here! Dastardly's too close for comfort," she exclaimed, watching Barnaby quickly punch in the data. They were off with a rumbling and the darkness and a jolt.

Unfortunately, Barnaby had sent the timeship off before his fellow travelers had buckled into their seats, and they were now lying around the floor of the timeship looking dazed.

"Well, we're here in the far past, when the footprints were made. What's that noise? What's going on?" Barnaby announced, helping Babette to her feet. The timeship was vibrating and shaking and there was a roaring in the air like an angry bull. They couldn't see much because of the rain.

"Would you believe a volcano? Erupting?" Beauregard explained matter-of-factly. Outside, the grasslands moved like a river.

"Look! It's animals!" Bridget gasped. She was right; the "river" was actually herds of many different types of animals, all stampeding away from the mountain that billowed smoke, ash, and bright orange flames angrily into the air. What looked like a family was heading their way, the child following behind in her father's footprints. The trio passed by their timeship, ignoring the huge boulder, intent on getting away from the spewing volcano. They were too far away to see their features, but the kids and Beauregard stood watching, fascinated, realizing they were watching early humans setting down marks that wouldn't be uncovered for millions of years.

"I'll take our footprint back out there in that softened ash," Barnaby suggested, his voice loud in the stunned quiet of the timeship's cabin. "Then we'd better get out of here before we're buried in ash or damaged by the volcano ourselves!"

"In-cred-i-ble! They truly do look human from this distance," Babette pointed out.

"Nothing like the Flintstones!" Bridget added.

"Flintstones," Barnaby groaned. He took the footprint out of the archyfactor and hurried out of the timeship with Beauregard behind him to help watch for stampeding animals. The family had wandered off with the disappearing herds of animals and were almost out of sight, leaving the trail behind them. Barnaby immediately found the hole where the footprint was missing in the trail, replacing it and thus preventing Mary Leakey and future scientists from puzzling over yet another mystery: how a footprint came to be missing from the middle of their trail. Beauregard used his tail to wipe their own prints out of the ash.

"RUN!" Beauregard yelled, as the earth began to shake and more ash showered down on them. "Hurry, run!" They turned to see a stampede of animals coming their way. They only had moments to escape. Running for their lives, for what felt like the third time that day, Beauregard and Barnaby made it back to the timeship.

More herds of the ancient animals came stampeding across the plains, crossing near where they'd been standing only moments before, but missing the trails of footprints.

"You could've been trampled to death," Bridget gasped.

"Whew, mission accomplished," Babette said, buckling into her seat.

"Mission has just begun!" Barnaby pointed out, lifting the sack.

"This adventure makes me feel . . . almost human!" Beauregard observed, also buckling in.

"Beauregard may feel human, but as the French writer Fernand Mery wrote, 'With the qualities of cleanliness, affection, patience, dignity, and courage that cats have, how many of us . . . would be capable of becoming cats?'" Babette laughed.

Beauregard puffed up importantly. "True. He also said that 'God made the cat in order that man might have the pleasure of caressing the lion.' But enough of this banter. We have so many things to return and time's going by without much progress, even if we're finally beginning our quest. Let's hurry!" Barnaby quickly placed the next artifact in the archyfactor, pushed a few buttons, and they were off.

⚐ACTIVITIES ⚐
Our Early Ancestors

1. How were the footprints found at Laetoli preserved for 3.8 million years? What are some other ways fossils and artifacts are preserved?

2. How do archaeologists decide where to excavate? Why did Mary Leakey and her team excavate at Laetoli?

3. List the ten characteristics of primates mentioned in this chapter.

4. How do you think the Ice Age climate affected bi-pedalism (walking on two feet)?

Word Puzzle.

See if you can find some of the words from this chapter in this puzzle.

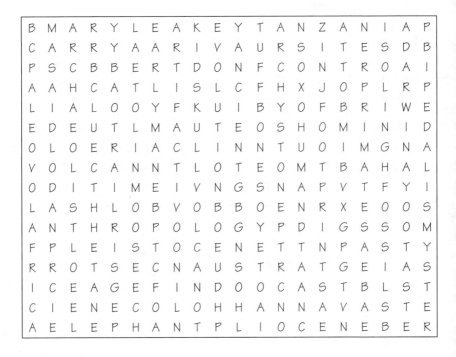

__A.D.
__Africa
__Ancient
__Anthropology
Archy Stone
__Artifact
__Ash
__B.C.
__B.P.
__Bipedalism
__Bones
__Carry
__Cast
__Cat
__Clue
__Darwin
__Dig
__Early Man
__Elephant
__Evolution
__Find
__Footprints

__Fossil
__Holocene
__Human
__Ice Age
__Kids
__Laetoli
__Mary Leakey
__Masai
__Old
__Paleo
__Past
__Pleistocene
__Primates
__Savannah
__Skull
__Tanzania
__Time
__Trail
__Tuff
__Volcano
__Zinj

Food for Thought

1. Create a knowledge chart, dividing your paper in two columns. In one column, list what you know about early humans, and in the second column, list what you want to learn.

2. List basic human needs such as water, food, etc. Then write a story about how you imagine the australopith hominids who made the Laetoli footprints met these needs. What do you think their lives were like?

Vocabulary

(Listed in glossary at back of book)

australopiths

bipedal

Holocene

Homo sapiens

Mary Leakey

Olduvai Gorge

omnivorous

Chapter 8
Cave and Rock Art: The Paleolithic

"How did you DO that?" Bridget demanded, standing in front of the cave and reaching out to grab the solid rock, as if to get her balance.

"Barnaby? Didn't you hear me? How did we get here? One minute you were pulling out that panel thing from the sack and putting it into the archyfactor. Now we're in front of a cave. This is a CAVE, Barnaby. We're not in the timeship. We're not in Africa anymore, at least I don't think so. Where's the *Archy Stone*? How in the world did you get us here, just like that?" Bridget snapped her fingers in front of the young scientist's face. "I feel like I blinked and everything changed. Whoa . . . this is moving a bit too fast for me. I don't like it."

"I agree, things have a way of getting stranger and stranger," Beauregard said, studying his manicured paw and looking remarkably calm despite their situation. Freezing rain was falling, obscuring the surrounding mountains and farming valleys below. They stood under the cave's overhang, shivering.

"One other thing . . . I am COLD. I am not dressed for this, Barnaby. However you did it, you REALLY did it this time!" Bridget continued.

"Um, anyone have any wild guesses where we are?" Babette wondered. "Pinch me, I think I'm dreaming. *Ouch!* Bridget, that hurt!" Babette whirled on the other girl, assuming her karate stance, a dangerous gleam in her eye.

"Wait, don't attack, Babette! You said to pinch you and I did." Bridget moved in haste away from her friend, careful not to get too close to the ledge. She put up her hands protectively. "Okay, okay, I'm sorry. I'll remember next time not to do what you tell me, okay? *Especially* if you tell me to pinch you, I won't! Really! I promise! Cross my heart and hope to eat Beauregard's mousaroni and cheese if I'm not telling you the truth!" She chewed her gum ferociously, hoping it would help her to think. She was glad she had her baseball cap on, as the wet sleet tended to sprinkle them when the wind gusted.

"I can always whip you up a dish, when I get back to a kitchen," Beauregard offered magnanimously, not understanding when the others laughed. Their chuckles broke the ice . . . or, rather, loosened the accumulation of sleet over their heads, for they had to jump back into the mouth of the cave to avoid it dripping onto their heads and, icy cold, down their backs.

"I deeply regret whatever I did to make this happen," Barnaby apologized, wiping the icy gray stuff off his head and neck. "Ah!

Look here! At least there's an umbrella and some packets of hand-warmers," he picked the items up off the ledge from around his feet. The others stared, wondering where in the world the things had come from. Barnaby continued, "In answer to your queries, we do appear to be in a cave . . . but where we are in time and how we got here, I'll confess I have NO idea." He opened the umbrella for all of them to huddle under together. It did seem to keep some of the mist off of them. Bridget and Babette warmed their hands with the little handwarmer packets that Barnaby informed them he had once invented in his laboratory, using thermomolecular theories, of course, but he professed amazement at finding his inventions here.

Standing close together was also warming. Barnaby wished he had his coat on, too. It was quite an environmental shock to go from the heat of the African savannah to this cold and wet environment in the blink of an eye.

"I believe we're at some time in the present, as I can hear sounds of a tractor or farm machinery from below the fog," Beauregard pointed out. "If it's machinery, it's at least the nineteenth century. I also think I detected a horn, like a car horn. Sound carries better through fog or over water. Therefore, we can take solace that we're not lost in time," the cat concluded, and began grooming his fur where the wet stuff had fallen on him.

"Thanks, Beauregard. That's some help," Babette sighed.

"Great scenario, huh?" Bridget grumped. "Tell me, what's wrong with this picture? Huh? Someone puh-leeze tell me what's going on!"

"I may have an explanation," Beauregard announced, holding up a thick archaeology textbook he picked up from the stone ledge next to where Barnaby had retrieved the umbrella and handwarmers. "Apparently our arrival at this cave jolted the book, and the other items, out of Barnaby's hair."

"Barnaby, can you give us some coats? Sweatshirts? Sweaters? Scarves?" Bridget pleaded, shaking her friend as if it would help. Of course, nothing happened.

Beauregard cleared his throat and pointed at the words with one perfectly manicured claw. "This book says some sites such as caves in western Europe provide important lessons about the early but fully modern members of your species. This evidence has existed for at least the last 50,000 years. Their hunting and gathering, migratory ways of life persisted widely throughout the world long after the climate shift of 10,000 to 12,000 years ago. That was when the most recent glacial phase of the Pleistocene, ended."

"Ply-stow-scene? I like it!" Bridget grinned, trying the word out.

Babette rolled her eyes, saying,. "Bridget, we learned about the Pleistocene in Africa."

"True. Now we're in the Holocene, as we also learned in Africa," Beauregard pointed out. "I can see someone was too busy chewing gum and must've missed that! Anyway, back to this book. Okay, the belief systems of these **hunter-gatherers** were artfully expressed in paintings and sculptures. The art in these caves demonstrates that humans used symbols at least 32,000 years ago, although humans clearly had language and other forms of symbolic behavior much earlier than that. The cave art is the earliest evidence of them. The art may also tell us about how communities used landscapes during the **Stone Age**, also known as the **Paleolithic**."

"*Paleo* means old and *lithic* means stone," Babette pointed out. "So we've obviously left the early human species like the australopiths back in Africa and moved on to the early humans of our species, homo sapiens sapiens. Don't you think it's interesting how science takes a simple word, like Old Stone, and makes it sound exotic by using Latin or some other language? Paleolithic is a good example. Pleistocene, Holocene, Pliocene, and all those terms are others!"

"Exactly! The late Pleistocene is the period when human beings developed into artistically endowed and socially complex hunter-gatherers," Barnaby agreed, somehow missing Babette's point, so intent was he on studying the panel he'd had in his hands when they were somehow transported to this cave from the *Archy Stone*. The animals on the panel were colored in, outlined in black, and looked like abstract paintings. Interestingly, they appeared to be painted at different times, for some overlapped others."

Barnaby's voice changed, becoming deeper, warning his friends he was going into lecture-mode. "The term 'Paleolithic' is used to cover the period of time beginning with the emergence of man and the manufacture of ancient tools some 2.5 million to 3.8 million years ago. The Paleolithic period lasted through most of the Pleistocene until the final retreat of the ice sheets in about 8300 B.C. It is usually divided into the Lower Paleolithic, with the earliest forms of humans (*Australopiths* and **Homo Erectus**), and the predominance of core tools such as pebble tool, hand ax, and chopper type. The Middle Paleolithic is the era of the **Neanderthal** humans and the dominance of flake-tools over most of Eurasia. The Upper Paleolithic started perhaps as early as 38,000 B.C. with *Homo Sapiens*, blade-and-burin tools, and the cave art of western Europe. During this stage, humans colonized the Americas and Australia."

"Yes, well," Beauregard said importantly. "The Pleistocene caves are decorated with images of animals and symbols. For more than 100 years people have sought the meaning of Paleolithic cave art. Yes, Babette, there are your 'exotic' words again," the cat smiled. "Some scholars believe the marks used in cave art represent records and counts of things, while others link them to rituals of hunting magic. Some interpret them as symbols of fertility and death, maleness and femaleness. Others think the art is random, while some feel there is a definite plan and structure to the drawings, and that the location in the cave is also very important. Most associate the art with religion and rituals. There's still no agreement on how to interpret the cave art. I think that's what Barnaby's holding—that panel with those images of animals on it is Paleolithic cave art. Though the art might look like what a young child would draw, their overall design of layout, style, and how they are made are actually masterful works of art. Cave art's function obviously goes far beyond mere decoration."

"Beauregard, you are quite an art connoisseur. Besides creating images, did these people also write out things?" Babette wondered.

"No, the earliest writing system known appears in the Sumerian culture of the Mesopotamian region of the Middle East, shortly before 3000 B.C.," Beauregard told them. "That's about 8,000 years after the Paleolithic cave art was created. Many generations of people and cats, when you think about it. Of course, just as we're finding out throughout other areas of archaeology, new discoveries, finds, dating methods, and other information could change any of this in the future."

"Well, I doubt THIS is the Middle East. Are you saying we're probably in Europe? Maybe even in France? Near home?" Babette asked, happily thinking of Paris and her home.

"Yes," Beauregard confirmed. "These caves are clustered in specific regions—Perigord, the Pyrenees in southwestern France, and Cantabria in northern Spain—so I believe we could be in France or Spain."

"That sounds accurate, yes." Two men walked out of the cave's dark depths and caused the kids and cat to jump, completely startled at their sudden appearance. Beauregard, who had been intently scanning the textbook, was most alarmed by the appearance of the man. He threw the book in the air, losing his balance and disappearing over the steep ledge.

"BEAUREGARD!" The kids yelled in unison, rushing toward the ledge and looking fearfully down onto the tops of trees far below. There was no sign of the cat.

"Everyone back, NOW!" The older of the two men ordered, lying on his stomach and reaching down to pull Beauregard, clinging only by his claws out of sight below, back up onto the ledge. Beauregard immediately began grooming his coat, trying to get the ruffled and wet fur to shine again. The kids surrounded him, petting him anxiously, relieved he was obviously okay.

"That was way too close!" Bridget said, relieved at the cat's appearance.

The man chuckled. "Cats have a way of taking risks, yes? But somehow they always land on their feet. Hello, I'm a French archaeologist, André Leroi-Gourhan. No thanks," he shook his head when Bridget offered him a fat piece of bubble gum. "And this is one of my students, Pierre Pouffant." The younger man nodded at them, happily taking Bridget's offered gum.

"You can call me Pierre," the man said, his words muffled as he chewed the bubble gum. "Formalities have a way of slipping away when you're in a cave," he joked.

Barnaby stared at the older archaeologist in sudden recognition. "My parents met you! But they said you died . . . um, never mind!" Barnaby said quickly, pausing when he realized how inappropriate it might be to tell the man that he had died, especially since Leroi-Gourhan stood before them looking very much alive. It dawned on Barnaby that they must be back in the recent past, but not the far reaches of time. If Barnaby remembered correctly, this man had died in 1986 when he was in his seventies. By no stretch of the imagination did he look like he was seventy years old at this point.

"What's wrong?" Bridget nudged Barnaby, thinking he was acting weird.

"Monsieur Leroi-Gourhan died in 1986," he said pointedly. "He was then in his seventies."

"In 1986? Then that means we're—" Bridget whispered back.

"—Back in time, yes." Beauregard pointed out, also whispering. "I would guess then that we're in the late 1960s or early 1970s."

"And who are your parents?" Monsieur Leroi-Gourhan prompted, raising his eyebrows inquiringly. When Barnaby told him, he nodded vaguely, obviously not remembering the two scientists.

"That's okay, they probably seemed *much* too young to have a son my age. But then again, people do seem to look younger all the time," Barnaby grinned. The scientist just looked puzzled.

"We did not mean to be impolite," Beauregard interjected. "This is our young scientist, Barnaby. I'm Beauregard and this is Bridget and Babette." The cat introduced the kids to Monsieurs Leroi-Gourhan and Pouffant. The archaeologist and his protégé didn't seem startled to meet a talking cat, just curious. They stared at Beauregard like he was an artifact of some sort. Beauregard ignored their interest. Instead, he waited until Barnaby caught their attention again, then discreetly took the art panel away from Barnaby and put it with the textbook into Bridget's backpack. Bridget was the only one of the four of them who had her backpack with her.

"Come into the cave and out of that wet," Monsieur Leroi-Gourhan suggested. The younger man held up a kerosene torch, lighting the large cavernous room, one wall covered with painted cave art.

Barnaby could barely contain his excitement. His eyes sparkled behind his glasses and he jumped from one foot to the other, his lab coat flapping. "Leroi-Gourhan! Yes! You conducted the first systematic approach to the study of cave art, working in the 1960s . . . ."

"Thanks, young man, for the credit. It has been an uphill battle to convince my fellow archaeologists and the scientific community. There are many skeptics out there," Leroi-Gourhan said, shaking Barnaby's hand.

Barnaby turned to his friends, explaining. "Now, if I remember correctly, before Monsieur Leroi-Gourhan, cave art was seen as random accumulations of individual images, representing simple 'hunting magic' or 'fertility magic'. This man has studied the positions and associations of the animal figures in each cave."

"Ah," Babette murmured politely.

Pierre matched Barnaby's enthusiasm. "Yes, he has, Barnaby," he hastily jumped in, stopping the flow of Barnaby's lecture. "And he's also established that the horse and bison are the most commonly depicted animals, accounting for 60 percent of the total figures in all cave art. They're concentrated on what seems to be the central panels of the caves, as you can see," the student archaeologist gestured excitedly, pointing at the art on the walls.

The archaeologist cleared his throat. It sounded like a roar as it echoed in the cave. "Forgive me, but I must return to my camp and some paperwork. I'll leave Pierre here as your guide. He should be able to answer any questions you have." The archaeologist bowed politely to them and left the cave.

"He's returning to base camp. There are several caves we've been working in, so the base camp is a hike from here," Pierre explained, as he led them deeper into the cave.

"Pierre, look! Is this a rhinoceros?" Barnaby asked, reaching towards the figure.

"Don't touch! Sometimes the art can be damaged simply by touching it," Pierre warned. Barnaby quickly stepped back, not touching the figure. "Ah yes, that is a rhino," Pierre continued. "Although rhinos, felines, cave bears, and other less common animals are usually painted in the cave depths, as I will show you. See, here in the center of the cave we have the horse and bison. I'm sure we've found the 'blueprint' for the way each cave has been decorated."

"Felines?" Beauregard echoed, dashing back into the deeper parts of the cave, obviously wanting to check out the cats Pierre had mentioned.

Though most of the cave was very dark beyond the light from Pierre's flickering torch, a lantern blazed on a narrow natural shelf on the cave's wall. It was damp and smelled of old fires and musty scents they couldn't identify. Caves were exciting in that one never knew what he was going to find. The kids followed Pierre into the gloom and darkness where Beauregard had disappeared, toward the back of the large cave. They all felt a mingling of adventure and mystery, but also fear. They had all seen too many films showing dangers in caves, from holes or rockfalls and other natural booby traps, to bats or bears or scorpions or even an outlaw or two.

The cave art stretched along the full wall of the cave, some of the shapes brighter and drawn over other animal shapes. They'd never seen anything like it before. It was almost as though the past was reaching out across the thousands of years and telling them something.

"You might want to take your sunglasses off," Pierre suggested to Babette.

"What for?" She responded. Bridget realized then that she'd rarely seen Babette without the shades. Pierre shrugged and continued his discussion with Barnaby.

"Handprints!" Bridget pointed out, intrigued to see a set of red stenciled handprints, small as if done by someone her age. Bridget lifted her left hand and placed it over the ancient red one, rough and cold from the rock. It was almost a perfect fit. "Wow, Babette . . . to think someone, thousands and thousands of years ago, put their hands in this exact spot." This sense of time and connections with people who had come before hit Bridget even harder than seeing those footprints earlier in Tanzania.

Babette put her hand on the right handprint, but her fingers were much longer and thinner than the one on the wall. "Well, Bridget. It obviously was your ancestor," she joked, "not mine. Let's hurry and catch up with Pierre, Barnaby, and Beauregard. We're not supposed to touch the art, remember?" Bridget ignored her, studying the handprints and wondering who put them there.

Beauregard was well ahead of the kids and their guide. He sniffed and searched for some proof of his ancestors. There were no cat paw prints for him. Undaunted, he went farther back into the cave where it narrowed, glad he was able to see in the dark.

"Barnaby? Pierre? You guys?" Babette's voice and footsteps echoed back to the main section of the cave where Bridget was studying the carvings around the handprints, trying to get some clue to who they belonged to.

Pierre's voice droned on. He pointed out shapes, discussing Monsieur Leroi-Gourhan's theories. "Other species, like these ibex, mammoth, and deer, are located in more peripheral positions as you can see. Very few humans and virtually no objects were drawn on the cave walls, with the exceptions of some handprints back in the main cave. Some figures are so tiny, while others are over five meters—that's sixteen feet—in length. Some works of art, as you can see, are easily seen and accessible, but others are hidden carefully in the farthest recesses of the cave where I believe your cat is exploring now."

Bridget heard the voices growing fainter and could no longer see the light from their torch. All was dark beyond the light from the small lantern not far from where she stood. She searched the wall for more handprints, but didn't find any, so she returned to the point where the original ones were. Had the person who made these prints lived here in the cave? What was life like for him or her?

Suddenly realizing it was too quiet, Bridget looked toward the darkness where her friends had disappeared. "Babette?" Bridget called nervously, pulling her baseball cap further down the back of her head. The cave made the sound of her voice echo Babette's name over and over, fainter and fainter. It seemed to bounce off the walls, but there was no response. She felt more alone than ever. The shadows seemed darker. In front of her were the handprints that Bridget was beginning to think of affectionately as her handprints.

"So cold, but so old," she murmured, placing both of her hands over the red prints again. She was surprised that the prints felt like they were growing warmer, almost sticky. She closed her eyes, leaving her hands on the prints, trying again to imagine what the person had been thinking of to put handprints here. She could almost smell the smoke from a cookfire and the smell of meat roasting . . . .

✎ ✎ ✎ ✎ ✎

"Meat?" Startled, Bridget opened her eyes and realized she really did smell meat . . . and strongly. Not only that, but the air was slightly foggy with smoke! She looked around the cave to see two fires burning several yards apart with people sitting around them. Over the closest fire, on sticks, some sort of meat was roasting slowly. Bridget began to wish she'd listened to Pierre and not touched the cave art. Not far from her, a guy was chipping an animal figure into the rock using stone tools. He had what looked like an oil lamp burning in some sort of bowl. He held it up to see the wall better as he worked.

Next to her handprints, a big square-shaped hole was gouged in the cave wall. It looked like someone had chipped the art right off the wall of the cave. She didn't remember that hole before. She was glad she was against the wall, away from the light. No one seemed to notice her yet, but she was worried what would happen if they did. Not daring to move, hardly daring to breathe or chew her gum, Bridget studied the rest of her surroundings.

She didn't get the feeling these people lived in this cave all of the time. Instead, it appeared they had just taken shelter here and were camping while on a trip or something. In the flickering firelight, the people looked remarkably like those of her own time, except they were smaller and wore what looked like leather clothing and they were barefoot. All of them had dark hair.

A woman worked scraping at an animal skin. Another appeared to be grinding berries or seeds in a bowl. Several of the men were repairing or sharpening spears and other weapons. All of them were talking to each other using gestures and a language Bridget couldn't understand. She wished Babette were here to tell her what they were talking about. She noticed a man holding an antler, like from some sort of deer. He was carving it with what looked like a sharp knife. She realized he was making some sort of animal carving, a piece of art.

He seemed to feel her eyes on him and looked up to meet her gaze, warning the others as he did so. Bridget felt her heart pounding as she leaned back against the cave wall in fright. What would happen now? The man stood up and grabbed a spear, coming straight at her and making angry noises. In her fright, she swallowed the entire wad of bubble gum in her mouth, coughing as it stuck in her throat. The others circled her threateningly, obviously seeing her as an intruder and possible enemy. He lifted up the spear as Bridget's eyes grew wide with terror. The entire cave became silent, and she could hear her own heart racing. Ba-boom, ba-boom, ba-boom . . . .

"H-h-help! Help!" She gulped out, still coughing, and in these moments wishing she could be transported back into the Archy Stone or that she had Babette's martial arts skills or Barnaby's solutions or Beauregard's feline wisdom, or anything, anything at all, only to get her out of this situation. Wishing didn't make it so. The man kept walking closer, his red-rimmed brown eyes staring into her own.

✎ ✎ ✎ ✎ ✎

Meanwhile, Babette stood behind Pierre and Barnaby, studying the drawings on the cave wall. "Did people live in here?" Babette asked curiously, then added, "Are we in France?"

"Ha ha ha," Pierre laughed, chewing and snapping his gum. "Just because you're in a cave doesn't mean you've left the country, Mademoiselle. Of course you're still in France! Early archaeologists had the wrong picture of these early cave communities. Unlike modern archaeologists, they didn't study how people settled and moved around, so they didn't get a complete picture of the people whose settlements they studied. Unfortunately, the early misconceptions from these studies have persevered. The vast majority of modern illustrations of the Stone Age depict prehistoric men and women living in caves. The primitive cave men and their submissive cave women. Common sense should dispel this notion, right Barnaby?"

Barnaby nodded, obviously impressed with the young man's knowledge. "Yes, plus wood and other materials for actual shelters would disintegrate over time. Clues to the lives of these early hunter-gatherers were better preserved in caves, so early archaeologists and historians thought their lives were in caves. It makes sense."

Pierre continued. "Now we know more. We've also developed a strong respect for the technology, survival skills, and adaptations of these Stone Age hunter-gatherers. We no longer think of them as primitive, for they were much more skilled and creative than earlier archaeologists imagined. In fact, much more like us than the stereotypical crude cave men and women."

"I'd think living in a cave would make it harder to get food and other needs. Besides," Babette said with a shiver, "it's damp and unhealthy in here. It's also very cold and dark. Brrr . . . I wouldn't want to live here."

"Right, that's the common sense I referred to," Pierre said. "Caves were rarely used as dwellings, but we know they were used for rituals or camping shelters. Not caves, but rock shelters were preferred for living places, and then only in bad weather. People were constructing shelters out in the open 1.75 million years ago and throughout the Paleolithic. Paleolithic tent remains excavated at Pincevent and Dordogne areas of France helped prove this. We did find that some hunters set up tents inside of caves, or rock walls, to try to make them more habitable, but it was for temporary shelter and not permanent dwellings. We find that shelters out in the open usually only leave their preserved garbage or **middens** behind. You'd be surprised how much you can discover about people from their trash."

"Lovely," Babette grimaced. "Finding only garbage. Ugh." They laughed at her expression.

Pierre continued. "People were hunter-gatherers for thousands of years. We think they stayed on the move, going where they could find game animals and gather plants and berries. The ice that covered parts of Europe for about 20,000 years finally began to melt after 13,000 B.C., or 15,000 years ago, changing the climate and the land. People, animals, and plants gradually returned to the newly uncovered land, including Britain, which stayed attached to Europe by a **land bridge** until around 6,500 B.C. These land bridges weren't actual bridges, just land exposed by lower sea levels that are covered today by water. Most early Paleolithic people lived a **nomadic** life, gathering food and making shelters from animal skins or tree branches. As the climate warmed up, the farming communities developed and people settled down."

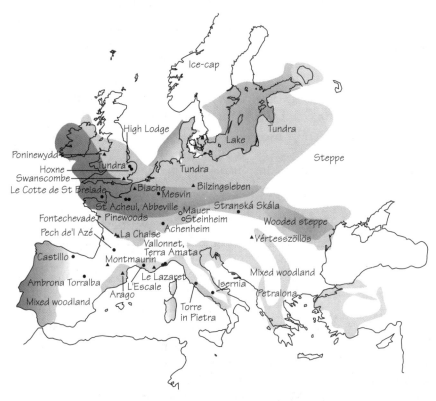

Barnaby nodded. He already knew most of what Pierre was telling them. "Didn't Monsieur Leroi-Gourhan conduct excavations at reindeer-hunting camps near Paris? Along with his work in the caves?"

"Yes," Pierre agreed. "He taught us some new ways of getting information about the past. We learned from studying everything in its place rather than removing individual objects."

"Like what did you study?" Babette prompted.

"Oh, everything—how they butchered game, made their tools and weapons, what materials they used, the wear and tear of the tools and weapons, and how they refitted **flints** and **cores**. Flints are hard but brittle stones found in chalk or limestone. They can be flaked and shaped easily in any direction. Flints are the commonest 'stones' used in the Paleolithic period," Pierre informed them. "Besides flints, **obsidian**—a hard volcanic glass that can be razor sharp when cut—was used for knives and other weapons and tools. In fact, obsidian is still used today for surgical knives or medical tools and other uses where an extremely sharp edge is required."

"What about cores?" Barnaby reminded Pierre.

"Yes, cores were chunks or pebbles of stone. The core was used as a tool or blank from which other tools or weapons were made. Often cores were carried everywhere and used to shape into tools by striking flakes off it. Although the core is the main tool produced, the flakes that are chipped off it can be also used to make knives, scrapers, and other tools. The history of stone tool technology becomes more advanced and refined over time. The first stone tools were simple choppers and flakes made by knocking pieces of pebbles to create sharp edges. Some of the oldest were found at Olduvai Gorge in Tanzania," Pierre told them.

"We know where that is," Babette pointed out, winking at Barnaby.

"Good," Pierre said, still intent on his description of cores and stone tools. "After hundreds of thousands of years, flaking both surfaces of the tool led to hand-axes that could be sharpened with a bone hammer. Usually people had to stay near a stone source, because their stone cores were too large to carry. Then around 35,000 years ago, people learned how to remove long, double-sided, or **bifacial** blades from round stone cores using a punch and hammerstone. This was a great advance because it was easy to produce a large number of blanks and more specialized tools like scrapers, burins, or borers. It also wasted less of the stone core. Most of the stone used was easy to work with, like chert or obsidian."

"I bet it was easier to carry the stone core when they could use more of it and wouldn't have to stay so close to a source of the stone, right?" Babette asked.

Pierre nodded. "Yes, Babette. Around 10,000 years ago, stone tool technology reached its peak when people learned to create several tiny tools from one core, called **microblades**. Smaller stone cores were needed and could easily be carried anywhere, so people moved around more and could live **nomadic** lives, following the game herds." Pierre concluded.

"Didn't Monsieur Leroi-Gourhan help change the early views that Stone Age people were primitive cave dwellers?" Barnaby asked.

"Yes," Pierre responded. "He and other modern archaeologists helped demonstrate that studying artifacts can teach us about human behavior, or **ethnology**. Even when it's only middens or ashes from an ancient hearth, Leroi-Gourhan helped change the emphasis in archaeological research to focus squarely on the life of prehistoric people and not just on the classification and arrangements of bits of stone and bone as earlier archaeologists did."

"I think that's awesome," Barnaby concluded, studying the representations of animals. Then he frowned. "Hey, where's Bridget?" He asked, turning to Babette, finally noticing she wasn't with them.

"Probably still daydreaming about those handprints," Babette laughed, pointing towards the front of the cave.

✎　✎　✎　✎　✎

Back in time, Bridget watched the man come closer. The others behind him were staring at her strange clothing and dark skin, though theirs was tanned from living most of the time in the outdoors. A young child reached out to touch her arm, obviously fascinated. His mother quickly pulled him back toward the hearth. In the flickering firelight, Bridget noticed how white their teeth looked.

"H-h-hello?" She gulped, when the man put the tip of the spear underneath her chin and made some sounds that appeared to be demanding something of her. Without thinking, Bridget popped more gum into her mouth. The man moved the spear threateningly again, causing her chin to sting where it broke the skin. She stopped chewing and reached in her pocket, pulling out another piece of gum and handing it to the man. He took it and studied it intently, pulling the spear away. He touched the thin paper covering the bubble gum reverently, showing it to the others.

"That's paper," Bridget told him, realizing he'd never seen paper before. She reached out to show him how to open it, and kept chewing, blowing a small bubble and then taking it back into her mouth. Everyone stared at her, fascinated.

"Gum," she tried to explain, "bubble gum."

"Guh-um," the man repeated, nodding and suddenly smiling. She was relieved when he pulled the spear away from her throat. The man gestured for her to sit down next to the closest hearth. She sat, the small cut under her chin burning like a paper cut. She knew she probably needed a bandage.

"Band-aid," she muttered, and reached around for her backpack. The man was chewing the gum slowly and smiling broadly, his few teeth looking strong and white in the firelight. He nodded happily as the people gathered around him, watching him chew, obviously enjoying the bubble gum. He kept chewing and chewing, obviously expecting the gum to start disintegrating like most food did.

Bridget searched for a band-aid and touched the cave art panel in her pack. She pulled it out. The people gathered around her, gesturing and pointing, talking excitedly in their language and pointing at the wall. Bridget looked from the handprints and the raw chipped square next to them to her panel, realizing it looked like it would fit. The man next to her took the panel and walked hurriedly over to the wall. A woman grabbed Bridget's arm, pulling her to her feet and with them as they all gathered to watch. The stone art panel fit perfectly. In fact, when it was placed against the cave wall, the seams disappeared and it looked like it had never been chipped away. The people began talking excitedly. The cave rang with their voices and Bridget felt like plugging her ears against the noise.

Instead, Bridget blew a bubble and let it pop. Instantly, all of the people ran away from her, huddling in obvious fear against the far wall of the cave. The pop! Oh-oh . . . Bridget grabbed the chance to quickly put her palms back on the handprints again, as she had before. She closed her eyes, hoping against hope she would somehow return to her friends and the cat.

✎ ✎ ✎ ✎ ✎

"Run! RUN!" Bridget opened her eyes to see Beauregard barreling out of the dark depths of the cave toward—and past— her. The air was clear, the smoke gone. Behind the cat, Pierre, Babette, and Barnaby raced, passing her without slowing.

Bridget stood stupefied. Was it the cave people? Had they all somehow gone back in time with her? She heard a lot of commotion in the cave, but instead of people, she saw the towering figure of a huge bear coming after them. The beast was angry. He roared, his teeth shining against the lantern's glare.

Bridget no longer hesitated. "Hey you guys, wait up!" she screamed rushing out of the cave to quickly catch up with the others. Beauregard was far ahead, much faster than the young humans. They followed the path down the mountainside, running for their lives.

"Here they are!" The friends stopped abruptly, facing the unwelcome sight of Dastardly Looter blocking the trail in front of them. There was no sign of Beauregard. "Ah ha! We tracked you back here to 1968 and these Ice Age caves of France," he laughed wickedly. "Okay now, where's my loot?"

"Who are you? What loot?" Pierre asked, bewildered, as the other three looked nervously behind them, expecting the bear to make an appearance any moment.

Barnaby didn't hesitate. He pointed up the trail behind them. "I . . . left the sack of artifacts up . . . up there in that cave," he quickly improvised. "We're just grabbing lunch."

Sneakers came growling up the path.

Dastardly looked suspiciously at them a moment, then ordered Sneakers to watch them while he hurried beyond them to the cave.

"Why not let Pierre go? He has nothing to do with this." Barnaby tried to reason with the dog. Sneakers just growled. There was no sign of Beauregard, Dr. Tempus, or the *Archy Stone*.

Bridget, now chewing quite a bit of gum after her experience back in time in the cave, began to slowly blow a bubble. Understanding, Babette and Barnaby reached out and grabbed hold of her tightly. All three of them rose upward into the air and over the trees. Sneakers went berserk below them, barking and jumping into the air, not noticing that Pierre was able to slip off down the path in the direction of their main camp.

"Look, the *Archy Stone*," Barnaby pointed at the huge boulder lying off the trail ahead.

"I'd like to know how that Dastardly Looter keeps finding us," Babette groaned.

"He's obviously developed a tracking system, or probably had Dr. Tempus do that, to find us. It doesn't seem to work very fast, though. He showed up much later than we did," Barnaby pointed out.

Bridget began to let air out of her bubble, as they slowly returned to the ground in front of the timeship. They entered the cabin.

"Welcome back," Beauregard grinned, holding a tray of soda pop and paper plates filled with sandwiches and potato chips. "Hopefully Dastardly will find more than he's bargained for in that cave," the cat chuckled. "Meanwhile, here's some sustenance."

Bridget rushed into the bathroom, not only needing to use the facilities, but also wanting to get some antiseptic on the cut that was still stinging underneath her chin.

"Thanks Beauregard, I was ravenous," Babette said. "But how do we return that panel of what we now know is cave art?"

"Okay, I'm searching the database for Paleolithic cave art . . . Ah!" Barnaby smiled, eating his lunch. "Here's what it says, 'Pech-Merle Cave in France—magnificent horse and handprint of Old Stone Age. New finds continue to be made on an average of one cave per year, including major discoveries in France. These include Cosquer Cave in 1991 near Marseilles where the Ice Age entrance is now underneath the sea, and Chauvet Cave in 1994 in the Ardéche, with its unique depictions of rhinos and big cats'."

"Cats?" Beauregard repeated, perking up his ears.

Barnaby ignored him. "In the 1980s and 1990s archaeologists found that cave art was sometimes produced in the open air. While most of it has succumbed to the weathering of many thousands of years, we have more of what survived inside caves. Only six open air sites are known so far, in Spain, Portugal, and France . . . but they comprise hundreds of figures, mostly pecked or chipped into rocks and called **petroglyphs**. Others are painted on and called **pictographs**. Their style and content are clearly Pleistocene in date."

"Can you skim the info, to help us identify our panel?" Babette urged, "Because that bear might've found Dastardly by now and he might come any minute. I don't relish the thought of another encounter with that man . . . or his canine beast."

"Hmm, true. Okay, I'll rush through here," Barnaby agreed. "Do you think it's cave art? Maybe it's a panel of **rock art**?"

"What's the diff?" Babette wanted to know. "I'd like to scrawl my name across stone, myself. It makes me feel immortal somehow, like it will stay there forever. I can understand why those early peoples did it and people continue to scribble on stone or other surfaces today. Look at graffiti."

"Okay, rock art is cave art or any pecking, incising, drawing, or painting of designs onto stone surfaces. Sometimes there are also **symbols**, representing something else from the pictographs and petroglyphs. Early peoples throughout the world created rock art in prehistoric times. Rock art occurs in caves, on cliff walls, or on boulders in every culture. Here in France, rock art is considered a national treasure. Every effort is made to insure not one flake of paint or chipped design is lost. By contrast, few ancient rock art sites are protected in the United States. Too many rock art murals have been vandalized by graffiti and gunshots.

"Do people create rock art today?" Bridget asked, coming out of the bathroom and catching the end of Barnaby's explanation. She wore a new bandage under her chin. She began eating her lunch, hungry after smelling all that roasting meat during her time travel.

"Yes," Barnaby agreed. "In modern America, the graffiti scrawls on concrete and brick walls, bridges, and rock faces of the artificial canyons of our cities and along highways are the most common modern kind of rock art. Based on my research and what the archyfactor told us about the quiver and arrows, I think we've tentatively identified the owner. However, we can't be sure it's the Iceman or that it's from the late Paleolithic. Remember what Dr. Tempus warned us about, that the archyfactor only provides an option for us where similar artifacts have been found, but it might not be the origin of our artifact? That's why I didn't even mention the Iceman to Babette. We need to do more research, Beauregard. Before we can return it, we have to absolutely identify where it belongs. I'm not sure this is a good idea, having us all break up like this," Barnaby pointed out. "What if one of us needs help?"

"Does the rock art tell stories?" Babette wondered.

"Rock art can't be 'read' like Egyptian hieroglyphics or a phonetic alphabet," Beauregard informed them. "In fact, most rock art seems to mean something different to each person who ponders it. Think what future archaeologists may think about our modern graffiti? We may never know exactly why it was created and what it means. You'd be amazed how many people became archaeologists, though, after seeing rock art for the first time and deciding they wanted to know more, understand more. They ended up making a career out of studying things like this from the past. Mary Leakey said that's what influenced her, remember?"

"True," Barnaby agreed. "Archaeologists analyze the figures and patterns. They often find different cultural groups create different styles of rock art. The cave artists used different techniques, from simple finger tracings and modeling in clay, to engravings and even hand stencils or paintings using two or three colors. Some Native American tribes and aborigines from other countries have oral traditions about rock art and its meaning. Many believe that the spirit of the makers resides in what they have created. They think rock art is living and has a spirit."

"I can believe that," Bridget agreed, thinking of the red handprints and her journey back to the Paleolithic hunter-gatherers.

"Eerie," Babette said, "Is our panel alive, then?"

"More alive than you think, Frenchie, but it's gone," Bridget said matter-of-factly, tipping the soda pop can back as she drained it, enjoying the stunned expressions on their faces. Time adventures made her thirsty.

"Gone?" Beauregard, Babette, and Barnaby all said at once.

"Yeah, I returned it. Hey, it's back on the cave wall in the Pleistocene. No sweat. Let's move on to our next adventure, huh?," Bridget suggested.

"You returned it?!" Barnaby exclaimed. "Bridget, you've got some explaining to do, but here comes Dastardly. He looks angrier than ever, and his clothes are all in shreds. At least the bear didn't make dinner out of him, maybe unfortunately for us." Hurriedly the buckled into their seats while Babette rushed to the door and assumed her martial arts position. Dastardly knew how to open the door, obviously having learned this from Dr. Tempus.

"Heeeeee-YAHHH," Babette screamed, pushing him solidly backwards onto the ground. Sneakers yelped when Dastardly landed on him with his full weight, causing the dog to hightail it through the trees with his tail between his legs. Dastardly lay on the ground stunned.

"Barnaby quick, get us out of here! I do believe Dastardly is NOT having a good day," Bridget giggled. Barnaby slid another artifact into the archyfactor, pushed some buttons, adjusted the tempometer to the date on the computer screen, and they were off, the strange vibrations, darkness, and dizziness overwhelming them.

⚐ ACTIVITIES ⚐
The Paleolithic Period
Quiz #3
Matching

Provide the correct words for the definitions below.

1. These people stayed on the move, going where they could find game animals and gather plants and berries: _____

2. The study of human races and their origins: _____

3. When ice sheets covered much of the Earth's continents, sea levels were lower. The land that is under water today between Russia and Alaska or between England and France was exposed when sea levels were lower during the Ice Ages and is called a: _____

4. Symbols or drawings pecked into a surface are called: _____

5. This archaeologist was the first to study the structure and context of cave art in depth: _____

6. A hard but brittle stone that can be flaked and is the most common "stone" of the Stone Age: _____

7. Pieces of stone used for making tools: _____

8. Ancient garbage heaps: _____

9. Beginning with the emergence of humans and the manufacture of most ancient tools some 2.5 million years ago, the _____ period lasted through most of the Pleistocene until the final retreat of the ice sheets in about 8300 B.C.

10. Volcanic glass: _____

Quiz #4

Choose the best word(s) to complete the sentences below.

1. During prehistoric times, natural caves were used by humans for temporary shelter and for
   a. government centers
   b. permanent shelter
   c. magic or religious ceremonies
   d. developing city structures

2. Items from the past would be best preserved in a
   a. dry cave
   b. damp grave
   c. sunny mound
   d. dark ship

3. The ways of living that are shared by a group of people are called its
   a. immigration
   b. community
   c. culture
   d. location

4. Neanderthal humans lived during this period or Epoch
   a. Pliocene
   b. Holocene
   c. Jurassic
   d. Pleistocene

Stories in Stone—Topics For Discussion

1. Why do you think ancient peoples created cave and rock art? What are the most common subjects?

2. Do you think early peoples lived in caves? Why or why not?

3. Using rock art symbols shown in this chapter, explain what you think the symbols represent. What do they tell you about the artists?

4. What is the difference between **petroglyphs** and **pictographs**?

5. Many rock art sites are being defaced and vandalized in our modern times. What are the results of destroying rock art?

6. Brainstorm uses for caves. Include hideouts, mushroom growing, scientific research, and tourist attractions. Try designing a modern cave with up-to-date and imaginative conveniences.

Make Your Own Cave Art Panel

Below are several ways you can create your own cave art or rock art panel and learn even more about them.

Bleach/Water/Construction Paper Method. Use brown construction paper, a cotton swab, and about 3 tablespoons of chlorine bleach diluted with 1/4 cup of water. Dip the swab in the bleach mixture and rub the swab on the paper to create animal symbols or other symbols.

Soap Etching Method. Use a bar of soap and some simple tools such as a nail file, a paper clip, or a stone. Etch your design into the soap using any of the tools listed.

Flour/Salt/Water/Paint/Pencil Method. Using flour, salt, water, black tempera paint, measuring cup, plastic squeeze bottles, cardboard, gray paint, paintbrush, and a pencil, do the following. Paint the cardboard with the gray paint and allow to dry. Mix one cup of flour, one cup of water, and a half cup of salt. Add the black tempera paint to the flour mixture and mix well. Pour the mixture into the squeeze bottles and attach their lids. Using the pencil, lightly draw the outline of an animal or human. Squeeze the black paint over the pencil-drawn lines. When dry, the black outline should glisten to resemble chalk used in cave drawings.

Mural on Butcher's Paper, Poster Paper, or Gray Construction Paper. Create a mural showing simple pictures of you and your friends at play, school, and in your home. You can use black chalk, charcoal, pencils, paint, wide markers, or any other writing tool.

Questions and activities to do with your cave or rock art panel.
Look at your finished cave or rock art panel as an
archaeologist would. What does the panel tell you about
the artist? The animals or symbols? List what features
you see (sizes, colors, subjects, position, and features such
as legs, arms, fur or hair, horns, tails, and so on). This
information has helped you to analyze the art.

Vocabulary

Bifacial

Cave Art/Rock Art

Cores

Ethnology

Flints

Homo Erectus

Hunter-Gatherer

Land Bridge

Microblades

Middens

Neanderthal

Nomadic

Obsidian

Paleolithic

Pectroglyphs

Pictographs

Stone Age

Chapter 9
Frozen in Time:
The Iceman

"Sleuthing again," Bridget said happily. She enjoyed these quests back in time. At the moment it was September 1991 and she was wearing one of Barnaby's white lab coats. She was standing in front of the Innsbruck Institute for Forensic Medicine.

Never mind that she looked nothing like a forensic scientist with her New York Yankees baseball cap, sneakers, and a backpack. She held a fluorescent clipboard with baseball stickers all over it and on top of that she was a bit young. Her disguise obviously puzzled the reporters clustered to one side of the building, watching her with indecision. Was she one of them or not? Would she know anything about the world-shattering archaeological find within the Institute's walls? Before they could make up their minds, Bridget hurried through the door, pulling out the credentials Barnaby had made for her on their computer. Behind her, she heard a reporter yell, "Hey, know anything about the Iceman?"

Meanwhile, a few days earlier in time and at the very top of the rugged, rocky, and snow-covered Tyrolian Alps, Babette held onto the rope tied tightly around her waist, dug her metal cleats into yet another icy slope, and held on for dear life. The two mountaineers she had been following disappeared on a skinny ledge below, around yet another dark crevice. Beauregard had transported her to the edge of the ice field only a few hours earlier. She had been following the couple ever since, trying to learn where the artifact Barnaby had identified as a fur quiver containing broken and unfinished arrows in it had come from. The archyfactor had identified the quiver's possible location as the Tyrolian Alps and Similaun Mountain, September 1991, as their destination and date.

"Don't do this to me!" Babette complained, her hands numb from the countless and difficult detours she had taken while shadowing the couple on their little-used route across the ice field. Her lungs hurt from the thin air. She knew from Barnaby that the two tourists ahead, Erika and Helmut Simon, had reached the Similaun Mountain's summit earlier, at midafternoon. They were now on their descent back to their little resort village in the Italian South Tyrolian Alps. She leaped down onto yet another heavy snow-filled ledge, moving along it in the direction the two tourists had taken and trying not to look down.

"I'm to do what?" Barnaby asked again, as Beauregard helped him into the insulated gear inside the Archy Stone's cabin. "Based on my research and what the archfactor told us about the quiver and arrows, I think we've tentatively identified the owner. However we can't be sure it's the Iceman or that it's from the late Paleolithic. Remember what Dr. Tempus warned us about, that the archyfactor only provides an option of us where similar artifacts have been found, but it might not be the origin of our artifact? That's why I didn't even mention the Iceman to Babette. We need to do more research, Beauregard. Before we can return it, we have to absolutely identify where it belongs. I'm not sure this is a good idea, having us all break up like this." Barnaby paused. "What if one of us needs help?"

Beauregard chuckled at the young human's hesitation. "Barnaby, this way there will be one of you involved in everything from the discovery to the analysis of the Iceman and his artifacts. What better way to research? We'll have our answers. Don't worry, Barnaby, I'm going to keep monitoring all of you from the *Archy Stone*," Beauregard reassured him reasonably, sighing. "Such are the responsibilities of a feline of my position and intelligence."

"Okay, okay, so I'm part of the unofficial official recovery of the Iceman?" Barnaby asked.

Beauregard nodded. "Exactly. I checked with my friend, Helmutty, from Innsbruck. Now that cat gets around! Anyway, apparently in Austria, responsibility for the recovery of bodies found in glaciers rests with the police and air rescue service. Your knowledge of science should help. Remember, none of them realize for days that the Iceman discovery is anything more than some unfortunate mountaineer that had a mortal accident. None of them even dream that the body and its belongings are over 100 years old."

"Okay, this is going to be a challenge, at a minimum, the quest of the quiver. We should all accumulate interesting observations. And where are Bridget and Babette again?" Barnaby asked, putting freeze-dried food into his backpack. He was unable to shake the feeling that he was a character in a spy film or something. He almost wanted Beauregard to pinch him so he knew this was real.

Beauregard switched his tail patiently. "You're all on time travel in the same month and year, but at different points of time and different locations. Babette's a few days earlier than you and will be there when the Iceman's discovered. Bridget's a few days later than you and will watch and learn about the analysis of the finds."

"A variation of days, I know," Barnaby agreed. "Though for us, time will move a little faster than for others, right? Especially if you keep transporting us ahead during the quiet times. Eventually we'll all meet up again?"

"Yes, I'll attempt to do that. I know we haven't tried this before, but I predict we'll get accurate results," Beauregard responded sleepily, thinking how he couldn't wait to have the timeship solely to himself to catch up on much-needed grooming and get some shut-eye. With all the excitement lately, he'd had no time to do his cat stuff.

The two looked out into the gully at the edge of the glacier where the Iceman had been found, an area called the *Hauslabjoch*. It was only a short distance from the Austrian-Italian border. A helicopter was approaching off in the distance. Whump, whump, whump, its sounds echoed loudly throughout the vast Alps. Freshly fallen snow covered the find. Barnaby exited the *Archy Stone* into the frigid air blowing off the glaciers.

After watching him on the monitor for a moment, Beauregard checked on Babette's and then Bridget's progress. It was like watching a picture-within-a-picture TV, except that three pictures were within the big screen of the computer monitor, all with running clocks and dates showing where they were in time. Beauregard planned to keep the *Archy Stone* in the middle with Barnaby for now. Each of the young humans looked fine and under control. Satisfied, Beauregard began grooming himself, at last.

Back at the top of the Alps, Babette realized they weren't going to make it back to the village before dark. Setting low on the horizon, the sun was turning the peaks a golden pinkish hue. It would be dark soon.

"Hey, *hallo!*" Babette was startled to see another mountaineer hailing her from up the trail. He reached her, holding out his gloved hand. "I'm Erik," the mountaineer announced, speaking German, "from Austria."

"*Ja*, Babette, from Paris," Babette gasped out in fluent German, still breathless from the thin Alpine air. She pulled her black scarf up over her numbed nose and slung the rope over her shoulders. The trail was now wider and less steep, clearly marked. She was relieved she wouldn't need to descend any ice walls for awhile. The young mountaineer trudged companionably at her side.

"We're heading for the Simalaun refuge, yes?" He asked. "I made reservations for two, but my partner headed back earlier today, so I know there's room for you. Let's catch up to those two ahead of us," Erik suggested, noticing the Simons. Not knowing what else to say, Babette nodded as Erik hailed the couple.

"So much for spying," Babette whispered, as the Simons waited for her and Erik. They all made their way quietly to the hut. Here, they were greeted by the innkeeper, Markus Pirpamer, and his wife, who served them a warm meal before they fell tiredly into their beds.

    ✎ ✎ ✎ ✎ ✎

In Innsbruck, inside the Institute of Forensic Medicine, Bridget pulled the bubble gum out of her mouth and let it snap sharply against her teeth, wondering what to do next.

"May I help you?" A young woman paused in the hall in front of Bridget.

"Yeah, I'm supposed to be helping with the Iceman," she responded, debating whether to offer the woman some bubble gum. Gum sometimes opened doors that I.D. cards never would.

The woman smiled in obvious relief. "Great! Most of the staff are either on some far-flung digs or on holiday. This Iceman find couldn't have happened when we felt less prepared, but we're scuttling to remedy the situation. There are only a few staff and students. I'm Julia, the secretary," she held out her hand.

"Bridget, from . . . ah . . . New York City," Bridget shook Julia's hand. "I'm just an assistant, a student, and was told you could use some help?"

"Definitely. Bridget, we sure can use you! Come," she beckoned down the hall towards the laboratories. "Dr. Konrad Spindler's the archaeologist doing the initial work, along with the head surgeon. We've recalled our archaeologists and techs from their dig on the Rennweg in Innsbruck's old town center. We're trying to build this all up from scratch."

"I'll do what I can," Bridget promised, feeling overwhelmed at what she'd stepped into. Barnaby should've taken this assignment instead. Oh well, it was too late now.

"I've begun the task of tracking down the people who visited the recovery site these past four days, though when Elisabeth gets here from the Rennweg dig, she'll take over the project. We have to reach everyone who visited the gully from the moment the Iceman was discovered to the opening of the recovery operation yesterday. Here's the lab, and that's the Iceman," she said, moving aside excitedly. The room reeked of a hospital smell, like disinfectant.

Bridget stared.

✎ ✎ ✎ ✎ ✎

Back at the Similaun refuge, Babette yawned. The night had been much too short. She didn't know Beauregard had shortened it for her to less than an hour. The radiant sun was hot against them at noon when Babette, Erik, and the Simons reached the 3,516 meter Finail Spitze mountain summit, where they ate bag lunches. Erik planned to head back to the parking lot to return home and to his job. Babette pretended to go with him, hiking down the trail until she was out of the Simon's sight.

"I've changed my mind," Babette told Erik. "I think I'll hang around up here awhile longer." She waited until he disappeared down the well-marked trail, then backtracked to a wide, slightly tilting snowfield, tracking the Simons's trail towards a rocky ridge. Hiking in the beautifully crisp and clear mountain air, Babette wondered what lay ahead.

✎ ✎ ✎ ✎ ✎

Beauregard again checked the monitors. His grooming finished, he curled up on his bunk, sipping happily from a mousehead milkshake. Everything was in control. Soon he could have another catnap and some sardines. The cat was fully enjoying his role in this adventure.

✎ ✎ ✎ ✎ ✎

"Hi, I'm Barnaby," Barnaby told the rescue team and camera crew, standing in the fresh snow when the helicopter landed. "Here to help with official recovery efforts," he added, relieved that no one questioned him further. It was bitterly cold and Barnaby's breath made white clouds in the frigid air.

The tall, lanky man shook Barnaby's hand. "I'm Markus Pirpamer, the innkeeper of the Similaun refuge," he said. "I reported the find to the police after tourists told me of the body last Thursday. My father is the chief of mountain rescue. We've been up here on and off over the last three days since it was found, working on removal. Let's get to work, shall we?"

Barnaby agreed, joining them at the white mound, the snow covering a cut black plastic bag Pirpamer had placed over the Iceman earlier. Whomp! Whomp! Whomp! The helicopter took off and disappeared into the distance. Barnaby helped the men scrape off the snow.

"Well, it's still there," Markus said. The camera crew was recording everything.

"But the body's already mostly out of the ice," Barnaby remarked, eyeing the damage to the body that looked new.

"Yes, we finally freed him from the ice on Saturday. The pneumatic chisel caused some damage when we first chipped through the ice," Markus explained. "We may have fractured some bones as well." Barnaby shook his head, having an extremely difficult time keeping the secret of what these men were working with. He knew the men still thought this was a recent accident and death. In fact, it felt like a crime not to handle the Iceman and his belongings with the care used in archaeological excavation. Barnaby sighed.

Whomp! Whomp! Whomp! Another helicopter arrived, sending snow flying around them like a blizzard, preventing them from seeing anything. It finally settled and more men were trudging through the snow to join them. Barnaby met Mr. Henn from the Forensic Medicine Institute. As the forensic specialist in charge of recovery, he had arrived with an assistant holding a body bag. Henn carried a black bag with special instruments and his camera, prepared to move the Iceman. The low amount of oxygen in the air at that altitude kept conversation to a minimum.

"He's still frozen in place!" Henn scowled, after trying in vain to move the Iceman. He took pictures, mumbling, "Overnight the body has (pant!) frozen into its base and can't be moved (pant!) nor shaken free, and is tragically damaged (pant!) from earlier efforts to move (pant!) him."

"Sir, if I may?" The reporter attempted to interview Henn. Henn ignored his questions until he asked about dating the Iceman.

"Very long periods of time are involved (pant, pant!) for the Carbon 14 method and other dating methods," Henn explained. The cameraman videotaped the body. "Teeth worn down from chewing (pant!). Partially mummified. (Pant, pant!) Must've been exposed to the air for (pant) some time before he got into the ice. Hmm, clothes? (Pause) Unfortunately it appears that there's nothing left on the body itself. If only we had an ice pick or something to extract the Iceman. That's all we can say at this point."

Barnaby studied the site. Icy meltwater from the glacier kept running just below the ice. "Glaciologists may be able to help by identifying the speed of flow of the glacier ice," he suggested. Henn nodded. Suddenly, the world went crazy.

"H-help!" Barnaby cried, slipping in the meltwater covering the ice around the Iceman. Items flew out of Barnaby's hair and into the soft snow. He would have fallen onto the Iceman if Henn hadn't grabbed his arm, steadying him.

"Thanks. Aha! Here's an ice pick and . . . um . . . a ski pole," Barnaby offered, retrieving the two things that had dislodged from his hair as casually as if he'd just dropped them. The other men began working to free the body with the ice pick. While they worked, Henn and Barnaby knelt down to recover tatters of leather, stacking them up beside the Iceman. Barnaby's woolen mittens became wet and heavy with the water, numbing his fingers. Gradually the body was loosened. They eased the body out of the ice and onto its back by the hole. It was a shocking sight. Everyone stared.

The large boulder that was the *Archy Stone* perched on the rocky ridge behind them. Beauregard could see Barnaby's footprints leading down to the site in the new snow. With his monitor Beauregard could hear and see everything going on. On the timeship's sound stereo system, Beauregard played the old rock song "Cat Scratch Fever" and hummed along.

Henn cleared his throat, turning to them grimly. "What matters now is that we bring out a few (pant!) more things for the archaeologist." They set to work, fishing out any items they could find in the flowing icewater where the body had lain. Barnaby noticed no one was mapping the site or locations of any artifacts. They recovered several implements: a miniature dagger with a short flint blade and wooden handle; a bow that was broken off when it couldn't be removed from the ice; pieces of leather clothing; and other odds and ends that they couldn't identify. Everything was placed in the body bag with the Iceman. Barnaby sighed.

There were no quivers or arrows. Maybe that was because they had the artifacts?

✎ ✎ ✎ ✎ ✎

Babette stopped behind a rock at the head of a small gully at the end of the ice field. Here, she waited for the Simons to move farther ahead. Mysteriously, they came to an abrupt stop. Babette saw a piece of brown sticking out of the ice not far from them. It looked like a piece of rubbish or a doll.

"But it's a man!" Babette heard Erika exclaim, causing shivers to run up and down Babette's back. It must be a dead man! Ugh!

Helmut Simon took one look at the corpse and ran back up the gully right toward Bridget. She panicked, looking hurriedly for a place to hide. She was able to slide down into a small crevasse in the midst of the boulders. Most people wouldn't fit, but Babette was double-jointed in every joint and able to squeeze in. Simon looked frantically around the empty snowfield they had just crossed, and saw no one. He returned to his wife and the body.

Babette took out her mini-binoculars, looking closely at the leather-brown bald skull with what looked like a hole or bruise on it. She could also see thin, bony shoulders and a yellowish back with its spinal column clearly visible, lying face down in meltwater against a rock. "Gross!" She whispered, repelled but at the same time fascinated. She'd never seen a dead body before, even if it did look more like a skeleton than a human being.

"Hmm, maybe it's a woman? It's very thin," Erika whispered, yet her words carried easily across the snow to Babette's hiding place. Helmut picked up a blue ski-clip, a rubber strap used for tying skis together.

"I rather think not, more likely a small man, a mountaineer. Poor chap. This must've happened maybe twenty years ago?" Helmut said. "We'll report it, but we shouldn't touch the body." They didn't and walked over to examine something small and dark in the snow. Through her binoculars, Babette watched Helmut pick it up, examine it, and then put it back. Helmut pulled out his camera and took a photograph as the couple discussed the directions they'd taken in order to memorize them to give to the authorities. Then they resumed their downward trek.

Babette watched them disappear and wondered if she should stay or follow, as they were obviously returning to the refuge. Overcome with curiosity, she decided to walk over and look at the Iceman herself. She didn't smell anything bad, as she had expected with a body that had been dead for who knew how long. She stared at the partially exposed yellowish body. Was this what Barnaby and Beauregard had meant her to find when they left her to follow the couple? Was this the owner of their quiver and arrows? Was her quest over?

"Beauregard!" Babette yelled at the mountains and then waited, wondering why the cat didn't respond and get her back in the timeship. Only her own words came back to her. "Beauregard . . . gard . . . gard . . . gard."

✏ ✏ ✏ ✏ ✏

In the lab at Innsbruck, Bridget looked away from the Iceman and upwards to meet Barnaby's familiar eyes on her. How could that be? She had left him in the timeship ready to set off on his own adventure. What was he doing here in Innsbruck? He winked at her.

In front of them on a slab was the shriveled corpse of a man. Though naked, the Iceman looked like a skeleton except for a strange, grass-filled shoe. Next to him was a long wooden thing, broken at the bottom, and a piece of green cloth filled with items. While Barnaby listened to the surgeon and archaeologist discussing the find, Julia beckoned to Bridget to examine the items laid out with the Iceman.

Bridget stared at an axe with a metal blade, a stone bead with a tassel, a small dagger with a wooden handle, some sort of strap-bag, a wooden stick with holes in it, a scrap of leather, and a nut-sized stone. On the other slab were all kinds of round and flat pieces of wood, torn cords, braided materials, bunches of hair and grass, two objects suggesting tree fungi, many remains of leather and fur, and several other items.

"More than seventy items," Julia said excitedly. "And we know it's from the late Stone Age, anyway," she confided, "the best **Neolithic** find of all times, we think!" Her excitement was shared by all of the others. Bridget listened to one of the most intense and heated scientific discussions she believed she had ever heard. In addition to Barnaby's usual lecture-mode with his bushy hair standing at full alert, they all were doing it—pacing and hopping excitedly and moving their hands around and acting absent-minded—everyone was speaking at once. It was wild!

"We're talking thousands of years," Dr. Spindler's voice rose above the others. The archaeologist was at least making some sense. "While it will take time for the dating to be complete, any first-year archaeology student could tell you the axe and flint blade of the dagger may be from the early Bronze Age. In fact, I would guess 4,000 years ago, and if the date is revised after more testing, it will be even earlier."

"Who would've thought? Truly, who would've?" the surgeon was saying, running his hands through his thick hair. "My, my, my..."

"Can you give us a briefing on what you've found?" Dr. Spindler asked the surgeon.

"Er, yes, of course." The surgeon began reading off his notes. "A dark-skinned male; aged between twenty-five and forty; cranial capacity of 1500-1560 cc; about 1.56 meters-1.6 meters or 5 feet 2 inches tall; weight is about 54 kg or 120 lbs.; teeth very worn, especially front incisors; no wisdom teeth; gap between upper front teeth; though bald, curly brownish-black human hairs about 9 cm long were found near the body and on his clothing; he may have been bearded; right earlobe has traces of a pit-like and sharp-edged rectangular depression where he must have had an orna-mental stone fitted there. Also, groups of tattoos, mostly short blue lines about a half inch long are on both sides of his lower spine, on his left calf, and right ankle. He has a blue cross tattooed on his inner right knee. These marks may have had therapeutic purposes; meant to relieve the arthritis we found in his neck, lower back, and right hip."

"Awesome, like totally awesome," Bridget whispered, excitedly nudging Barnaby.

"Cut it out!" Barnaby teased, poking her back with his elbow.

"What about the body scan?" Dr. Spindler prompted.

"Ahem, yes. The brain, muscle tissues, heart, liver, and digestive organs are in excellent condition. The lungs are in good shape, but are blackened by smoke, probably from open fires. He has hardening of the arteries and blood vessels. His left arm is fractured above the elbow but appears to be a recent fracture during recovery efforts." The surgeon glared momentarily at Barnaby, one of the recovery team.

"Continuing," the surgeon said as Barnaby squirmed, "The analysis revealed not only that he undertook manual labor, but also went through periods of reduced nail growth during times of serious illness—four, three, and two months before he died. His nails had dropped off, but one fingernail was recovered that gave us this information. Skin structure shows fatty tissue is very weakly developed, showing he didn't carry extra fat reserves at the time of his death. Several healed rib fractures and a once-crushed thorax are old injuries. The fact that he was prone to periodic crippling disease and arthritis may help explain how he fell prey to bad weather and froze to death."

"Did he have any cavities?" Bridget asked curiously.

"No," the surgeon answered, "No cavities."

"This Iceman's the first prehistoric human ever found with his everyday clothing and equipment. We think he was just going about his normal business. Other ancient human remains have either been carefully buried or sacrificed. Bridget, I suspect strongly that the quiver and arrows we have should have been discovered with the skeleton. If Dastardly hadn't stolen it, it would be adding even more information to what they've discovered here." Barnaby said solemnly.

"Next?" Dr. Spindler prompted.

The geologist intern raised his hand nervously. "After death, the Iceman was most likely dried out by a warm autumn wind before becoming encased in glacial ice. The depression holding the body protected it from the movement of the glacier above it. He had to have some protection from sunlight to avoid decomposition. A storm from the Sahara desert must have laid a layer of dust on the ice, absorbing sunlight and finally thawing out the area imprisoning the Iceman. Now we've got to deal with how to preserve the Iceman and the artifacts for the future," the geologist said.

The geneticist stepped forward. "Preliminary analysis of the Iceman's DNA confirms his links to northern Europe. However, we need more time to complete the tests. Over a long period of time, DNA molecules are broken up by chemical action. As some of you may not realize, it is now possible to work out family relationships through DNA analysis. We can also determine blood groups from soft tissue, bone, and even from tooth dentine up to 30,000 years old. We are working on that."

And the forensic specialist said, "No one realized how old this Iceman and his belongings were, so the recovery was done in a most unprofessional manner from the beginning until his arrival here. Those fractures and deep incisions by the pneumatic chisel could've been avoided if we'd only known, if we'd only—"

✎　✎　✎　✎　✎

Back in the *Archy Stone*, Beauregard left the galley holding a steaming cup of hot mouse chocolate topped with a mountain of whipped cream and a strawberry and sprinkled with cinnamon sugar. He glanced at the monitor.

"Ah! Barnaby's caught up with Bridget in time. I'm glad I speeded time ahead for him by cutting out the helicopter travel time and taking other shortcuts." Beauregard said, impressed with his own ingenuity. He felt totally in control and liked the feeling.

Beauregard considered what he needed to do now. Should he move the timeship or remain where he was? Soon he would need to transport each of the young humans back, as they obviously had a target date to return the quiver and its contents. It was time to get Babette back, and then he could take the Archy Stone to Innsbruck to get Bridget and Barnaby.

Beauregard activated the transporter and Babette appeared in the cabin.

"Get buckled in, we're going to Innsbruck," he told her. "You can get out of that mountaineering gear when we get there." She buckled into her seat. Beauregard turned again to the controls, but before he could do anything, the timeship jolted as if an earthquake hit it.

To the cat's horror and amidst Babette's furious screams, the rounded vehicle began to roll. It rolled through the gully and down the rocky mountain slopes. Far below, but closing in fast, the treeline began. Totally horrified, Beauregard grabbed the seatbelt and let go of his cup, causing hot chocolate and whipped cream to splatter through the timeship and over Babette. During the rolling, topsy-turvy pandemonium, Beauregard caught a glimpse of something tall and shiny up at the top of the gully where the Archy Stone had been parked only moments before. In those few seconds, he realized that it was Dastardly Looter and the *Money Probe*.

Bridget scanned the computer screen at the Institute. "Okay, there have been fifteen radiocarbon dates obtained from the body, the artifacts, and the grass in the boots. They all fall within a range of 3365 to 2940 B.C., averaging at 3300 B.C. or 5300 years B.P.," she read to Barnaby. "That should give us an idea of where we have to go to return the quiver and arrows."

Barnaby nodded. "Exactly, if Beauregard ever remembers us and returns us to the Archy Stone," he pointed out. They had been trying for hours to get the cat to transport them back to the timeship, with no luck. "At least we've learned a lot about how those things found with the Iceman and his body have told us so much about the man and life over 5,000 years ago. Now the entire world knows!"

"True," Bridget conceded. "It's amazing how the specialists were continually surprised at their findings—"

"Right from the beginning, when everyone thought Iceman had only been dead and frozen in the ice for ten or twenty years, huh?" Barnaby nodded. "But considering that it was four days before full recovery of the body and over seventy artifacts was completed, it's amazing things were still in as good shape as they were by the time it got to the laboratory, huh?"

"Yeah. The more they found out, the more excited everyone became," Bridget admitted. "In fact, the frozen man and his things turned out to be older and older . . . until everyone was stunned with dates showing he lived about 5,300 years ago!" Bridget and Barnaby walked to the outside of the Institute, sitting on a park bench and hoping Beauregard would return them to *Archy Stone*.

"Barnaby, you know what else is cool, huh?" Bridget asked.

"That many of the things discovered were different from the way scientists thought during the late Neolithic period, when the Iceman lived?" Barnaby said, kicking his sneakers against a clump of dirt on the edge of the sidewalk, trying to break it up.

"Nope," Bridget said, refreshing her bubble gum and stretching sleepily. Time travel was fatiguing. "I'm referring to the Iceman Wars! Can you believe Italy, Austria, and even Germany kept fighting over which country had rights to the Iceman and his things? I mean, really ! Though he was found near the borders, but it was a big dispute. They're still arguing and investigating to determine if he was discovered inside Italy or Austria."

Barnaby chuckled, standing up to stretch. "Meanwhile, they've got the Iceman in a freezer at -6 degrees Celsius with 98 percent humidity. They have to closely monitor the temperature and humidity at all times, trying to replicate the glacial ice conditions as closely as scientifically possible. Just think, if he thaws out, he'll start decomposing like any frozen organic matter does. Yuck! Remember, he's a **permafrost** mummy."

"Yes, he is," Bridget nodded. "Weren't you amazed that Dr. Spindler could put together a story of the people of the Neolithic time and the life of this man just from what was found?!"

"Er, what exactly are you referring to?" Barnaby pushed his glasses back up on his nose, looking more the mad scientist than ever.

"Well, all those things . . . like the Iceman was strong and worked outside, probably as a shepherd working with his dogs to look after a herd of goats and sheep. His clothing was perfectly suited to the high mountain climate and is the first complete set of Neolithic clothes recovered in our time," Bridget recounted.

"His clothing did fascinate me," Barnaby admitted. "Though apparently it had fallen off by the time he was fully recovered from the ice, he was resting in the ice fully clothed. Not all of his clothing was completely preserved, with the hair having fallen off the fur items making it look like leather and tear too easily. The wind blew much of his clothing off him as the ice melted around him. The clothes contained no woven materials. The Iceman's clothing included a cap, his upper garment, a pair of leggings, a loincloth, a pair of shoes, and a cloak. He also wore a body belt with a pouch. Most of his clothing was sewn cut pieces of fur or leather made from the fur."

"Don't forget his equipment!" Bridget said, rolling her head and shaking her shoulders in an effort to loosen up a bit. She'd learned these yoga moves from Babette.

"Yes, his equipment," Barnaby echoed, slumping back on the chair and stuffing his hands in the pockets of his lab coat.

Bridget was able to continue her yoga exercises and talk at the same time. "With his equipment, the Iceman could survive for several months away from regular supplies. They found the bow, axe, backpack, animal bones, two birch-bark containers, a dagger with its scabbard, a belt pouch full of items, an amulet consisting of a tassel with a stone bead, a net, stag-antler fragments to make carved arrowheads, and many other things. The largest piece discovered is part of an unfinished bow made of yew wood. Just think, Barnaby, that bow's unlike any found before. Though Dr. Spindler told me most prehistoric and historic bows are fashioned from yew, the Iceman's bow was unfinished, making it unique."

"If you say so," Barnaby shrugged, growing seriously worried that the cat hadn't returned for them yet.

"Yes Barnaby. In fact, the Iceman was pretty self-sufficient," Bridget pointed out. "He could hunt game with the weapons he had and defend himself and his animals against animal or human predators."

"Speaking of animals and self-defensive, where is Beauregard?" Barnaby glanced at his watch, realizing how silly that was since he'd been zipping around time and space. New York time was not where he was at the moment.

"I did find the axe most intriguing," Barnaby declared. "Another first! The only prehistoric axe discovered complete with the handle or haft, blade, and binding. When they found the axe, they thought it was an iron ice pick, not a copper axe. The Neolithic craftsman who made it had an excellent knowledge of working with copper and produced an exceptional tool!"

"Don't forget the backpack! Can you believe he actually carried a backpack?!" Bridget said. "Tied to a u-shaped frame by several cords made from woven grass? Fur scraps discovered near the axe are thought to be parts from a sack that was tied to the backpack. Though the backpack was more disintegrated than the Iceman, that's because it was dropped at a higher location and came out of the ice earlier."

"Right. Becoming a victim of both the sun and wind once it lost its ice cover, huh?" Barnaby said. "Wasn't another thing that surprised the experts was the wood or organic stuff the Iceman used to make his equipment? Though normally organic things wouldn't be preserved over time, but it happened with this permafrost mummy and the glacial ice. I believe the Iceman used a lot of organic, mostly vegetable, materials to make his equipment. He selected specific woods for his tools and weapons, cording and binding material, bark for containers, and grasses used in parts of his fur clothing. Even pollen was found sticking to his clothes and deposited in the ice. The variety of trees he gathered wood from for his tools is astonishing. The type of wood was selected for the type of tool or weapon he planned to make."

"Wait until I tell Babette that capricorns really exist!" Bridget marveled.

"If we ever see Babette again," Barnaby pointed out, a bit discouraged. "What's this about capricorns?"

"Capricorns are also named ibex. The ibex was once common in the mountains of Eurasia and North Africa. It had magnificent horns and was a sort of deer with excellent climbing skills. Only a few survive today. Two small ibex bones were found near the Iceman and are thought to be left over from meat the Iceman gnawed off. That would also partially explain why his teeth were so worn down, from a regular diet of dried meat. The ibex bones indicate the Iceman survived long enough to reach the gully and eat his last piece of meat, spitting out those ibex bone fragments. I learned ibex were also used for medicine."

"Beauregard, Beauregard, wherefore art thou, cat!" Barnaby said.

Bridget ignored his mood. "We also know the Iceman wasn't an outcast, but spent time away from his kin for months at a time. He wasn't a shaman or a priest, but his amulet was to protect him against misfortune and bad luck."

"I definitely could use that lucky amulet right now," Barnaby responded wryly, "or maybe the horn of a capricorn?"

"Well, Dr. Spindler thinks a disaster or violent conflict happened in the Iceman's village that caused him to flee. He thinks the villagers were in the midst of harvest time. In the process, he would have lost some of his equipment or damaged it," Bridget shook her head. "The poor man! It would also explain his rib fracture. He was probably chased, with his flight and the pursuit taking place over several days and weeks. Possibly he got caught in a bad storm or blizzard and fell. He died at a site along the route that herds used to cross the main ridge of the Alps, near the end of the summer grazing season. Another find has shown violence existed at this time in prehistory and possibly the Iceman was running from great danger."

"Theories, theories, theories," Barnaby chanted.

"Ah, but Barnaby," Bridget reminded him, "some of these explanations may change in the future if more becomes known. Dating methods are improving all the time. The archaeologists did say they were disappointed not to find any arrows or a quiver to go with the unfinished bow, though they suspect they may still be buried in the ice. Barnaby! I'm sure we have our man! We need to return the quiver and arrows to his lifetime so they can be found with the Iceman and fill in even more of the story!"

Barnaby sighed heavily. Too much enthusiasm was becoming tiring. Waiting was becoming tiring. In fact, he was feeling overwhelmed with weariness.

"I know, Barnaby, I'm also ready to go," Bridget acknowledged. "I have this terrible premonition that some awful has happened, but I've no idea what. What will we do if something's wrong? How will we ever get home? It's years in the future!"

Barnaby gave her an awkward hug, no longer knowing what to say.

No way could he or Bridget know that a catastrophe of monumental proportions had fallen upon their two friends and the timeship!

_____

⚒ ACTIVITIES ⚒
Frozen in Ice: Stopping Time

1. How were the Iceman and his belongings preserved for 5,000 years?

2. What were some of the clues that helped scientists and archaeologists figure out that the Iceman was from the late Stone Age?

3. Go to the dig RECORD SHEET used in chapter 5 for the sandbox dig. Fill out all of the information possible for the Iceman discovery.

4. Make a list of the dating methods you've learned about so far. What methods were used to help figure out how when the Iceman had lived? Some dating methods are listed in the glossary.

5. What if the kids and Beauregard returned to New York City and found a living Ice Age Neanderthal human was brought into this century? What inventions and technologies do you think would impress him or her the most? How would you communicate? Do you think she or he would be happy here? Why or why not?

6. While on a dig you have just uncovered a small skeleton. What is the age and sex of this skeleton? How can you tell? One member of the dig thinks the skeleton may have been damaged during excavation. How can you be sure?

Food for Thought

1. **Glaciers**. Research how a glacier forms. You may want to prepare a presentation to give at school or with your friends about glaciers. Do you think more fossils or artifacts may be preserved under existing glaciers? Why or why not?

2. **Creative Writing Exercise**. Imagine what life was like for the Iceman in his time and write his story the way you think he would tell it. You may want to research the Iceman on the Internet to get more

facts. You may also want to write a short story and research about life 5,000 years ago in other parts of the world and compare it to that of Stone Age Europe.

3. **Geography/Mapping**. On a map of the world, identify where the ice sheets covered the continents and where the land boundaries were when sea levels were lower.

4. **Carbon 14 Dating**. Research radiocarbon, or C14, dating and explain why the early dates on the Iceman based on that method may not have been as accurate as they would be today using that method.

5. **Sequence Dating**. Sequence dating is a method employed to show how objects have changed over time. With a friend, choose a modern object such as the television, telephone, computer, or automobile. Draw pictures of your chosen object from the first model to the present , showing how it has changed over time.

6. **Understanding European Time Periods**. In Europe, archaeologists divide the history of most sites into three distinct periods: (1) the Stone Age (2) the Bronze Age, and (3) the Iron Age. Make a list for each period of time of the different tools, weapons, and other artifacts that might be found during each age.

Chapter 10
Carved in Stone: Megaliths and Mysteries

"Babette? Are you all right?" Beauregard asked tentatively, wiping whipped cream off his eyes so he could see, then licking it off his paw. "Hmmm, still tastes great. What a mess! Babette?"

A groan filled the timeship's cabin. "Beauregard, what happened?" Babette asked from underneath the bedding that had fallen off their bunks. She shoved the sheets and blankets off, unhooked her seatbelt, and tried to stand on the sloping floor. Everywhere there were gobs of white and chocolate.

"Dastardly Looter again, of course. He landed the *Money Probe* directly on top of us, causing the *Archy Stone* to barrel down a mountainside in the Alps," Beauregard sniffed. "That man continues to affect life's equilibrium. Sometimes it's more than a cat can stand."

"So where are we?"

"Oh, Babette. I grabbed the tempometer just before we hit the tops of those trees, and was jolted wildly. This you can see from the remnants of my hot mouse chocolate with whipped cream, not to mention the rest of the disheveled mess." Beauregard began grooming the sticky stuff from his fur so intently that he didn't see the fear in Babette's face.

"I take it you don't know where we are? Beauregard! How are we ever going to get Barnaby and Bridget back from Innsbruck? They must be waiting for us by this time," Babette said, trying to clean up the cabin. "We didn't land flat, wherever we are. The whole floor is tilted."

"And it's dark outside. Can't see much through those windows. Still have the quiver and arrows to return to the Iceman's time, too. Oh no!" Beauregard stopped licking his fur and stared in dismay at the computer console.

"What's wrong?" Babette asked, alarmed. "No! Don't tell me. It can't be good news," she added hurriedly, but too late. Beauregard held up the tempometer from where it had landed on the floor.

"Looks like the tempometer has dislodged from the computer. We might be stuck here a bit. I can transport us using the achyfactor, but that's all. However, since we didn't smash up and crash in our fall down the mountain, I rather suspect that we moved into a different time period and had a much gentler landing. I wish Barnaby or Dr. Tempus were here to fix us up."

"There's some light, Beauregard!" Babette said, pointing out the windows into the dark night. It appeared that the lights were approaching them. They looked like fireflies almost against the dark, moonless night. As they came closer, Babette and the cat could see people holding lit torches. The light wasn't clear enough to see the people fully, but it appeared they were all dressed in dark gowns of some sort. Only their faces reflected the torchlight. It reminded Babette of pictures of monks she had once seen.

The people solemnly passed in single file by their timeship, not realizing it wasn't just a big boulder. Their lights hit on some huge, light, upright stones.

"Stonehenge," Beauregard whispered in awe, their location dawning on him.

"In England?" Babette asked curiously. She'd heard of Stonehenge, of course, but had never been there. "Are you sure?"

"I think so. Those rocks look like a **megalithic** monument," Beauregard explained. "But I'm not sure if we're back very far in time or closer to our own present. Many megalithic monuments are older than the Egyptian pyramids! Since the people who built them had no written language, we have to rely on archaeology to tell us how and when they were built. If I remember, no one has ever had a satisfactory explanation of why Stonehenge was built. Lots of theories, though."

"Splendid." Babette said. "We're somewhere in England. Meanwhile, Barnaby and Bridget are probably stuck in Innsbruck, waiting for the timeship. Beauregard, this isn't a cool scene at all."

Beauregard wasn't even listening. He was playing around with the computer, reading the screen out loud. At least the computer still worked. "Theories on the origins of megaliths such as Stonehenge include religious fervor; evidence of coercion by powerful religious elites; instruments to predict tidal cycles by charting phases of the moon; astronomical-scientific or calendar inventions. Hmmm, in other words, no one knows. I smell controversy again," Beauregard licked his lips, craving another hot mouse chocolate with whipped cream. After all, he didn't exactly get to enjoy his first one.

"Can't you find out from the computer where we might be? I mean in time?" Babette appealed to the cat.

"Shhh, I'm still researching," Beauregard said, his tail twitching as he kept scrolling the computer screen. "Stonehenge is one of the most impressive Neolithic structures in Europe. Okay, okay, we're duly impressed," he said to the screen. "Though we might need to wait for daylight to be fully appreciative," he chuckled. "Hey! Listen to this! Some English archaeologists even have a bumper sticker: 'Love is fleeting, but stone tools are forever.'"

Babette groaned. "Right! No clues on our time frame?" she asked again.

"Ah! Here we are!" Beauregard exclaimed. "Spectacular mega-lithic monuments were built from 4500 to 1500 B.C. They're found throughout western Europe and on Malta and Gozo. Megalith means—"

"Huge stone," Babette said dispassionately. "Usually rough, used in prehistoric cultures as a monument or building block. Now that I know. Continue, okay?"

"Sure thing," Beauregard agreed. "The monuments include large tombs, stone circles and avenues, and single standing stones, sometimes called menhirs. Some tombs, such as one at West Kennet in Wiltshire, England, were used over many centuries for burials and possibly in ceremonies for the dead. The stone circles, avenues, and menhirs are more mysterious."

"I think where and when we've landed is a bit more mysterious at the moment, Beauregard. Maybe we're at a different place than Stonehenge. Nothing you've said has either given me clues to that or convinced me yet," Babette pointed out impatiently. She cleaned her sunglasses and put them back on—having a gob of whipped cream on them wasn't helping her see things clearly. It was better now.

"I'm reading about the stones themselves. Many of the monuments have the stones specifically placed to relate to the positions of the Sun, Moon, and Sirius, the Dog Star, at various times of the year, especially midwinter and midsummer. They may have been used as vast outdoor calendars or astronomical observations. The Sun was probably important in religious beliefs at this time, as it enabled farmers to predict the seasons." Beauregard paused and looked longingly at the galley. Should he stop to prepare another hot drink? One look at Babette's anxious face and he decided his palate could wait a bit.

"Babette, there's more," Beauregard tried to smile reassuringly. "Some monuments were built from local stone, but even this had to be quarried, cut into the right shape using only simple tools made from stone, bone, or wood, and then placed upright in the soil. Other stones were transported over long distances, probably by a system of sleds, rollers, and ropes. This involved large numbers of people, which suggests that society was very well organized at this time, but we know nothing about its rulers."

"I don't know much about the Stone Age, really, though apparently the Iceman came from that time," Babette pointed out.

"Well, the ice that had covered parts of Europe for about 20,000 years began to melt after 13,000 B.C. People, animals, and plants gradually returned to places such as the Alps, Scandinavia, and Britain. Interestingly, Britain stayed attached to Europe by a land bridge until around 6500 B.C. Most people lived a nomadic life, gathering food and making shelters from tree branches and animal skins. When the climate warmed up, settled farming communities developed. People quarried stone for making tools, and some of these were traded. This was the beginning of the Stone Age. Around the 4000s B.C., copper mining started in the Balkans and knowledge of metalworking grew. Oh!" He read the screen to himself. "This is interesting!"

"What, Beauregard? Does it tell us anything more about where we might be?"

"Not really, but it's intriguing," the cat smiled. "It's about games. The people who lived off the northeast coast of Scotland during the late Stone Age may have played games in their spare time. Archaeologists have discovered a pair of dice, carved from bone, at the Skara Brae site. There were few trees, so houses were constructed entirely from stone. The people gathered driftwood for fires but made their furniture and tools from stone. Even the beds and cupboards were built from stone. Hmmm, that adds a new meaning to "a firm bed," wouldn't you say?"

Babette nodded, giggling. "That would be a bit hard, I would think." She couldn't imagine living surrounded by stone. It sounded cold, but definitely sturdy. It was easy to see why this period in past history was called the Stone Age, at least in Europe.

Beauregard continued to read out loud. "The Skara Brae houses were built partly underground for protection against the cold and were linked by narrow passageways. Six houses were built in 3100 B.C., about the time of the Iceman back in the Alps. But in 2450 B.C., the houses were completely buried in sand by a sudden, violent storm. Another storm, in A.D. 1850, uncovered them. Today, archaeologists continue to study them and learn more about people at that time."

"That's interesting, Beauregard, but I still don't think it tells us much about Stonehenge or wherever we might be. Those stones didn't look like the remains of stone houses," Babette observed.

"True, let me keep scanning here," Beauregard said. "Okay, here's some information about tombs. From around 4500 B.C., farming communities around Europe built tombs for their dead from massive stones. Bodies were placed in a room, or chamber, inside the tomb. At Newgrange in Ireland, the entrance to a megalithic tomb is marked with a massive stone carved with a design of spirals and diamonds. During daylight, if we find tombs, we can look for spirals and diamonds and it might help us know if we're in Ireland," Beauregard pointed out. "How about making a list of what we can look for to help us identify where we've landed and when? Ready?"

Babette held up her notebook and nodded, scribbling the clues they'd already uncovered.

"Okay, at Carnac in northwest France, avenues of standing megaliths stretch for several miles. The stones almost certainly have religious significance. It sounds like they won't be in a circle like at Stonehenge. People were still building megalithic monuments in Europe during the Bronze Age, which started around 2300 B.C. and lasted until about 700 B.C. At first only a few tools and weapons were made from bronze, but by 1200 B.C., bronze had completely replaced stone and flint, even for everyday objects. Bronze was traded over great distances, as the copper and tin needed to make bronze were not found in all parts of Europe. Axes from Brittany have been found in Switzerland. Swords from Hungary have been found in Denmark."

"Wouldn't it be hard sometimes to figure out if a piece of stone is an artifact or not?" Babette asked, changing the conversation. Beauregard looked thoughtful, hit a few more computer keys, then nodded.

"Yes, when studying an object the archaeologist must first decide whether it was made or used by people in the past. Although for most periods the answer will be obvious, for the Stone Age— or Paleolithic (especially the Lower Paleolithic)—judgment can be less straightforward." Beauregard pointed at a timeline and chart showing up on the computer screen. "See, Babette? Here's a chart showing the different time periods so we have a better idea of what we're talking about," Beauregard pointed to the computer screen.

Babette again nodded. The chart did make it easier to understand.

"For many years a vehement debate raged in archaeology concerning the problem of **eoliths**—pieces of stone found at the beginning of this century from the early Stone Age in eastern

England and elsewhere—believed by some scholars to have been shaped by early humans, but by others to have been products of nature. The controversy led to early attempts to establish criteria to help recognize human-made stone items, such as characteristic bulges or bulbs on pieces of flint purposely struck off. Thus, the eoliths were pronounced to be of natural origin."

"Great! So maybe these stones we can see outside are not artifacts after all?" Babette said, sounding disappointed.

"Those stones were different. Megaliths, not eoliths. Okay, obviously if the stone objects were discovered with fossil human remains or animal bones with signs of cutmarks made by stone tools, then we can assume humans used the stone and they are artifacts," Beauregard pointed out.

"Back to the computer. I'm searching stone tools now. Here we go," he said, again reading his findings to Babette. "It has traditionally been thought that tool-making separated humans from apes. The past thirty years of field research have revealed that wild chimps make and use tools of wood and stone. Chimps use hammers and anvils to crack nuts. In fact, American primatologist William McGrew believes that without museum labels some artifacts can't be attributed to human or chimp species. This makes the identification of crude, humanly made stone tools even more difficult, but also offers archaeologists the chance to 'observe' in chimps some of the possible tool-making, tool-using, and tool-discarding behaviors of early hominids."

"It sounds like we really are close to chimps," Babette agreed. "Is this helping us to identify where we are?"

"Um, not really, but I never knew this stuff before," Beauregard responded, finding it easy to get distracted while searching the computer. "See, what it tells us about tools and early humans and the use of stone is all part of where humankind came from and developed," the cat tried to explain. "From the first recognizable tools, dating back about 2.5 million years, up to the adoption of pottery-making, dated to 14,000 B.C. in Japan before it was found in other areas, the archaeological record is dominated by stone. How were stone artifacts, from the smallest microblade to the greatest megalith, extracted, transported, manufactured, and used?"

"Beauregard, those are huge stones out there, not tools. Why are you reading so much about stone tools?" Babette sighed. She was tiring of the computer search and wished it were daylight so they could explore outside. She didn't see any more torches or people.

"Stone tools are among the most enduring objects ever to be fashioned by human hands," Beauregard pointed out. "They easily last millions of years. Stone tools have become the main criterion for defining the basic periods of prehistory. The Stone Age lasted 2 million years while stones dominated human technology. To understand stones from the viewpoint of prehistoric people, keep in mind that stone tools were not made to exact shapes planned in advance."

"I think it would be almost impossible to make things out of stone. Rock is so hard," Babette said, studying her notebook and trying to see more of their surroundings out of the window.

Beauregard joined her, holding a rounded palm-sized stone he pulled out of the artifacts sack and showing it to her. "Babette, prehistoric people were confronted with basic problems they had to solve in order to get food: How to point the end of a stick so it can be used to spear an animal? How to cut through the tough hide of an animal to get to the meat? How to make a wooden spade that will dig up tubers and roots? A stone tool became an important part of the answer. Stone edges were the foundation of technology for those 2 million years—as long as they were convenient to hold and their size and weight were appropriate for the job."

"That stone looks easy to hold," Babette agreed, hefting it like a baseball.

"Yes," Beauregard agreed. "With stone, what was important was not its shape but the nature of the edge. Some stones had very fine crystal structures, like cherts or chalcedony. Others didn't, like obsidian. Those without crystal structures are easier to shape and excellent for cutting hides and meat because of their very fine, razor-sharp edges. Obsidian was very valuable because of this. Rock salt, sheet mica, or slate fractures when it's cut. To select the right stone, grain size, brittleness, toughness, hardness, internal cracks, or flaws were all considered."

"Of course, they couldn't just go into a store and buy the right stone." Babette commented. She shined a flashlight out on the huge stone rectangular structure outside. It looked shaped, not natural. "I think I'm learning more than I ever knew about stones and maybe more than I ever wanted to know. I wish Barnaby and Bridget were here; then we could go exploring. Someone needs to stay in the timeship, and without knowing what's out there, I don't dare go alone."

"Wise decision," Beauregard agreed, returning to the computer. "Okay, I've got more for your notes on the Stone Age. Early Stone Age peoples left behind three types of artifacts related to tools: (1) hammer stones —rocks that knock rocks off of rocks; (2) cores— rocks that had rocks knocked off them by other rocks; and (3) flakes or blades—rocks that have been knocked off rocks by other rocks. Whew! Did you get that?"

"Yeah, hammer stones, cores, and flakes or blades, three types of Stone Age artifacts related to tools. I bet they made spears to hunt animals, huh?"

"Well, according to this research, stone-tipped spears were a myth." Beauregard said.

"A myth?" Babette grinned. "The Myth of the Stone-Tipped Spears . . . ." she laughed. "Sounds like a horror movie title."

"Hardly," Beauregard said. "Early hunters didn't need stone-tipped spears to kill large animals. If you remember from the Colorado field school, archaeologists usually call arrowheads or spearheads projectile points. Projectile points of stone are not essential for good hunting. In fact, in Australia hunters of kangaroos and emus hunted with wood-tipped projectile points. Stone-tipped arrows were never used in New Guinea. Today, the pygmies in Zaire hunt elephants with wood-tipped spears, as their ancestors did. In Washington State, back in the good old U.S.A., a majority of well-preserved arrows found were wood-tipped. Those are just a few examples."

"Can you summarize things? I'm confused a bit about all of this," Babette admitted.

"Sure!" Beauregard replied. "Okay, during the Paleolithic, especially the early Paleolithic—and you can translate that into Stone Age—the stones are chipped or cracked rather than ground. During the Late Paleolithic or New Stone Age, also called the Neolithic, stones were ground into shape."

"How do you date a stone object or material like flint or obsidian? Even ceramics, for that matter?" Babette wondered, hefting the rounded stone in her hand.

"Sophisticated techniques are used to date stones, ceramics, and bone tools," Beauregard read, after searching for on the computer for "dating methods" and "stones." "This is good to write down in the notebook, for we didn't cover all of this in our archaeology training. Chemical analysis of minute traces of blood and or other residues on the stones can be done. Examining the physical properties such as sizes, shapes, colors, etc., and applying design theory is another method. Dating of not only the stones but also the areas and surrounding artifacts or features in which they were found is important. Other clues to look at in dating include the availability of the materials used, how they were used, how easy they were to use and manufacture, how efficient they were, how much they cost to produce, how costly were their raw materials and maintenance, and other such things. These clues are helpful to date most things, not just stone. Did you get all that?"

"Yes, but you didn't mention if how they were made can help in dating or classifying them," Bridget said.

"Well, good tools usually can be made in more than one way, so that criterion doesn't always work," Beauregard said, yawning. "All this stuff about tools! I suspect that round stone you're holding is a core, used to make flakes or points. See how it's had some chips knocked off it?"

Babette studied the stone. She could see flat grooves where small pieces of the stone had apparently been chipped away or knocked off.

"I'm going to try to fix the tempometer, though I wish Barnaby were here," Beauregard said, getting out a screwdriver and removing the screws from the computer casing.

Several hours later, Beauregard pushed back from the console, a satisfied grin on his face. "Babette? I think I fixed it! Ta-da! Mission accomplished! This calls for a toast with berry punch, wouldn't you agree?" The cat turned to his friend, surprised to find her deep asleep in her bunk. His stomach still growling, Beauregard headed for the galley. He'd toast his accomplishment on his own.

He chuckled moments later as he sat back in one of the seats and sipped the very berry liquid, turning his pink tongue a deeper shade of red. He stared out at the huge megalith, the stones in a perfect circle around the timeship. He knew all along that they were at Stonehenge, for he could see so well in the dark, which Babette couldn't do. Ah! But he liked educating the young human. Besides, he thought computers were fascinating. Look at what he'd uncovered!

What he didn't know, but hoped daylight would tell them, was where in time they'd landed. That was going to be the zillion dollar question. Maybe he should take time for a catnap while he had the chance. He's probably need his wits about him to-morrow.

$\diamondsuit$ $\diamondsuit$ $\diamondsuit$ $\diamondsuit$ $\diamondsuit$

Whack! Beauregard sleepily opened an eye, wondering what was causing the terrible racket.

Whack! Whack! Whack! "Beauregard?! What is it?" Babette jumped off the upper bunk, squatting into her martial arts stance. Outside, the sun was barely touching the sky, causing a bright reddish glow on the horizon beyond the huge stones, the sky a deep, deep blue.

Whack! Whack! Beauregard hurried to the window and stared out, watching a man and his younger son hitting their timeship again and again with rocks similar in size to the one sitting by the computer, where Beauregard had left it last night.

"Oh! Oh, yes," Beauregard said, nodding his head. "They think we're a boulder, Babette," he added. Apparently they're trying to chip some pieces of stone off of our timeship. The timeship shook with their increasing efforts, as the stone exterior refused to chip. Little did they know that it was a modern metal Dr. Tempus had used to fortify the timeship. If falling and bouncing down the side of an Alpine mountain hadn't chipped it, these two humans were not going to be able to.

"This is Stonehenge!" Babette said, watching as the sun came directly between two of the stones, its rays hitting them squarely on the window. The timeship sat in the middle of the circle.

"Yes, and I think it's rather new. All of the stones are up, and there are no ruins lying around," Beauregard agreed. Whack! Whack!

"I wish they'd stop that horrid racket. How's a cat supposed to sleep around here?"

"Beauregard! You fixed the tempometer! Great! Now we can get out of here and go rescue Bridget and Barnaby!" Babette said happily, noticing the instrument back in place next to the computer keyboard. "What are you doing?"

Beauregard was standing at the timeship's door, opening it, as it wasn't near where the father and son were still hitting their timeship. He threw the round stone he had out at the man's feet, then hurried back inside. The man kicked it before he noticed it, but bent down to pick it up and studied it, grinning as he showed his son.

"Well, I'm taking a big chance that we're somewhere back in time where that stone belonged," Beauregard winked. "One less artifact. I believe we only have the bust of Cleopatra and two other artifacts to go. Of course," he amended, "after the Iceman's quiver and arrows."

"Let's do it, Beauregard!" Babette urged. "Let's return the quiver and its contents to the Iceman, then we can be that much further ahead when we get Barnaby and Bridget!"

"Get ready," Beauregard suggested, already setting the quiver and arrows in the achyfactor and the tempometer to August of 3100 B.C and the Neolithic. Babette hurriedly buckled into her seat.

✎   ✎   ✎   ✎   ✎

Again they experienced the rumbles, flashes of light, and usual slight dizziness that came from time travel. Then the *Archy Stone* settled down abruptly. Outside appeared to be an alpine meadow, dotted with a few stunted evergreen trees. Snow-covered, rocky peaks were in all directions. They were back in the Alps.

Babette took the reddish fur quiver and her archaeology backpack, and to the door. "Let's find him," she said, and then noticed that Beauregard wasn't hurrying to follow her. "Aren't you coming?"

"As before, I'll monitor you, then if there's trouble you can still get transported back here to the *Archy Stone*," Beauregard suggested, reminding her that someone should always stay in the timeship.

In the meadow, Babette saw a man hurrying towards her, walking as if he were in pain or had been injured and glancing back over his shoulder fearfully. He was so busy looking behind him, he didn't see Babette coming toward him. She couldn't see who or what he was frightened of. When he finally did notice her, he quickly lifted up a long stick threateningly. Was this the Iceman? Behind him, Babette could hear sounds echoing through the hills that sounded like a battle of sorts. He had curly, dark brown hair and a full beard. He appeared to be bleeding in several places, and his clothing and backpack appeared dirty and stained. He'd obviously been in the battle behind him and had narrowly escaped. Right now, he was staring fiercely and defiantly at her, ready to attack. Babette realized her clothing, shades, and height probably made her very conspicuous, for he was about the same height as she was. He stared fiercely into her eyes, ready to defend himself. She could fight him, but that wouldn't serve any purpose. Instead, she dropped the quiver and turned, sprinting for the timeship.

Beauregard stood at the windows, watching, ready at any moment to transport Babette back to the cabin if the Iceman attacked. He gulped when the Iceman swung his thick brown stick directly at Babette, hitting empty air where she had stood only moments before. The Iceman made as if to run after her, but stumbled on the light brown fur quiver and the arrows sticking out of it. Picking it up, he quickly began pulling out the contents as if to reassure himself they were still there. Beauregard smiled. The Iceman obviously recognized the quiver as his own. He'd never believe in his wildest dreams the journey those items had been on.

Babette returned to the timeship, glad the man was so involved in his things that he didn't notice she disappeared into the boulder. Too late, he remembered her and looked around suspiciously, obviously wondering where she'd disappeared to. He made his way across the meadow, continuing to look everywhere and obviously expecting an ambush any second.

"Another mission accomplished! Bridget and Barnaby? Back to 1991 Innsbruck?" Beauregard asked. Babette nodded. Just as she could see what looked like a group of rugged men on the edge of the meadow, the Iceman quickly ran down into the trees. They were obviously in pursuit of the Iceman.

"I think we got here, and are getting out of here, just in time, Beauregard," Babette observed as she quickly buckled back into her chair. Nothing happened. Beauregard sat at the controls, fidgeting with them, watching the men outside spreading out across the field and wondering if perhaps they shouldn't have helped the Iceman and hid him inside the *Archy Stone* to keep him safe. But then he might not have stumbled into that gully and been found 5,300 years or so from now, when the glacial ice retreated and melted around him.

"Well? Beauregard, what are you waiting for!? HIT IT!" Babette screamed. She knew Bridget and Barnaby had been kept waiting wayyy too long.

Apologizing, Beauregard quickly set the tempometer. With a whir, some more flashing lights, and that sudden lift and butterfly-in-the-stomach feeling like on a fast elevator, they traveled briskly through time and space.

✏ ✏ ✏ ✏ ✏

Back in Innsbruck at the Institute for Forensic Medicine, Barnaby and Bridget sat in a theater listening to Dr. Spindler lecture about the Iceman find to archaeologists and university students. They didn't look happy and were barely listening. Both were feeling very depressed because they had lost hope that the *Archy Stone* was going to return for them. Bridget kept pulling her bubble gum out of her mouth with her fingers, seeing how far she could stretch it before it snapped. Barnaby, lost in his own world, was writing out the chemical formulas involved in his research for the biofriendly essence of the dirty socks pest inhibitor.

"What's important is that the quiver, lying about five meters from the corpse, did not begin to emerge from the ice until the preceding day," Dr. Spindler was saying, flashing slides on a large screen with pictures of the leather-like fur quiver and its contents spread out on a lab table.

"Quiver? QUIVER!?" Bridget repeated too loud. Barnaby ducked down in his seat when everyone's eyes turned to them, and Dr. Spindler paused in his lecture, frowning at them.

"Ahem. Where was I? Oh yes," Dr. Spindler attempted to return to his lecture. "There can be no doubt that the quiver with its contents had lain immobile in the ice from the time it was placed there over 5,000 years ago . . ."

"What got into you?" Barnaby hissed, "That little episode was embarrassing!"

"But he said . . ." Bridget began, her voice defensive.

"Ohhh, quiver! The quiver! Do you suppose . . . ? Of course, it has to be . . ." Barnaby jabbered, unaware of the irritated glances from those around them who obviously didn't appreciate the distraction from the lecture.

"Definitely, it's our quiver, Barnaby. Look!" Bridget pointed at the large screen where their quiver lay in all its recovered glory, no longer soft reddish fur, but appearing leathery. However, it was definitely the same quiver they'd removed from Dastardly's sack.

". . . As you can see, the quiver consists of a fur bag, stiffened by a hazel rod knotted to the side," Dr. Spindler pointed. "Though the hairs have almost completely fallen out, there were a few still embedded in the bag. Projecting at the top are the ends of the fourteen arrow-shafts. All damage to the quiver occurred during the Iceman's lifetime, as it was extremely well preserved over the 5,300 years or so that it was in the ice. The upper part of the quiver, with its semi-circular flap, are here." He again pointed at the rounded top. "In this next picture the contents were removed. The carrying strap of the quiver had been torn off and lost before the Iceman"s death . . ."

"Our quiver had a carrying strap, didn't it Barnaby?" Bridget asked.

"Sure did!" Barnaby agreed.

"We believe the fur the quiver is made from belonged to a stag-like animal such as red deer or roe deer. It's less likely it's elk, though some elk were native to the meadowlands of the Tyrolean river valleys in prehistoric times, so we're not ruling out that possibility. The main sack is made up of a trapezoid-cut piece of fur. This was folded over and sewn up along the sides with fine leather bands. For some reason, this seam faces outwards, while the seam at the lower, short end of the quiver is turned inwards..."

"This is amazing , I mean, how they analyze it. I just saw this narrow sack to hold arrows, didn't you, Barnaby?" Bridget whispered, intrigued at all the details of the archaeologist's analysis and what it told them about the Iceman.

"Shhh, I want to hear this," Barnaby shushed her.

"...Along the side seam is the hazel rod which stiffened the sack so it wouldn't collapse when it was laid down. This rod is 92.2 centimeters long and 1.4 centimeters in diameter. The rod was carefully stripped of its bark and smoothed. A long groove was cut into the rod. It is interesting that the Iceman carried with him all of the tools necessary to make the quiver: a blade scraper for cutting off the ends and removing the bark, the drill-like flint tools for routing out the groove, and its point for making the perforations needed to sew it together. The top of the rod is level with the quiver-mouth, which is, as we shall see, of complex construction."

The two adventurers were no longer bored.

Dr. Spindler paused to take a drink of water, then continued. "Because the middle piece of the quiver was missing when the item was recovered, and was found later still firmly lodged in the ice, that told us that when the quiver was laid down over 5,000 years ago, this middle piece was already missing. The man was carrying it separately, presumably planning to make repairs when he could. Again, let me point out that the quiver was put down by the Iceman about five meters from the boulder on which the corpse was found. Before removing any items from the quiver, we used X-rays and **computer tomography** pictures to see inside. We found that in addition to the fourteen arrow-shafts visible in the quiver-mouth, it contained a number of other objects. You can imagine how excited we were for the actual opening that took place on December 19, 1991, in the workshops of the Roman-Germanic Central Museum in Mainz in the presence of myself and numerous scholars involved in the Iceman project. It held some astonishing surprises . . ."

"Barnaby, have we been here four months?! Impossible!" Bridget said. "He mentioned December and I thought this was September!"

"I don't know," Barnaby admitted. "But we'll discuss that later. I want to hear what they were so surprised about!"

"The quiver contained two arrows ready to be shot, twelve partly completed arrow-shafts, a coiled string, four bundled stag-antler fragments, an antler-point, and two bundled animal sinews. Let me stress again that the quiver and its contents are unique finds unlike any recovered anywhere else in the world at this time. We're still evaluating and interpreting, which is going to take some time. Therefore, think of this as a preliminary interpretation."

Dr. Spindler went on to give extensive analyses of each of the items found in the quiver, including the types of wood or materials used to make them, how he thought they were made, how these compared to other finds from the same time period, and how he thought they were used by the Iceman. It was all very interesting, but Bridget couldn't enjoy it as much as Barnaby. She felt an overwhelming sense of homesickness and loneliness for Beauregard and Babette, her friends and family back in New York City several years in the future, and everything they were missing by staying stuck in some fast-moving timeframe here in Innsbruck.

Suddenly, Dr. Spindler wasn't speaking anymore. In fact, they weren't in the theater anymore. Was it? Could it be?

The *Archy Stone* cabin?!!!

"Welcome back!" Babette smiled, running to her friends to hug them. She waved a sack of bubble gum in the air, rightly guessing her friend's supply was getting low.

"Babette! Beauregard!" Barnaby and Bridget shouted happily, truly unable to believe they were finally back in the timeship. Bridget gratefully took the bubble gum and hugged her friend. It had been too long.

Beauregard even did a little dance, entertaining them while singing an adapted theme from the old T.V. sitcom "Welcome Back, Kotter". "Wel-come baackk, to that same old place you've been dreaming about. Wel-come baackk, to *Archy Stone* and Babette, myself and tempo-meters . . . don't forget the archyfactor, yes, wel-come back, welcome back, well . . . wh-what?" Beauregard abruptly stopped singing and dancing and stared out the windows.

"Huh?" Barnaby echoed, wondering what had interrupted the cat's little jig and his pleasant baritone.

"Uh-oh!" Bridget groaned.

"Not AGAIN!" Barnaby complained.

"It IS," Beauregard confirmed. "Dastardly P. Looter himself, right on schedule." They watched the man walk determinedly up the sidewalk and through the doors into the Institute for Forensic Medicine, not yet having discovered their timeship.

"What now?" Bridget said anxiously.

"What else? Quickly, what's our next destination?" Babette urged, resigned that Looter would continue to find them eventually. He was like a bad penny that kept showing up.

Barnaby reached into the sack and pulled out a carved, sharp projectile point. "This is it," he told them, placing it in the archyfactor and pushing the buttons.

"UN-be-liev-able!" Barnaby said, reading the computer screen.

"What? What's wrong?" Bridget asked, joining the others in buckling in their seats for another takeoff.

"Not wrong! You mean, what's RIGHT! Alaska, that's what. We're heading for Alaska!" Barnaby laughed. "Mesa Site, Brooks Mountain Range, Alaska," Barnaby read again. He'd always wanted to go to America's Last Frontier.

"King Crab? King Salmon? Halibut? Ah! A cat's dream come true," Beauregard said, grooming his whiskers back and perking his ears up in anticipation.

Barnaby pushed a button and they were off . . . just as Dastardly Looter came running out of the double doors of the Institute and caught sight of the timeship in those split seconds before it disappeared.

Shaking his fist at the empty area where a huge boulder had rested only moments ago, he screamed at the sky.

"I'll get you yet! All I need is just one artifact, just one! It's not over until it's OVER!" He threatened. He couldn't figure how they'd gotten away again. He thought the freefall down the mountain had destroyed the timeship and its occupants. He knew Barnaby and Bridget were stuck here and hoped to recover the quiver and arrows, but once again he was just moments too late. Once again, his prey had eluded him. Once again, he was left staring off across time and space after a timeship that was proving more elusive than he had ever thought possible!

There was no time to waste. Dastardly ran back to the *Money Probe*, intent on his pursuit.

✍ ACTIVITIES ✍
Quiz #5

Select the correct definition for each of the terms below.

__ 1.Eoliths

__ 2.Megaliths

__ 3.Projectile points

__ 4.Flakes

__ 5.Cores

__ 6.Hammer stones

a. Arrowheads or spearheads

b. Rocks that had rocks knocked off them by other rocks

c. Large stones used as building blocks or in monuments

d. A term used for what were once thought to be the oldest human-made tools consisting of roughly chipped flakes and cores, but may have been naturally made

e. Rocks that have been knocked off rocks by other rocks

f. Rocks that knock rocks off of rocks

Pondering Stonehenge

1. Why do you think Stonehenge was built? You may want to research astronomical uses of Stonehenge. Lines drawn between pairs of Stonehenge's Station Stones have long been known to show midsummer sunrise and midwinter sunset. A new Stonehenge astronomy began in the 1960s involving the moon-rise and moonset. By using a computer, a whole pattern of alignments in solar and lunar astronomy were discovered for Stonehenge, including the possibility of predicting eclipses of the moon. However, this is still controversial today. Research and discover more about this.

2. Research how Stonehenge and other megalithic monuments or tombs were built. How would they be built today? Compare the suitability of various building materials. Are structures still built with stone?

Food for Thought—What If?

1. You and a friend go hiking. You cross a peat bog, and stumble on bones of a fully preserved saber-toothed cat. Also nearby is a large stone knife and an axe. With these clues in mind, tell what you think might have happened to the saber-toothed cat? Describe your initial reactions—are you frightened, surprised, excited, etc.?

2. An unexpected flood, mudslide, volcano, tornado, or other natural disaster buries your house and its contents. Two hundred years later the site is dug up by archaeologists. Tell which artifacts or fossils in your house will have survived and explain why.

3. What types of games do you think the people of Skara Brae, Scotland, played with a pair of carved bone dice that archaeologists found there?

Chapter 11
First Peoples of the Americas: Mysteries at the Mesa

"Alaska!" Bridget exclaimed, pointing out the windows at the animal herds spread out across the rolling arctic tundra. Treeless plains stretched as far as they could see, broken only by the grazing reindeer.

"Reindeer!" Babette laughed, intrigued. "I've always wanted to see real reindeer. Look! It's like they have soft, white scarves and socks on! Many even have those racks of horns—"

"Antlers, Babette, not horns. The antlers branch into three slightly flattened tines, one extending over the brows. Reindeer are also called caribou," Beauregard told her, taking his apron and floppy chef's hat out of his overnight bag. "Their habitat is northern forests, bogs, and of course, tundra. Unlike other deer, both male and female caribou usually have antlers, though the males' are much larger. Caribou have another peculiarity; when one moves, a tendon in its foot rubs against a bone and produces an audible 'click'. You really notice it when you're near a herd," Beauregard chuckled. "These caribou migrate, wintering in the scattered spruce-fir forests south of their summer range. When they migrate, as many as 100,000 of the caribou may band together. It's awesome to see them on the move. However, usually they're in smaller herds like we can see here. The reindeer of the **Old World** are considered by many to be the same species as the American caribou."

"What else lives on the tundra?" Bridget asked.

"Arctic fox, musk oxen, wolves, ptarmigans, and lemmings, to name a few," Barnaby said.

Then Beauregard announced, "If you'll all excuse me, I'll fix lunch." He disappeared into the galley.

Beauregard didn't begin cooking at once. Instead, he peered curiously through the small galley's window. Smacking his lips, he was unable to shake his powerful craving for freshly caught Alaskan seafood. There was just one problem. Where was the Bering Sea? Instead of the Arctic Sea, a small, clear stream passed close to the timeship. Beauregard could see the stream zigzagged through tundra to its glacial headwaters in the snow-capped Brooks Mountain Range, more than fifty miles away.

"Drats!" Beauregard muttered dejectedly, talking to himself. "Obviously no salmon, king crab, prawns, shrimp, or any other decent seafood delicacies."

Then he stared. How had he failed to notice the scrubby tundra plains weren't flat after all? For there, just a few hundred yards beyond the stream, rose a dark, steep, treeless mountain towering up and up. "Amazing! It must be over 200 feet high!" Beauregard whistled, tilting his head back and straining to see the top.

"Yeow!!!" Beauregard let out a cry of anguish when he whacked his head against the window frame. So much for trying to see gigantic things from small windows!

"Beauregard, what's going on in there?" Babette yelled.

"Are you okay?" Bridget's head appeared in the doorway to the galley.

Beauregard quickly began noisily shuffling the pots and pans around. "Oh, hi, Bridge . . . please pardon the distraction. I was... uh... just looking for the pizza pan," Beauregard reassured her, knowing his explanation of looking for the Bering Sea would sound really stupid.

"We thought something was wrong," Bridget explained.

"Come see this!" Barnaby called out. Leaving Beauregard to his pizza, Bridget took the stuff Barnaby had just printed from his Internet search.

"DNA testing traces ancestry of British teacher back 9,000 years through links with the Cheddar Man skeleton," Bridget read. "The teacher's name is Adrian Targett."

Babette chuckled. "I guess Mr. Targett has a good sense of his roots, huh? Talk about having your family history go way back!"

"Did someone say cheese?" Beauregard stuck his head out of the galley, holding a mozzarella ball and cheese scraper.

"No, not really cheese, Beauregard. It's what scientists named a prehistoric man's skeleton, Cheddar Man. He's an ancient human fossil found in a cave near the British town of Cheddar," Babette explained, "and dated to be about 9,000 years old!"

"Okay, no cheese then. I've got a pizza to make," Beauregard said, disappearing back into the galley.

"How'd they trace Mr. Targett's ancestors back to the Stone Age?" Babette said, intrigued.

"The scientists extracted DNA from Cheddar Man's tooth," Bridget skimmed the article. "He's older than the Iceman, so he was probably a Paleolithic hunter-gatherer. Archaeologists seem to name their finds with the location where they're found, huh?"

"Yes, sometimes," Barnaby confirmed. "That's quite common, to name new finds after the site, like the Laetoli footprints or the Mesa Verde Anasazi. Does the article say why they tested Mr. Targett's DNA in the first place? This discovery demonstrates what modern testing methods can do, doesn't it?"

"Sure does! The scientists were doing other research on the skeleton and came up with the idea that genetic testing might show a modern link with the Cheddar Man. They tested fifteen students and some of their teachers at the Kings of Wessex school in Cheddar. An astounded Targett said he thinks testing many others from the Cheddar area will identify more genetic links to Cheddar Man. The school's only a half-mile from the cave where the Cheddar Man was discovered," Bridget summarized. "It worked!"

"Great! With today's knowledge of DNA and genetics, it isn't that hard to do," Barnaby informed them. "It's the same as what they do to match the DNA of criminals to DNA found at the crime scene. Modern blood samples are compared with Cheddar Man's genetic material, the DNA. Matches establish the link. In this case, the mitochondrial DNA matched."

"Barnaby! You lost me, what's mito—?" Bridget looked bewildered.

"Aptly called the powerhouses of the cell, mitochondria are the organelles responsible for most of the cell's energy production and respiration. They are located outside of the nucleus and possess their own DNA. Mitochondria DNA is different from the DNA that makes up chromosomes of the cell nucleus. The mitochondrial genetic material is only inherited from the mother. When Mr. Targett's mitochondrial DNA matched Cheddar Man's, the results showed Targett was a descendent of Cheddar Man's mother or sister." Barnaby finally stopped lecturing and took a big breath.

"In-CRED-i-ble!" Bridget exclaimed. "I can see genetics are going to provide even more clues to the past. There's so much we keep learning about that they don't know! But, I really like the idea that I'm passing on DNA that you're not, Barnaby. Go figure, huh?" She popped a bubble.

Babette looked thoughtful. "There always more questions than answers in archaeology, did you notice that?"

"Frenchie! They're waiting for us to become archaeologists and figure out the answers for them," Bridget joked. "Anyway, on to more important things. I'm STARVING!"

"Pizza, pizza, pizza!" Beauregard announced right on cue, dancing into the main cabin and holding the pizza aloft on one arm over his head like a waiter in a fine restaurant. Its scrumptious odor wafted over them.

That's when the timeship began to shake and rumble, buffeted by gusty winds. While not an earthquake, it was a bit of a jolt. Startled, Beauregard lost his balance and fell, doing what most cats do when they fall. He landed firmly on all four paws. The pizza pan went flying up toward the ceiling, twirling slowly, as the kids gaped. Then the pan flipped completely over and began its descent. All of its hot cheesey, tomatoey, mushroomy, pepperoni, oniony, green peppery, and crispy crusted glory splattered onto the chef's exposed fur, right onto his back.

"YEOWWWWWWWWWWW!!!" Beauregard's primitive cry caused the kids to cover their ears. Still howling, the cat ran for the door and disappeared outside. A cloud of thick black smoke appeared in his wake, entering the cabin and surrounding them. It was a moment before the reality sunk in.

"Ouch! They bite!" "Owww!" "He got me, the rotten dude! They're all over me!" "Do something, somebody!" "Helppp!"

All three kids wailed, cried, screamed, and swatted at the air and each other, blinded by the swarm of the largest mosquitoes they'd ever seen in their life filling the cabin. Then, abruptly, the cloud disintegrated and disappeared out the open door. The mosquitoes were gone.

In their wake, Beauregard came barreling back into the timeship, gooey pieces of pizza and sticky strings of mozzarella cheese clinging everywhere. He slammed the door shut and deliberately covered his nose with a linen handkerchief.

"Wh-where'd they go?" Bridget asked, looking in disgust at the black insects stuck all over her bubble gum. They had even flown into her mouth, for crying out loud! This was just too much, too fast, and wayyy too painful. She felt mosquito bites everywhere. She noticed Babette's face was swollen and Barnaby's eyes were all puffy. Red, swollen, burning, itchy welts polka-dotted everyone's skin. They looked like they had a bad case of the chicken pox.

"That odor!"

"That horrible, awful, terrible stench!"

Bridget and Babette grabbed their noses, now understanding Beauregard's strange behavior.

"It works! It actually works!" Barnaby exclaimed triumphantly, pulling out his notebook and scribbling furiously. An open test tube, minus its cork stopper, stuck out of his lab coat pocket. The overwhelming odor of dirty socks reeked through the cabin, becoming absorbed into every porous surface. Their clothes. Their bedding. Their backpacks. No wonder none of the bugs had hung around!

"I don't know what's worse." Babette said, ruefully. "The stink or the bites? At least the stink is so horrendous, it completely numbs your senses of smell and taste."

A bit later, as they finished eating the burritos Beauregard had warmed up for them, Beauregard addressed the young scientist.

"Barnaby?" Beauregard began, meticulously wiping his whiskers with his large white linen handkerchief. With Bridget's help, the cat had restored his fur to its usual pristine perfection.

"Beauregard, I've really had enough food, thanks," Barnaby said, patting his full belly and looking up from his notes. He had light pink spots all over him from the calamine lotion.

Barnaby beamed at his friends. "This is the best feeling in the world, guys! To have theorized that the essence extracted from soiled socks, namely the perspiration absorbed from the sweat glands or pores of feet, entombed in porous materials forming a layer between the epidermis and . . ."

"No, no, not what I was going to ask at all," Beauregard denied, trying to ward off an impending Barnaby-lecture. "What do we know about our artifact, the projectile point? Remember? Why else would we be here, in the Alaskan arctic? During my brief excursion outside, I didn't see any excavations underway to give us any clues on why we're even in this place, nor was there an archaeologist to be found."

Beauregard shook his head sadly, ruminating. "Of course, it's possible those reindeer have a few other characteristics than I'm familiar with. According to popular folklore, some of these deer fly, live at the North Pole, and one is even rumored to have a luminescent red nose. Whether they also have interests in archaeology, that I don't know. There's certainly reindeer here, I'll not dispute that. Plenty of mosquitoes, too, if you can call those dipteran female flies with proboscis adapted to puncture the skin and suck the blood of their hosts and who are vectors of serious diseases that make each one a potential murderer—"

"*Musca* comes from the Latin, meaning fly—" Babette contributed.

"What's more to the point," Bridget said, "is why this place? The arctic tundra?"

"Thanks, Bridget, that is what I was getting at," Beauregard admitted sheepishly, realizing he was getting a bit carried away against the mosquitoes. "I can't help conceiving the notion that possibly the archyfactor was damaged in that freefall down the mountain in the Tyrolian Alps. Do you think it may have sent us to one of the remotest places still existing on Earth due to a malfunction? Barnaby, I presume you've been researching while I pursued my culinary endeavors?"

Barnaby reluctantly returned his research notes from his dirty sock experiments to his backpack and turned to his friends. "Do I think the archyfactor malfunctioned? No, and I'll tell you why. I think we're in Alaska to learn about the origins of the first Americans. I've come to that conclusion because in order to return our artifacts, we've learned about the probable origins of early humans, then about people throughout the Paleolithic in Europe. The fact we have come to Alaska and North America, not to other continents, makes me think we'll learn about the first peoples to settle in the Americas. If so, let me see if I can put this in some sort of order so it makes sense, but forgive me if I ramble a bit."

"Barnaby ramble ?" Bridget echoed, as the others chuckled, and chorused, "Never!"

BANG, BANG, BANG, BANG! Someone or some thing was pounding the Archy Stone.

"Who is that?" Barnaby asked, pointing through the mosquito-splattered windows at the man. He was using a hammer and chisel, pounding away at their timeship.

BANG! BANG! Barnaby hurried out the door. "Hey! You! Hey! What are you doing?!" Barnaby confronted the man. He seemed oblivious to the swarms of mosquitoes surrounding him.

The man stopped pounding the chisel and faced Barnaby in obvious bewilderment. Inside the timeship, Beauregard turned on the microphones so they could listen to Barnaby and the man talking outside.

"Who are you?" Barnaby demanded.

"Who am I? I should be asking who are YOU and where did you come from?"

"I'm Barnaby, from New York City."

"Hello 'Barnaby-From-New-York-City', I'm 'Chilkoot-From-Kotzebue', a federal archaeologist, though you can call me 'Chilkoot'. I'm on contract with the U.S. Bureau of Land Management's Kobuk District Office in Fairbanks," the man said, pushing the wide brim of his hat back and removing his work gloves to shake hands. "B.L.M. manages millions of acres of public lands, mostly in the Western U.S. and Alaska. Imagine meeting some New York tourist in a lab coat out here on the remote tundra," Chilkoot mused. Barnaby smiled politely.

"Yes! Our archaeologist!" Bridget said happily, holding her hands palm-up for Babette to give her five. Beauregard did one of his little dances.

"Now we're getting somewhere," Babette laughed, "though we're being silly. All this dancing around and hand slapping."

"I've never met anyone named 'Chilkoot' before, and where's Caught-Sue-Buoy?" Barnaby asked, wrinkling up his face at the strange names.

"Believe it or not, everyone asks me about that. I'm named after my granddad, Chilkoot Taylor. He was named by my great-granddad, an Alaskan gold miner, after Chilkoot Mountain where the Indian trail pass crosses on a route to the Yukon River, where great-granddad struck gold. He got out before the place went bust, moving the family to Nome. Later, my dad moved to Kotzebue, that's K-O-T-Z-E-B-U-E, not a place to 'catch Sue by the ocean buoy', but it does sound like that, eh? Kotzebue's the largest Inupiat Eskimo village in northwestern Alaska. It's located north of Nome on the Chukchi Sea's Kotzebue Sound," Chilkoot explained. "Barnaby, any ideas how this big rock got here?" The man asked, beckoning at *Archy Stone* with his chisel.

"Did you say there are federal archaeologists?" Barnaby asked, quickly changing the subject.

"I hope so, or I need to start looking for a job," Chilkoot joked. "Though I suspect there should be more of us. Yes, the federal government has many archaeologists working in its agencies. We spend a lot of our time doing archaeological and cultural surveys of land before it is developed. While there are about 3.5 million cultural sites in the United States, very few have been excavated and surveyed. Most of our time we're doing surveys on lands prior to any development or construction work. When we survey, we're looking for any artifacts or signs of human habitation that might have archaeological significance, or rather, be important sites. That's a law now, these archaeological/cultural surveys before development on public lands."

"Sounds interesting," Barnaby replied, his eyes a bit glazed. For someone who loved to lecture, Barnaby didn't like to listen very well. Instead, he seemed to absorb information through osmosis instead of his ears.

"I like it," Chilkoot said. "Sometimes we get to do education projects with schools and the community. If I come to your school, remember to have plenty of cookies and invite me to lunch in the cafeteria," he joked, then continued.

"With summer field seasons, we get to do what I like best—working at sites solely to learn more about prehistory. We've been lucky here at the Mesa Site. I've worked with archaeologists Richard Reanier, Michael Kunz, and Sergei Slobodin on the Mesa Site excavations. Michael Kunz discovered the site during a routine archaeological survey almost twenty years ago, before the area was to be opened for oil and gas exploration. Since then, and especially since 1990, we've spent summer field seasons excavating, sample collecting, and conducting or awaiting analysis before the discovery could finally be announced. The Mesa Site is one of the oldest well-documented archaeological sites in North America. Hm, I wonder where this immense rock came from?" Chilkoot tapped the timeship again.

"I came to investigate, too." Barnaby explained, careful not to say what he was actually investigating. "You said the oldest site?"

"Yes, one of them. There's others, of course. Would you look at this rock, though? It's got me stumped. Just appeared out of nowhere!" Chilkoot marveled, slapping the camouflaged windows and splattering more mosquitoes, some of which had obviously fed recently because blood smeared when he killed them.

"Gross, gross, GROSS!" Bridget complained, revolted along with Babette and Beauregard by the squished bugs smeared across the surface and moved back away from the windows.

Chilkoot's voice continued through the speakers. "I thought I was hallucinating when I saw this rock from the top of the mesa. I hurried down here after getting the students going on the digs, and then I couldn't even chip a piece off from it . . ." Chilkoot shrugged. "The stone's cold and there's no crater, so it's not my first thought—a meteorite or something from outer space. There's no erupting volcanoes nearby and the stream is too small. This is definitely a dilemma. Very puzzling."

"You're excavating at the top of the mesa?" Barnaby prompted to change the subject from the timeship.

"Uh huh, we're doing that," Chilkoot agreed. "Quite a view up there, 360 degrees for more than 50 miles in all directions. It's easy to see why hunters used the mesa as a lookout near the end of the Pleistocene or even earlier. I hope we'll solve more of the mesa's mysteries this summer field season. We're going to scout out possible sites down here, around the base of the mesa. But really, I couldn't help but notice this boulder. Barnaby, how did you get here? I would've remembered if you'd arrived with the archaeology students from the University of Alaska. I know I wouldn't forget your hair!"

"I can see why you're a bit puzzled . . ." Barnaby stalled, crossing his fingers behind his back. "I came with a later group." That much was true.

"Did another helicopter arrive from the landing strip? Didn't hear a thing!" Chilkoot replied, puzzled. "The chopper must've arrived after I hiked down here to check out this boulder, huh? How many came with you?"

"With me? Oh, there's four of us," Barnaby said.

"Come on, then," Chilkoot turned to hike back toward the mesa. "I'll check out this rock later. Let's go to the Mesa Site for your team overview and then get you going on the excavations, okay?"

Barnaby followed Chilkoot across the shallow stream and through the scrubby tundra towards the back part of the mountain.

"Babette, Beauregard, I think we'd better hurry!" Bridget urged. They grabbed their backpacks, dabbed on more of Barnaby's dirty sock essence like it was suntan lotion, then quickly ran out the door. Beauregard covered his head with a mosquito headnet, looking like a martian.

"Yoo-hoo! Hey, Barnaby? There you are! Wait up!" They called, rushing to join the young scientist and Chilkoot. While Barnaby looked relieved, Chilkoot frowned, obviously wondering how they appeared out of nowhere.

"We're with Barnaby's group," Babette explained, grinning. "I'm Babette, hi!"

"Chilkoot," Chilkoot said, shaking her hand, then Bridget's. He wrinkled up his nose, faintly sensing a strange odor around the kids, worse than the standard government issue deep woods insect repellent. "Hope you brought work gloves?"

Bridget handed Barnaby his pack and they all removed and put their work gloves on.

"Hi Chilkoot, I'm Bridget and that's Beauregard behind us, he's sort of into tundra plants," Bridget said, offering the man some gum. He took the piece and plopped it into his mouth.

Behind them, Beauregard continued studying the ground. He was talking to himself. "Look at these tundra plants! Purple monkshood, red bog rosemary, and even yellow tundra roses! All these mosses, lichens, herbs, and dwarf shrubs; and clumps and tussocks of sedges and grasses! Not a bad selection for a gourmet chef, not at all." Beauregard pulled at the scrubby plants, stuffing his selections in his backpack. Their roots were cold, some even icy, growing as they did in the thin layer of dirt over the permafrost, the permanently frozen layers of earth.

The three kids and Chilkoot continued their hike. Black clouds of mosquitos continued to hover around them, growing worse between spurts of wind. The wind was loud, making them feel like they had to shout.

"Never, never, never in my wildest dreams have I ever seen bugs like this!" Babette groaned. She whipped her arms around like a human windmill to try to break up the swarms.

"Definite bugfest," Bridget agreed, swatting at the clouds, though Barnaby's essence of dirty socks worked so effectively that none landed or bit them. "Hey guys, without Barnaby's experiment, we'd be gulping down bug protein big time," she pointed out.

"Experiment?" Chilkoot echoed, puzzled.

"How do you stand these bugs?" Babette asked the archaeologist.

"Oh, our Alaskan State Bird? That's what residents call the Alaskan mosquitos. There's twenty-six different kinds in Alaska. They're everywhere and cover everything all summer. They're really hardy insects and travel in huge swarms! We even have competitions to see who can get the most in one swat. The current record is 165 at once!" Chilkoot laughed.

"One hundred sixty five mosquitos with one swat?" Barnaby gasped.

"Yeah," Chilkoot laughed. "That's called density. We've learned to face into the wind because then the mosquitos are behind you. When you work, you try to face into the wind. We also get snow occasionally during the summer, and we like that because at least some of the mosquitos are usually gone for a day or so after the snow melts!"

"Snow? In summer? Brrr," Babette shivered, remembering how cold she was so recently in the Tyrolian Alps.

While there had been no trail to the mesa from the timeship, when they approached the back of the mountain, they saw several trails leading upward. Hiking in single file, they followed Chilkoot up one of the steep trails, having to use their hands at times.

"Excuse me?!" Beauregard yelled over the sound of the wind, barreling past them. They watched him easily climb upwards and disappear from sight.

Finally, they reached the mesa top. A dozen college students were busy at work in different excavations, surrounded by hovering clouds of mosquitos and a couple of archaeologists. Most, like Beauregard, wore netted headgear. In fact, they couldn't tell if Beauregard was among them.

"Wow! What a view!" Barnaby exclaimed, looking at the tundra in all directions, only broken by the glacial white peaks of the Brooks Range and Alaska's North Slope. "It feels ancient here, very old."

"We're 350 miles from the nearest city, Fairbanks, and 160 miles north of the Arctic Circle. The only way here is by air, as you probably discovered. We all take a bush plane to that old oil exploration airstrip and then the short helicopter ride," Chilkoot told them. "This view probably looks much like it did when the **Bering Land Bridge** existed during the last Ice Age." The kids had never noticed how noisy gusts of wind could be.

"But we're really in the middle of . . . nowhere!" Babette said. "Is the Bering Land Bridge named after the Danish navigator and explorer Vitus Bering?"

"What?" Chilkoot asked. Babette repeated her question. "Yes, Babette, the land bridge is named after Vitus Bering. I'd like to think this is a very important site," Chilkoot said, leading them over to one of the excavations. Nearer to the ground, it wasn't as difficult to talk. "Let's see if I can explain why. I assume you've been studying some archaeology?"

"We went to the Eagle Mesa Archaeology Field School," Barnaby informed him. "We've also got our own archaeology kits and tools."

"Good! Let's start at this plot over here, okay?" The kids nodded, getting their notebooks out of their backpacks. A pile of large manila envelopes sat in a box under a large rock to keep them from blowing away. Chilkoot pointed at them. "These envelopes are for any artifacts you find. Include a complete written description of where it was found. Check carefully for charcoal, small flakes, or any pieces of tools. Anything significant, alert me right away!"

Where was Beauregard? That cat definitely had a mind of his own. He always was disappearing on them, especially when they were beginning the nitty-gritty work.

"Chilkoot, you mentioned a land bridge?" Barnaby asked, as he began to brush away the layers of soil in their plot. Babette and Bridget spread out and began to work at different locations.

"Yes, I did. Have you learned about the first peoples to migrate into the Americas?"

"A little bit. We know now it wasn't Christopher Columbus," Bridget said, "though before the archaeology field school that is what I believed. That's because we celebrate Columbus Day and learned about him in school as if he were the first to discover this land. I guess he did prove the world wasn't flat, but I know he wasn't the first to discover the Americas."

"Columbus did have a big impact on the people he found here, who he called Indians. He didn't know he'd landed on the Caribbean islands of Hispaniola and San Salvador, and mistakenly thought the people were from the Orient, India." Babette added. "He didn't find exotic spices, just tobacco that the local Arawak people rolled into cigars. The whole Columbus-discovering-America thing was all a big blooper. Columbus didn't arrive in the New World on purpose. I blame Marco Polo for Columbus's mistake," Babette announced.

"Why?" Bridget asked, carefully removing small stone flakes and putting them in a manila envelope.

"Ever since Marco Polo returned from the Orient loaded with spices, gold, and fantastic tales of the mysterious East, Europeans had lusted after the riches of the Orient," Babette explained. "Overland trade routes between Europe were opened up, but Constantinople fell to the Turks and brought an end to the spice route. That's why Columbus was searching for a direct sea route to the Far East . . ."

"Frenchie! I think Chilkoot knows about Columbus. He asked who the first Americans were, and we told him we know Columbus wasn't it. They had to be Indians, right?" Bridget asked the archaeologist. "And if humans originated in Africa and gradually migrated throughout through the Eastern Hemisphere, or **Old World**, there had to be a few who came to the Western Hemisphere first, the **New World**. They were here thousands of years before Columbus. But where did they come from? Who were they? When did people begin living in the Americas?"

Chilkoot nodded. "Yes, you're right, Bridget, though the answers to those 'who, where, when, and how' questions are still not fully known. In fact, the settlement of the Americas is among the most heatedly debated issues in modern archaeology."

"Pardon me," Beauregard asked, making one of his abrupt appearances. His mosquito net head covering blew wildly in the wind. He looked really funny. He sat down next to Barnaby. "I couldn't help overhearing a discussion about Christopher Columbus. Did I ever tell you my family's tale about Christopuss? Our ancestor cat who helped control the rats and mice on the voyage of the Santa Maria, Columbus's ship? After the ship's voyage from Spain to the West Indies, Christopuss stayed behind on Hispaniola with the native peoples when Columbus returned to Spain. Christopuss discovered . . ."

The kids groaned. Bridget rolled her eyes. "Beauregard, not now, another time, puh-leeze? Chilkoot was just telling us about the first peoples to settle in America, not Columbus!"

"Forgive me wholeheartedly, I was merely. . ." Beauregard stammered, then stifled a yawn with his paw. He obviously was due for a catnap.

"There's been plenty written about earlier 'discoverers' or voyages to the Americas, though the one best supported by archaeological evidence is that the Vikings. The Norse captain Leif Eriksson reached North America almost 500 years before Columbus and started the colony of Vinland in present-day Newfoundland around A.D. 1000. Even then, the Vinlanders reported problems with the local Inuits."

"Then Inuit peoples were in the Americas before the Vikings!" Bridget pointed out. "It's amazing how history's been recorded as if the people already living here weren't human because they were different from Europeans."

"That has been the case," Chilkoot agreed. "History tends to be recorded from the recorder's point of view. As many as 100 million people representing some 2,000 cultures inhabited the Americas at around A.D. 1500. There's a myth about Irish small boats called curraghs arriving in North America, but no archaeological evidence has proved it. An oriental ship's bell was discovered off the California coast, suggesting Japanese or Chinese fishermen may have sailed as far as the Pacific coast. However, these 'discoveries' are all between 500 and 1200 years ago, when native people had been settled throughout North and South America for many, many generations."

"Like the Anasazi! We learned about those people at Mesa Verde and others from between A.D. 700 and A.D. 1300 at the field school," Babette explained. The kids carefully began the excavation procedures they'd learned in their sandbox dig, under Chilkoot's watchful eyes.

Chilkoot nodded. "We know people have lived in the Americas since the Pleistocene. However, until people settled down, it's more difficult to find evidence because they left few remains. The small populations of early peoples moved often, harvesting wild plants and hunting animals. Erosion, burial, decay, and disturbance by future generations make it even more difficult to discover clues about these first peoples. This site is no exception. We've mostly found stone lance points and hearths."

"You've found points here? Are lance points like a projectile point?" Bridget asked, having a hard time to contain her excitement. Could this be where their projectile point came from?

"Before I get into that, let me share the most widely accepted explanation for how people first settled into the Americas, based on archaeological, geological, and genetic evidence," Chilkoot suggested, noting Bridget's suddenly downcast face. She was impatient for answers, as usual. "We believe that the first peoples crossed into Alaska from Siberia and Eastern Asia. They probably didn't realize they were even on a different continent, and simply walked from Asia to North America. This was possible because the floor of the Bering Sea was not covered by water . . ."

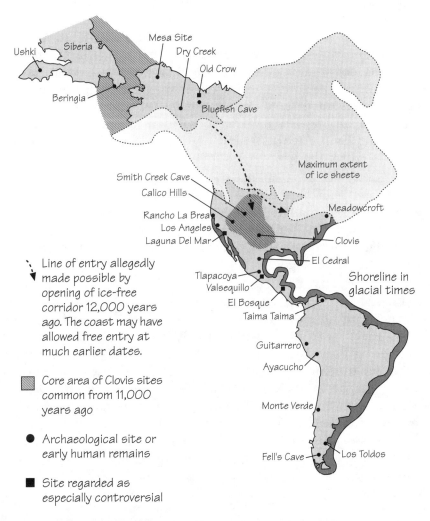

Ushki
Siberia
Mesa Site
Dry Creek
Old Crow
Beringia
Bluefish Cave

Maximum extent
of ice sheets

Smith Creek Cave
Calico Hills
Rancho La Brea
Los Angeles
Laguna Del Mar
Meadowcroft
Clovis
El Cedral

Line of entry allegedly
made possible by
opening of ice-free
corridor 12,000 years
ago. The coast may have
allowed free entry at
much earlier dates.

Tlapacoya
Valsequillo
El Bosque
Taima Taima

Shoreline in
glacial times

Core area of Clovis sites
common from 11,000
years ago

Guitarrero
Ayacucho

Archaeological site or
early human remains

Monte Verde

Site regarded as
especially controversial

Fell's Cave
Los Toldos

The Americas, showing the Bering land bridge, the maximum extent of
ice during the last glaciation, and early sites.

"During the Ice Ages!" Babette guessed, causing Chilkoot to grin. He could tell they'd done some homework. The kids were working well together and had already found a small chip of something that might be a flake from tool-making. They labeled it and put it in a manila envelope, carefully labeled.

Not to be outdone, Barnaby stood up and spoke in his lecture voice, loud and clear above the sounds of the wind. "The land connected the continents at different times due to continental **ice sheets**. We know the ice sheets covered almost all of Canada, the northern third of the United States, much of Europe, all of Scandinavia, and large parts of northern Siberia. At times, glacial ice covered 30 percent of the world's land area and then, during warm periods, the ice cover may have shrunk to less than its present extent. Today, glacial ice stores about three-fourths of all the fresh water in the world and covers about 11 percent of the world's land area. If all existing ice melted, it would create the world's sea-level to rise about 90 meters . . . "

"Barnaby? Uh?" Chilkoot tried to stop the flow of Barnaby's lecture, not realizing he was unstoppable. Barnaby's pacing and waving his arms about bewildered Chilkoot, who looked afraid Barnaby might be seriously cracking up or in the midst of a psychotic fit of some sort. Unperturbed, Bridget and Babette kept working at their dig.

"At times," Barnaby continued, "sea levels were 130 meters, that's 426 feet or 142 yards, lower than they are today. They began rising about 15,000 years ago, but didn't reach current levels for almost 7,000 years, slowly creating the Bering Sea. The Bering Land Bridge was covered by water for the last time about 8,000 years ago, near the end of the Pleistocene Epoch. Today, the Bering Sea is not that deep, averaging only 98-164 feet in depth and is only 53 miles wide at its narrowest point between Alaska and Russia. . . AH CHOO!" Barnaby sneezed when some mosquitos managed to find his nose.

"Thank you, Barnaby, that was really informative. The land between Alaska and Siberia is called **Beringia**—" Chilkoot hurriedly said, before Barnaby could recover to resume his lecture.

"If the sea level was so low, what about the Eastern coast back home, you know, New York City?" Bridget asked curiously. "Was it just the land between Alaska and Siberia that was uncovered?"

"No," Chilkoot answered. "Much of the continental shelf on the coasts of the Americas was exposed as dry land. In fact, it is thought that at one time, an ice sheet a mile thick covered what is now New York City! Underwater archaeologists have even discovered mammoth or mastodon teeth off the eastern coasts of Canada and the U.S. to further verify this."

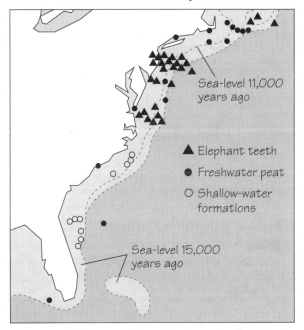

Sea-level 11,000 years ago

▲ Elephant teeth
● Freshwater peat
○ Shallow-water formations

Sea-level 15,000 years ago

Bridget nudged Babette and pointed toward the far corner of mesa. There, Beauregard had dug deeply, with only his tail showing above ground. Behind him was a tall pile of stones and debris. Worriedly, they glanced from Chilkoot to Beauregard's pile, knowing the archaeologist would be furious if he saw what the cat was doing. Beauregard was a wonderful digger, but he wasn't following the right procedures and was destroying the site without doing any paperwork. Though most of the pile looked like rocks, they hoped none of the stuff was actual artifacts or remains of a hearth or something or they'd definitely be in big trouble.

Chilkoot was still talking. The two girls quickly moved their attention from Beauregard back to the archaeologist. "The exposed plain of the Bering Land Bridge was hundreds of miles wide. These plains were not covered by the continental ice sheets. They were dry, cold grasslands, whipped by dusty winds blowing off the glaciers. We think most of the people who migrated across the land bridge were very strong peoples because the climate was very harsh at that time. From what we've found, we know different hunters would camp here on the Mesa Site, work on their tools, and look for animals to hunt."

"How do you know that?" Bridget challenged, pulling her baseball cap lower so she could watch Beauregard's progress without Chilkoot noticing so much.

"Over 85 percent of the tools recovered here at the Mesa Site are stone points of spears, throwing-stick darts, or other tools for hunting," Chilkoot told them. "These, and the remains of eleven hearths, helped us create a sketchy picture of these early hunters. We found obsidian and charcoal."

Barnaby asked. "From just points and hearths? How?" The kids stopped digging, intrigued.

Chilkoot smiled, enjoying their interest. "Yes. When we made our discoveries, we thought our artifacts looked like those others had found in the Lower 48, that's the continental U.S. To test our hypothesis, we had our site dated. Most early cultures can be identified by their projectile points—how they're styled, how they're manufactured or made, what they're made out of, their sizes, and other related details."

"Attributes, yes. Projectile points can be very important to an archaeologist." Barnaby said.

Chilkoot continued. "The points we found here make us think they are the kind associated with **Paleo-Indian** stone tool technology. Archaeologists learned about Paleo-Indians, or Big Game Hunters, back in the 1920s when they discovered projectile points stuck between the ribs of bison at sites near Folsom, New Mexico. In 1932, a similar spear point and bones of extinct animals were found near Clovis, New Mexico, dated back 11,000 years. This tells us that people lived below the farthest extent of the continental ice sheets in the Americas at least that long ago. Paleo-Indian points are the most common type of points found at sites in the Lower 48 for this time period, but never before had they been found in Alaska or Russian Siberia."

"So those points from Clovis and Folsom look like the ones found here at the Mesa Site? Are they identical?" Bridget asked. "What did the dates show? Did you have them radiocarbon dated?"

"The Mesa points are made from chert, a stone found nearby in Iteriak Creek. The points do look similar to Clovis points. Both have sharp points and upper edges, lancelike shapes, overall symmetry, a slightly narrower base than midsection, a lentil-shaped cross section, and heavy edge grinding on the base," Chilkoot explained, showing them one of the points he discovered. The kids had all they could do to contain their excitement, for it did look very much like the projectile point still inside the archyfactor back in the timeship. "However, see this shallow lengthwise channel on the front? That's not on the Clovis point, that fluting."

 Plano Points, about 7500-5000 B.C.

 Clovis Points, (Paleo-Indian) 13,000(?)-9000 B.C.

 Plainview Point, 8000-5500 B.C.

 Sandia Points, 23,000(?)-10,000 B.C.

 Folsom Points, 9000-7000 B.C.

 Pre-Projectile Points, 36,000(?)-20,000 B.C.

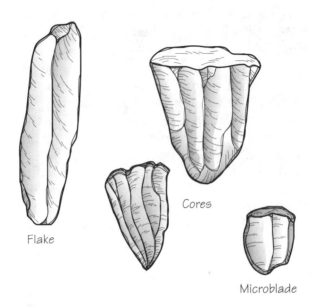

Flake

Cores

Microblade

Babette was obviously trying to mentally compare their point to Chilkoot's. "What about the dating method?"

"Radiocarbon dating can only be done to organic materials," Barnaby reminded them. "All living organisms absorb carbon 14. Once an organism dies, it loses carbon 14 at a fixed rate. By measuring the amount of carbon 14 remaining, scientists can determine the date an organism died. Artifacts such as charcoal, papyrus scroll, linencloth, bone tools, wooden bowls, and oyster shells can be dated using this method, but metal tools, stone statues, and ceramic vessels cannot. That's why the excavation site and context becomes so important . . ."

"Thank you, Barnaby!" Chilkoot roared, abruptly stopping the young scientist from the whole thing with flying arms and pacing around again. He returned to the dig. "The charcoal fragments in the hearths and in fractures caused by fire in some of the stone tools gave us a connection between the artifacts and the charcoal used to date them. We confirmed the hearths were human-built, not remains from a bush fire or lightning strike. A geochemical analysis on the obsidian showed it came from a source more than 320 kilometers away. This suggests the Mesa people may have traded with other cultures or migrated over long distances in search of big game. When obsidian is made into a tool, the freshly exposed surfaces will begin to absorb water from the surrounding environment and a hydration 'rind' will develop. Scientists can measure the width of this rind beneath a microscope. This test on the obsidian found here and the radiocarbon dates on the charcoal were very close."

"What were those dates again?" Bridget pursued, causing Babette and Barnaby to stop their excavating to listen attentively. After all, they wanted to return their point to the correct place in the past.

"The carbon 14 dates for the Mesa site reveal that it was used between 9,700 and 11,700 years ago. This period is very close to the dozen or so other Paleo-Indian cultures that were active between 8,000 and 11,200 years ago." Chilkoot concluded. "Though some archaeologists have controversial dates they claim prove Paleo-Indians were living in the Americas 30,000-50,000 years ago and had spread throughout North America by 20,000 years ago. We still haven't found enough evidence to settle the debate once and for all!"

"Are you saying, then, that the same people who used this site for a lookout also lived in New Mexico about 11,000 years ago?" Babette asked.

"We think these hunting artifacts are not the products of any known Paleo-Indian cultures, but are made using Paleo-Indian style and technology. We also suspect the Mesa people may be the ancestors of the Paleo-Indian Agate Basin hunters who lived on the American plains around 9,000-10,000 years ago and made points the closest to those found here at the Mesa site. None of the other artifacts discovered in Alaska or Siberia from that time period are Paleo-Indian, except for the Mesa site."

"If they're not Paleo-Indian, who are they?" Bridget asked curiously, rising to sift the dirt she'd removed to make sure she hadn't missed any small pieces of artifacts.

"The **Paleo-Arctic** people. They used small-blade stone tools made from wedge-shaped stone cores, or **microblades**, that have been found throughout the arctic, including Alaska. Their sites have been dated from 8,000-11,000 years ago and similar type tools have been found in Japan and Siberia. Sites discovered in Alaska's Tenana and Nenana river valleys dating from 11,800-11,000 years ago do not contain microblades, but their tools are similar to those found in northeast Asia and not like the Paleo-Indian tools. Archaeologists call these people the **Nenana Complex** peoples."

"What about the Eskimos? Weren't they living in Alaska?" Bridget asked.

"We know the Inuit cultural groups, who you're calling Eskimos, were among the last groups of people to migrated into the Americas from Asia about 8,000 years ago, where they settled along the arctic coast. The Inuit group consists of a number of arctic peoples, mostly the Inupiat and Yupik and the Aleut people. These people spread across the frozen arctic from Alaska to Greenland."

"I think it looks clear that the Paleo-Arctic and Nenana Complex people crossed the land bridge and lived as hunters in Alaska," Bridget concluded. "But I don't know what to think about this Mesa Site discovery, how does this fit into the picture?"

Chilkoot smiled, understanding Bridget's confusion. "Until we found these artifacts, many archaeologists believed only the Paleo-Arctic hunters made the earliest migrations into Alaska from Asia. They also felt all Native Americans are descended from this Northeast Asian culture and **Mongoloid** race. The Mesa discoveries open the possibility that more than one cultural group crossed into Alaska. But where the Mesa people, the Nenana Complex people, and the development of the Paleo-Indian tradition all fit together, we haven't figured it out. We need to know more and find more evidence."

"All this talk of cultures and groups of people and making tools sounds confusing to me. Is there another way you can explain this?" Babette asked.

"Yes," Chilkoot responded. "The theory was that as these early Siberian hunters migrated from Alaska further into North and South America, they adapted to their new environments. Gradually, they changed many of their Paleolithic or Old World culture **traits** and adapted to new lifeways. Major changes in the climate as the Ice Age ended also caused changes in how these people hunted and foraged for food. This is how the new cultural tradition, Paleo-Indian, began, and about a dozen distinct cultural groups of people continued that tradition until the big game animals became extinct and they had to change their lifeways to adapt to their new food sources and environment. Different plants grew, causing changes in foraging. Forests grew back where only ice had been before, making it more difficult to move around freely. People were learning to make more efficient tools and build better shelters. Settlements became permanent as people learned to gather more plants like wild wheat and barley, and to grind seeds to make flour."

"Traits, Chilkoot? You said they brought many Old World traits to America?" Bridget asked.

"Yes, besides the stone implements like spear throwers, harpoons, and simple bows," Chilkoot said, "the first peoples migrating across the Bering Land Bridge brought the use of fire and the fire drill; domesticated dogs; cordage, netting, and basketry; and various rites and healing beliefs and practices."

"Maybe the Paleo-Indian hunters changed their lifeways while hunting along the Bering Land Bridge, which is why no Paleo-Indian points have been found in Siberia?" Babette suggested.

"True. Or maybe Paleo-Indian hunters did live in Siberia, but the evidence hasn't been discovered yet," Bridget pointed out.

"Don't forget the original theory. It's possible the Paleo-Indian cultures developed in the New World and didn't spread back to the Old," Barnaby said.

Chilkoot was impressed with his pupils. "I agree with all three of you," he told them. "Based on the results of radiocarbon dating for the artifacts found here, we do believe prehistoric hunters maintained a lookout at this site around 11,700 to 11,200 years ago and again around 10,200 to 9,700 years ago. Because only hunting implements and fragments left from making projectile points have been found, we suspect the site was not used as a camp but was a lookout. No animal bones have turned up, though they are subject to decay and probably wouldn't survive for 12,000 years in the shallow arctic soils."

"From here the hunters could scout out giant bison, mammoths, American horse, and other Ice Age animals crossing the surrounding tundra," Barnaby guessed. "I bet while they scouted or waited for the herds to come within hunting range, they probably made and repaired the tools needed to fell the big game. I think these hunters probably migrated to Alaska across the Bering Land Bridge, because I don't think they would've migrated North to this colder, arctic environment if they were already in milder environments throughout the Americas."

"We still have a mystery," Bridget pointed out. "If you haven't found anything to indicate that these people used this site after about 9,700 years ago, why not? Did they just stop using the mesa as a lookout? Why did the Paleo-Indian hunters abandon this mesa?"

"Do you think the Paleo-Arctic people killed them off or chased them out?" Babette wondered.

"I think if these Paleo-Arctics evolved into Paleo-Indians who spread and settled throughout the New World, including here in Alaska," Bridget reasoned, "then they are the Indians, the first Americans, right? But Native Americans are all different tribes and groups with different lifeways. They all look different. How can they come from the same Ice Age ancestors or have once lived the same way?"

"I love these debates!" Chilkoot grinned. "Today's descendants of these earliest Americans are divided geographically into North American, Middle American, and South American Indian peoples and Native Hawaiians and Alaskan Natives. The differences in appearance today of the various New World tribes and cultural groups have happened over roughly, the last 8,000-12,000 years. These differences are due to: (1) genetic variation of their Asian ancestors; (2) isolation from their original Old World people and adaptation to the New World environments; and (3) since the Columbus era, native peoples have mixed genetically with people of European, African, and Asian origins. Their isolation and these differences have created a separate, distinct group from any in the Old World, generally called the American Indian geographic race."

"Can I get a clearer picture of the chronology here?" Barnaby asked. "Are you saying the first peoples crossed into the Americas about 11,000-12,000 years ago?"

"We think a little earlier, and others think a lot earlier. However, the earliest widely accepted dates for human arrival based on confirmed evidence in the Americas are in the 12,000-14,000 years ago range, or between 10,000 B.C.-12,000 B.C." Chilkoot responded. "Some archaeologists argue for 30,000-50,000 years ago and even thousands before that because the sea levels fluctuated throughout the Pleistocene Epoch, not just with its last Ice Age. They think people could have crossed the land bridge whenever the land was exposed. The date of arrival has not been accurately established with current archaeological evidence. It gets complicated . . ."

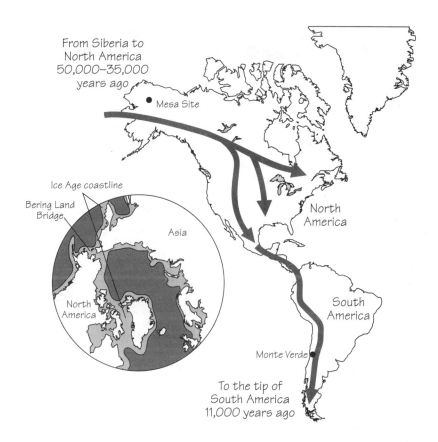

From Siberia to
North America
50,000–35,000
years ago

Mesa Site

Ice Age coastline

Bering Land
Bridge

Asia

North
America

North
America

South
America

Monte Verde

To the tip of
South America
11,000 years ago

During the ice ages, coastlines changed because large
areas were covered with ice

"How so?" Bridget asked. "I'll say," Babette agreed.

"Improved dating methods mean more accurate dates are being discovered for old and new archaeological finds. Most archaeologists are still skeptical about anything dated more than 14,000 years ago because of the extent of the continent ice sheets and the confirmed finds throughout the New World. Recent confirmation of dates in **Monte Verde**, Chile of about 12,500 years ago has added a new element to the settlement theories," Chilkoot said.

"Monte Verde's dates match our Big Game hunter theories," Barnaby pointed out.

"Yes, and mastodon remains were found. Their tusks were shaped, split, and used for tools. Radiocarbon dates on bone and twigs are about 13,000 years old. The 12,500 B.P. date is more than 1,000 years earlier than the artifacts discovered at Clovis, New Mexico and the Meadowcroft rock-shelters in western Pennsylvania dated between 11,000 and 12,000 years ago." Chilkoot told them.

"Chilkoot, if people crossed the land bridge near the end of the Pleistocene, how did they get all the way to South America during the same time period?" Babette asked.

"This isn't as simple to answer as you would expect," Chilkoot warned. "It is also not known exactly how these early Paleo-Indian hunters migrated throughout the Americas before the end of the Ice Age. We do know that the people who probably migrated in small groups and probably crossed the Bering Land Bridge into Alaska, probably followed the animal herds. Like people moving today, they probably used different routes and means to migrate, many of them moving again and again before settling down. They may have used corridors through the ice sheets and along the coasts, or boats. We're not really sure."

"Did the people here in the Americas develop their technology and culture the same as those in the Old World? Was there a Stone Age, Bronze Age, and Iron Age in the Americas?" Babette asked.

"Actually," Chilkoot replied, "the peoples of the New World developed much different cultures and lifeways from those of the Old World since the Ice Age. Old World practices such as the use of the wheel, plow, and use of iron implements did not emerge here. Yet pottery-making and the development of towns and cities reached high levels of sophistication in the Americas. Many New World cultures depended on hunting and gathering for food. After A.D. 800, agriculture came to be the economic base of more advanced civilizations. The focus in the New World was on corn (maize), beans, squash, and tubers as the staple crops. In the Old World, the reliance was on cereal grains such as wheat, barley, and rice."

"Um, Babette? I think we've established enough information to return our Paleo-Indian point," Barnaby whispered. "Let's figure out how we can make our exit, huh?" Babette nodded.

"Hey! Come look at this!" One of his colleagues beckoned to Chilkoot, who ran over to examine Beauregard's pile.

"Oh no! Beauregard, come quick! We'd better get out of here!" Babette called to the cat.

"Dastardly Looter! What timing! Look, the *Money Probe*," Barnaby pointed. The silver bullet-shaped timeship was parked on the opposite side of the mesa from where they'd parked the Archy Stone., by the B.L.M staff's tents and living quarters.

"We've gotta Scram!" Babette yelled, already running. Barnaby, Babette, and Beauregard were right on her heels. They reached the timeship, relieved to see no sign of Dastardly. Hurriedly, they strapped themselves in. Barnaby set the tempometer for 11,700 years B.P. Immediately, they experienced the by-now-very-familiar rumble. The timeship shook, lights flashed, and their ears popped. They landed with a jolt.

"Wow! That's a rush!"

The three kids and cat stared out the window. Small herds of strange animals roamed in thick grasslands over what had been tundra only moments before. The clear creek was now a silty river of glacier melt. The timeship appeared to have set down in almost exactly the same place. Thankfully, there was no sign of *Money Probe*.

They had no time to lose! Hurriedly, they climbed out of the timeship. The wind whipped against them, heavy with dust. Barnaby began sneezing fitfully. A solid ice wall rose, as high as the mountains of the Brook's Range had been. Happily absent were the swarms of mosquitos.

"Look! Over there!" Beauregard pointed at the small group of people moving towards the Mesa Site.

"But they look so small, those people, compared with the animals," Babette pointed out.

"AH-CHOO! Yes, we've got to get this spear point to them and see if that's where it belongs. If they don't seem to recognize it, we'll have to move on," Barnaby said, wiping his nose. His dust allergies were making him miserable. Barnaby returned to the timeship's door. "Beauregard? You coming?"

The cat appeared at the doorway, stretching sleepily. "Um, I think I'll stay behind here. That saber-toothed cat might not realize we're cousins of sorts . . . might even be twins if not for those slightly larger canines. He might want to sample modern, domestic cat cuisine, if he spies me."

"Saber-toothed cat?" The kids momentarily panicked, searching out the wild predator. Though Beauregard's eyesight was better, they saw the single feline crouching through the grass quite a distance away.

"Hellooo, hey! You there! Is this yours?" Barnaby screamed to the people making their way to the Mesa Site, holding up the Paleo-Indian point. Babette and Bridget jumped up and down, waving their arms to get the people's attention. It worked. A lance came flying powerfully at them.

"Yikes! DUCK!!!" Barnaby yelled, diving into the tall grass.

"Barnaby, they're attacking us!" Bridget pointed out disgust-edly, pulling her baseball cap down on her head as if it would provide extra protection.

"Stay cool, we'll get through this," Barnaby promised. The air was raining weapons, some hitting the timeship. Barnaby picked one up and examined the point. "Yup, looks like ours all right," he said, showing the weapon to Bridget and Babette, who were cowering in the grass next to him.

"Who cares, Barnaby! Let's just leave it and get out of here! Our lives are in danger, Barnaby!" Bridget screamed, already trying to wriggle on her tummy closer to the timeship.

Babette and Barnaby slithered after her. Luckily none of them had been hit yet, but the rain of weapons hadn't let up either. "I feel naked! We've nothing to protect ourselves."

"Beauregard, TRANSPORT, TRANSPORT!!" Babette yelled, following Bridget's feet around the timeship and hearing Barnaby's sneezes right behind her. They finally reached the timeship door.

"Beauregard!" Barnaby thundered, as the three stood shakily looking at the cat. Beauregard was curled up on a bunk, catsnoozing. He didn't awaken.

"Figures," Babette said. Outside, they watched the early peoples, dressed in brown fur clothing, retrieving their weapons and warily circling the timeship, looking for the three kids who were there only moments ago. They looked slightly confused.

"This was too close, Barnaby. We might have been killed," Bridget pointed out. "This was too much adventure for me," she admitted. The timeship jerked sharply and began rocking.

"No! Oh, oh, oh noooooooo!" Beauregard awoke screaming, as the timeship tilted off the riverbank and hit the grayish silt-filled rapids. The *Archy Stone* pitched and rolled like a rollercoaster ride. The timeship began to swirl and they could see behind them, on the banks of where they had originally landed, the silver exterior of the *Money Probe*. Dastardly and crew had again arrived, too close, and again seemed intent on destroying them and the timeship.

Quiz #6
North American Archaeology

1. **Definitions:** Test yourself and match vocabulary words with their definitions. Check the glossary if you're not sure.

   A. The continents of Europe, Asia, Africa, and Australia and all associated land in the Eastern Hemisphere is called the _____. The continents of North and South America and all associated land in the Western Hemisphere is called the _____.

   B. Wide plains between North America and Russia that became submerged by water after the last Ice Age are named the _____.

   C. Big Game Hunters were called _____.

   D. Some of the earliest people who lived in Alaska's interior from around 12,000 years ago and whose artifacts were found in the Tenana and Nenana River Valleys were called _____.

   E. The group of early people who spread out across the arctic about 7,000 to 10,000 years ago, from Alaska to Greenland, and made similar stone tools including microblades are _____.

   F. The site where the dating of its artifacts showed that people lived in South America at least 11,800 years ago is _____.

2. **Artifact Classification:** The way early people made their tools and weapons tells us a lot about who they were and helps us identify when they lived. Using artifact classification helps answer questions about prehistoric lifeways. What clues about the Paleo-Indian spear point found at the Mesa Site tell you about the people who made and left the spear point behind?

3. **Hunter-Gatherers:** How different do you think life was for the hunter-gatherers of the Mesa Site and the Anasazi people you learned about in chapters 5 and 6?

4. **Interpreting Artifacts:** Five stages or activities related to artifacts tell archaeologists about human behavior:

(1) acquisition of materials to make the artifact

(2) manufacture of the artifact

(3) use of the artifact

(4) what's discarded and not used

(5) where it is found in a site (context, location)

You are given:

(a) a hammerstone

(b) projectile point attached to a stick

(c) charcoal in a circle of small stones

(d) waste such as small flakes and pieces of stones; and

(e) broken spear points

List which of the five stages or activities listed (1-5) you think are represented by each artifact (a-e). Some could have more than one answer. What might these artifacts tell us about human behavior? Explain why you made your choices. (Answers to a-e in back of the book in the answer key).

Research You Can Do

5. Where did the first Americans come from? How did they get here? How did people spread all across the western hemisphere? Why did people settle in particular places? Write a skit to demonstrate this.

6. The more ice sheets and glaciers exist on the lands, the lower sea levels are. You may want to research glaciers and how there were continental land bridges during the Ice Ages with a local meteorologist or by researching the Internet. Currently, glaciers in Antarctica are melting and breaking off into the ocean, some in chunks as large as the state of Connecticut. How do you think this will affect sea levels in the future?

Plan An Archaeology Week At Your School.

Some activities may include:

a. Invite an archaeologist to come and speak to the class and review your projects.

b. Do some of the research projects listed throughout this book.

c. Create posters to hang around the school or class-room showing your archaeology projects and what you've learned.

d. Write and perform skits about different cultures.

e. Compile a resource directory of cultural sites, ar-chaeologists, and museums in your area. You may want to use a looseleaf notebook for this.

f. Develop displays showing the various stages of human development and timelines showing differ-ent cultures and major events.

g. Review materials available in your library on ar-chaeology. Discuss building these resources with your teachers and librarian.

h. Research archaeology and anthropology on the Internet. Create an Archaeology World Wide Web directory listing interesting archaeology web sites and topics.

i. Write to an archaeologist who has recently been involved in a major discovery and ask if he or she can tell you about it in a letter to read to your class or to post on your bulletin board.

j. Research the prehistory and history of your area and make a presentation of your findings.

k. Using a camcorder, create a video about the past and topics you found interesting as you learned about archaeology. Share the video with your class or family/friends.

l. Have a contest at your school to design an Archaeology Week poster.

m. Have a culture day where you research a culture and then dress in a costume, prepare foods, and discuss a way of life that's different from your own. How did the people live? Where did they get their food? Where did they find shelter? How did they communicate? How and where did they travel?

_____

Chapter 12
The Imperial City: Alexandria, Egypt

Bright light filtered over them, and the kids and Beauregard blinked against the glare. Groaning, Beauregard tentatively touched his head where he'd banged it on the floor.

"Are you okay?" Bridget asked the cat anxiously, as she stood up and tried to straighten her rumpled clothing. She reached down and helped Babette to her feet.

"I . . . I think so. It's tough to kill us cats," Beauregard chuckled, wincing a bit at his headache. "I think I've still got about five lives left or so. Barnaby? Are you there?"

"What did I do?" The young scientist asked, standing up and untwisting his lab coat. "Where are we?"

"Looks exotic to me. Greece or somewhere," Babette pointed out, as they gazed out at the bluest water they'd ever seen and the brilliant white plaster of the city's buildings surrounding the harbor. Statues adorned the high gates into the homes. "Do you think this might be where Lyle the Great, King of Littledot, and his daughter Equinia live? Remember, from our adventures in *Word Smart Junior*?"

"Yeah, I remember them. They lived on a small, deserted island somewhere around Greece. Or possibly we'll bump into Brother Owain and Brother Gruffydd, the two monks from the same adventures. They lived on the island of Cyprus. We could use some of their wisdom. Ah! 'Time is a labyrinth, full of twists and turns—and sometimes dead ends.' Yes, they were wise. I wonder if that's an ocean?" Babette said, glad to be wearing her shades as the sunlight reflected in thousands of points of light off the waves.

"I strongly suspect it's a sea . . . the Mediterranean Sea," Beauregard said hastily, recognition washing over him like a blast of wind.

"So this is Greece?" Bridget said happily.

"Could be," Barnaby agreed. "Or Turkey?"

"You're both wrong. It's Egypt," Beauregard said, leaving no room for argument.

"How can you be so sure, Beauregard?" Bridget asked, surprised that the cat seemed to know exactly where they'd landed, and possibly even when. "I thought there were supposed to be two long obelisks like the one in Central Park."

"I've been here before," Beauregard told them. "You must mean Cleopatra's needles? It's true that in our time one of the obelisks is located on the Thames River's banks by the Waterloo Bridge in England and the other, as you've seen, is in New York City's Central Park. However, when Cleopatra ordered the obelisks built to honor Mark Antony, she had them originally set up by Thothmes III in Heliopolis, near Cairo. They were transported to Alexandria and adorned the Caesarium temple only after Cleopatra's death."

"So this is Egypt? Of the Pharaohs?" Babette asked excitedly.

"Well, yes. This is Alexandria's Golden Age under the Ptolemies," Beauregard explained.

"I thought Ptolemy was Greek?" Barnaby said, confused.

"He was. Egypt has already been ruled by a foreign power, Greece, for more than 270 years. Greece created a huge empire in the lands surrounding the Mediterranean Sea, long before Rome created the Roman Empire. **Alexander the Great** conquered Egypt by marching his armies across the Sinai Peninsula, the land bridge between Asia and Africa. He built this port city at what was a small fishing village on the westernmost edge of the Nile River delta. Alexander dreamed that trade caravans from the east could meet the ships of the Mediterranean here and his vision came true. This is Alexandria, named by Alexander in honor of himself," Beauregard told them.

"Sounds like that man had a healthy ego," Babette pointed out. Beauregard nodded, agreeing.

"Okay, so you've been here and this is Alexandria. Um, is it still Greek? If Alexander founded it . . ." Barnaby asked curiously, as he picked up their archaeology packs, the bedding, and other things that had fallen loose during their wild ride on the river rapids and then time travel to Egypt.

"The main language and culture here were Greek, but now in Alexandria's Golden Age, this is truly an international and cosmopolitan city, full of people from every country around the Mediterranean Sea. Alexandria is divided into three main districts: the Jewish quarter, the Egyptian or *Rhacotis* quarter, and the Royal Greek or *Brucheum* quarter," Beauregard informed them. "We've obviously landed in the Royal Quarter. Look at all these splendid buildings!"

The *Archy Stone* was parked on one of two large, wide boulevards where they crossed at right angles. Temples and palaces, long colonnades, statues, and fountains lined the boulevards. Across the harbor, they could see a series of paved dikes protecting the inner harbor. "What's that?" Bridget pointed toward the western part of the harbor.

"*That* is one of the **wonders of the ancient world**—a lighthouse built on the island of Pharos. The fire that burns in the lighthouse is magnified by a series of mirrors, making it incredibly bright. In fact, I believe the light is visible to sailors forty miles out into the Mediterranean. It's the equivalent of our modern skyscraper to those of this world, and it is the tallest building at this time." Beauregard said, grooming himself almost frantically.

"What's the rush?" Babette asked as she put her backpack on. "What's left in the artifact bag, Barnaby?"

"Just this sculptured bust of Cleopatra," he said, carefully pulling it out of the sack. "And this rolled paper full of **hieroglyphics.** I'll leave the paper roll here for now. Our quest is almost over, and returning the Cleopatra bust looks like it will be easy. Since we're already back in time, I guess we don't have to try to figure out where to bring the bust to return it. Somehow that was done for us," Barnaby headed for the door. Warm Mediterranean breezes wafted over them and through the timeship.

"Beauregard, whatever are you *doing*?" Bridget asked, watching the cat's grooming become more intense.

"Where do we return this Cleopatra bust, Beauregard?" Barnaby asked, standing at the door with the stone bust.

"Probably should start at the library," Beauregard said absently, busy checking his reflection in the windows of the *Archy Stone's* cabin. "The Alexandrian Museum and Library, that is." He put on a red velvet vest with shiny gold buttons and a matching red fedora on his head. He seemed to glow with excitement, from the top of the fedora and the tip of his moist, wet nose . . . to the strange slippers he wore on his feet.

They didn't know it, but he looked like he had just stepped out of the dream he had earlier where he frolicked with Cleocatra in Cleopatra's palace. "Ah! I think this will do," he grinned, apparently satisfied.

"Beauregard?!" Bridget and Babette echoed, amazed at the cat's costume and puzzled by the cat's behavior.

"And *where* is this library?" Barnaby prompted, obviously only interested in returning the artifact.

"Hey, Beauregard? What's up? Why are you dressing up and acting funny?" Bridget pursued, outspoken as usual. Her bubble gum almost fell out of her open mouth when she caught Beauregard coming out of the galley holding a dish of mousaroni and cheese and a bottle of sparkling cider. The cat was truly acting weird.

"Oh, the library? It's here somewhere," Beauregard pointed down the wide boulevard, carefully carrying his mousaroni and cheese. "Alexandria is considered a center for learning and learned people from all over come here. It's the intellectual, cultural, commercial, and scientific center of the ancient civilized world. The library was started by the Greek ruler Ptolemy. It is the stuff of legends. Stories of the library's destruction have persisted throughout history. In fact, these stories have been retold so many times in so many forms, it's hard to know exactly what happened."

"Why would anyone care and change the story?" Babette wondered.

"Because of politics, mostly," Beauregard said. "Historically, the blame for the library's destruction has been attributed to many different rulers and groups usually as political slander, not as efforts to record the library's history. Ancient writers report that Julius Caesar torched over 40,000 volumes of scrolls housed in grain depots near Alexandria's harbor when he burned Cleopatra's brother's fleet. Other historians such as Livy reported that the fifth century scholar and mathematician, Hypatia, was dragged from her chariot by an angry mob of monks. The monks flayed her alive and then burned her on the remains of the old library. This story created even more legends, as you can imagine."

"Wow!" Bridget responded. "I hope we're not in danger of getting dragged from a chariot and flayed or burned?"

"That was about 400 years from now," Beauregard pointed out. "Anyway, one of the three libraries was the Serapian, located in the Temple of Serapis. That library was destroyed in A.D. 391. The main library is next to the palace grounds. I believe it has over 700,000 volumes in many languages, such as Greek, Latin, Hebrew, and Aramaic. The Caesarium, built by Cleopatra, later will become a cult center for worshiping Augustus and his family. The Caesarium held a third library and, we think, held the 200,000 books of Pergamon that Antony gave to Cleopatra."

"That sounds romantic, 200,000 books," Babette said. "So we've gone from Ice Age caves to actual books and written language now, huh?"

Beauregard laughed. "You could say that. This library and museum idea was a first for this time. Its founders were able to draw on the techniques of Aristotle and Greek thought, applying these methods to classical Greek literature and science. By its location, Alexandria not only was a center of trade, but also a major exporter of writing material. Grammar, manuscript preservation, and even trigonometry became new sciences. Writing was translated into Arabic and Hebrew. Even though modern scientists lament all of the information lost over the centuries from the museum and library, it's amazing how many Alexandrian discoveries and theories are still the basis of research in many fields. That's especially true of mathematics and geometry. People have continued to use the methods of research, study, information storage, and organization developed here through to our time."

Barnaby nodded. "Yes, and just as scrolls gave way to books, in our time we're watching the transformation from books to electronic documents."

Beauregard smiled. His anticipation was infectious. "Yes. As you can see," he gestured at the Royal Quarter and city all around them, "In addition to the library, Ptolemy I also built that sumptuous palace. He built these temples and monuments to both the Greek and Egyptian gods." Beauregard gestured grandly, as if he himself had built it all. They walked with him, gaping at the bustling crowds, beautiful fountains, statues, sphinxes, and gardens.

Beauregard pointed at the beautiful palace they were walking toward, built along the edge of a long quay or road on a dike leading out to the Island of Pharos. "That palace looks across the water at the residence of Mark Antony, Cleopatra's great love, who tragically ends up committing suicide with her in 30 B.C."

"Suicide! Ugh! Makes you wonder if there was something we could do to stop that from happening, huh?" Babette murmured. "I remember reading the French poet Théophile Gautier in 1845 wrote that Cleopatra is a person to be wondered at . . . whom dreamers find always at the end of their dreams."

"Oh, brother," Bridget mumbled. "At the end of their dreams, huh? I don't expect to find her at the end of *my* dreams. Also, we can't change history or we'll be in big trouble. Cleopatra didn't want to submit to the Roman conqueror, Octavian, so she killed herself. That was the end of the Pharaohs. Alexandria becomes a province of the Roman Empire. Okay, let's find that library."

"I think she was a great romantic, one of the greatest the world has known!" Babette declared, causing Bridget to smirk even more.

"Um, Beauregard, what period of time is this?" Barnaby asked curiously, surprised to see such a grand civilization in a time he thought was less advanced, more primitive. This city was one of the most beautiful he had ever seen. He felt he was definitely wrong in his assumptions. The sculptured bust of Cleopatra that he held even looked crude next to some of the magnificent water fountains, sculptured sphinxes, statues, columns, and architecture surrounding them.

"Oh, this is the time of the last Great Pharaoh, that of Cleopatra. It's about 40 B.C., I think, under Cleopatra's reign. Cleopatra is descended from the same Greek ruler Ptolemy, who founded the library, so she isn't truly Egyptian. She was only fourteen when she became Pharaoh. I think she's done really well."

"Does any of this exist in modern-day Alexandria?" Barnaby asked curiously.

"Well, this whole section of Alexandria was only recently discovered by marine archaeologists in our time, for it became buried under the Mediterranean Sea. The archaeologists used military satellite technology to survey and pinpoint the ancient royal city of Ptolemies and to make accurate maps, for the first time in over 2,000 years. Earlier maps of the Royal Quarter were found to be inaccurate," Beauregard explained, waving his paws expansively and accidentally sideswiping a man leading a camel.

The man merely bowed apologetically and pulled his camel out of the way. Behind him, a little boy kept scooping up the camel's droppings and depositing them into a sack, keeping the boulevard clean.

"What do they think happened? Did this city just sink naturally over time?" Barnaby pursued, intrigued.

"No," Beauregard shook his head. "Archaeologists think major earthquakes caused tidal and flood waves, sinking this part of the city. All of this grandeur—the city's palaces and holy temples— was submerged. Even these columns, statues, and sphinxes along these boulevards and side streets were left exactly where they are on the bottom of the sea. The underwater archaeologists uncovered more than 1,000 artifacts over the course of more than 3,500 dives. They gained a better appreciation of all of this grandeur when they caught some glimpses of the reality. They said these discoveries are only the beginning; they're still searching for Cleopatra's and Mark Antony's tombs. Archaeologists expect the excavations to take at least 50 more years before all is recovered, catalogued, mapped, or identified. If you become marine archaeologists, you might be involved in this project."

"Whew! Fifty years? I can't imagine doing archaeology underwater, where you can't plot and dig. How did they mark their finds?" Bridget asked.

"The divers labeled the location of each architectural feature and artifact using radio receiver buoys," the cat told them.

They stood in the midst of the boulevards, surrounded by activity that felt strangely like the busiest sidewalks back in New York City, hundreds of people all around them, intent on going somewhere, and all speaking different languages. Many were dressed in beautiful silks or richly embroidered tunics. Most wore fabulous jewelry and ornaments of precious gold and stones, obviously the wealthy and elite of Alexandria. When people spied Beauregard, they immediately fell before him onto their knees, raising their hands over their heads and bowing again and again in obeisance. Beauregard beckoned for them to stand. Although the cat was embarrassed from the unusual attention, he smiled a little bit, too.

"Why are these people treating Beauregard like he's royalty or something?" Babette asked, as they looked for the library. Barnaby carried the bust of Cleopatra in his arms.

"Not royalty, a . . . ." Beauregard mumbled something unintelligible.

"Did you say a dog, Beauregard? Why in the world would they associate you with a dog?" Babette said, amazed. "You're more cat than any cat I've ever known!"

"Not dog, a god," Beauregard clarified. "Cats are sacred here, some are even worshiped. I'm a bit larger than most cats, especially cats of this time, so they think I'm a . . . a . . . god," he sniffed, trying to act like it was nothing out of the ordinary.

"No wonder you knew where we are, Beauregard! This must be one of the best places and times in the world for a cat such as yourself," Bridget pointed out, snickering. "Maybe we'll just have to leave you here when we return to our time and our lives!"

"Well, we will see," Beauregard murmured, stunning Bridget as she'd been half-teasing him. "Anyway, I'm afraid I'll be leaving you for a while. I've got to . . . er . . ." Beauregard looked unusually flustered.

"Must be a female cat," Barnaby laughed, shaking his head. Beauregard looked away, maintaining his dignity.

"You could say that," Beauregard said mysteriously, wondering how to explain that he had actually visited this place and time in a dream before. He hoped Catra wasn't just a figment of his imagination. He had to find out for sure.

Then, in what seemed a blink of an eye, Beauregard had disappeared into the terraced gardens of the palace.

"Looks like we're on our own," Bridget pointed out unnecessarily. "Let's ask someone where the library is."

"I'll return the bust for you," said a man sitting in the shadows, his face hidden by a sky blue silk robe flowing around him. He held his hand out toward them.

"Ikiko?" Bridget said, feeling this couldn't be the wise old Asian man they'd met in earlier adventures who recited Haiku poetry and spent his time hanging out by a fish pool and plum and orange trees.

"What is that noise?" Babette scrunched up her face.

"The zoological park," the man responded. He pointed. "That way. It's part of the palace. Animals from all over the world."

"Ikiko?" Bridget repeated, trying to see if the old man had a thin white beard and white hair, but youthful features. But she couldn't see because of his hood.

"How did you know we're returning that bust?" Barnaby asked suspiciously.

"I am a seer. I know all, I see all," the man explained in a raspy voice, very unlike Ikiko's. "I will return that bust and you'll be free to leave to return to your present."

"He *knows*!" Bridget whispered, amazed. Barnaby lifted the heavy stone bust outwards and gave it to the man. He quickly covered it with his robe and stood up, turning away from them. Just as he did, Babette caught a glimpse of his face.

"It's Looter! Dastardly Looter!" She screamed, pointing as the man in the robe rushed back down the boulevard, a dog appearing where the hump on his back had been only moments before. They disappeared out of sight.

"He's got the bust of Cleopatra! Oh no!" Bridget wailed, running after the thief. Barnaby stood shell-shocked, unable to believe he had just given Dastardly Looter an artifact.

✎ ✎ ✎ ✎ ✎

"Catra," Beauregard said softly, peering into the huge, open terrace over the water outside of Cleopatra's palace. Soft silks rustled in the breeze and moved aside as Beauregard entered.

"You have come!" Catra responded, as if expecting him.

"Then it wasn't just a dream?" Beauregard said, plopping down onto the pillows just like he'd done before.

"No, I called you here the first time, and knew you would return to me one day, this time to stay," Catra said, purring loudly and blinking her beautiful eyes at him. "What's *that*?"

"Er . . . what?" Beauregard answered, tongue-tied in the face of this beauty.

"That?" Catra said, pointing at the dish in his lap.

"Oh, some mousaroni and cheese, my favorite. I thought you'd like to try some," Beauregard said. Catra nodded, sniffing the delicious aromas and sitting next to him on the pillows. The cat poured the sparkling cider into two goblets.

"You *are* here to stay, aren't you Beauregard?" She asked as she licked daintily at the mousaroni, still purring.

"Um . . . we'll see," Beauregard said anxiously, still holding back and not sure why. He didn't hear the kid's screams as they chased and then lost Dastardly Looter and the stolen artifact. He didn't know they returned in hopeless defeat to the *Archy Stone*, only to be met by Dr. Tempus, who had escaped from the *Money Probe* at last. In fact, Beauregard heard nothing but the soft purrs and slurps next to him as Catra helped him finish the mousaroni and life felt very good indeed.

———————————————

✍ ACTIVITIES ✍
Putting It in Perspective

1. Egypt was among the first places in the world to begin farming and then develop cities. Identify different stages in the transition of humans from hunter-gatherers to farmers and then to city-dwellers. List the different travels the kids and Beauregard went on in their quest. Identify how the people at each place got their food.

2. How has modern archaeology affected what we know about Alexandria in the time of Cleopatra? Refer to this chapter for recent findings and list what you think those findings contribute to our understanding of the history and peoples of Cleopatra's time.

3. Using a world map, outline the boundaries of Alexander the Great's Hellenistic Empire and compare it to the boundaries later of the Roman Empire.

4. You may wish to read William Shakespeare's tragedy about Antony and Cleopatra and compare it to what you now know from reading this chapter.

Food For Thought

1. Who was Cleopatra? What famous people did she meet? When and how did she die? When and where did she live?

2. Research the Seven Wonders of the Ancient World. List what you feel are Seven Wonders of the Modern World. Your wonders can be human-made or natural, but you must be able to explain why you chose what you did.

3. From its beginnings as a small fishing village, Alexandria became a powerful city. Why do you think the city thrived? What geographical features make the city strong? Would Alexandria have been as powerful if it had been landlocked?

4. Develop a timeline for Alexandria. Include major events, rulers, wars, architecture, and other accomplishments.

5. Write a story that begins, "When I first met Cleopatra . . . ."

6. When was your city or town founded? Who were its founders? Why was the city or town built where it is? Why did it grow? List five important events in its history. What changes have you seen? What changes do you predict in the future?

7. Alexandria was first part of the Hellenistic Empire, then the Roman Empire. You may want to research both the Greeks and Romans. What did each of these cultures contribute to Alexandria? Can you give some other examples of places today that are ruled by other countries?

Research Alexandria and its history on the Internet. List interesting sites and share with your friends or classmates.

Vocabulary List

Alexander the Great

Antony

Caesar

Cleopatra

Hieroglyphs/Hieroglyphics

Pharos Lighthouse

Ptolemy

Underwater Archaeology

Wonders of the Ancient World

Chapter 13
The Journey Home: A Last Adventure

"FREAKY!" Bridget exclaimed, when they entered the timeship. "Things don't look so great, do they? Dastardly's got our Cleopatra bust. We've lost Beauregard, and time is running out. We need to get back home and stop Dastardly, but how can we just leave Beauregard here?"

"True," Barnaby agreed, "Where's our cat? He's not crossed our path in far too long. I'm checking if there's any way I can transport him back here." Barnaby got busy at the computer console, pushing buttons and sighing when nothing happened. Finally, as a last resort, he turned to the instruction manual he hated to use. He liked figuring things out on his own, but Beauregard's absence called for extreme measures.

"What's left?" Babette asked, looking out at ancient Alexandria and feeling that somehow their visit there had all been a mistake. What had it accomplished?

"Just this papyrus scroll with scribbles and drawings all over it," Bridget said, pulling the rolled paper-like scroll from the limp sack. "Don't know what good it's going to do, now that Dastardly recovered one of his artifacts he has the proof he needs. Soon the world will know Dr. Tempus's secrets of time travel and Dastardly will grow rich. Even worse may be the consequences of stealing it out of the past and out of its context. Do you think he'll let Dr. Tempus go now?"

Babette shrugged. "Time will tell, it always does. Can I see the scroll?" She looked it over, shaking her head in confusion. "The Egyptians have two different kinds of writing: **hieratic** and **hieroglyphic**. Hieratic writing is a kind of shorthand, used for everyday business. Hieroglyphic writing is the older kind. It's used for important writings, religious writings, and inscriptions on monuments. Hieroglyphs are about 2,000 years old and were at first a picture language with a little drawing for each word. People who made the inscriptions were called **scribes**. As time passed, the writing became more complicated and signs began to represent sounds. It was more like our alphabet. Words could be made up of several signs. It will take me awhile to figure out what this scroll says. I can tell this is in hieroglyphic symbols and is a mixture of sound signs and word signs."

"How can anyone figure that stuff out?" Bridget complained. "I wish we had Ms. Hedda Gabbler and her husband Frizzy. Remember them from when we visited the Better Letter Inn in that old west town? They were experts on letter writing? I bet they could figure it out." Bridget reminisced, remembering these friends from their earlier adventures in *Writing Smart Junior*.

"Actually, the lost language was **deciphered** from the **Rosetta Stone**," Babette informed them. "That's a huge stone that was dug up in 1799. It had Greek and both kinds of Egyptian writing on it. Jean François Champollion, a French scholar, compared the hieroglyphs with the Greek text. It took him fourteen years, but he figured out the meaning of a single word and that turned out to be the key to cracking the Hieroglyphic Code. It looked like this:"

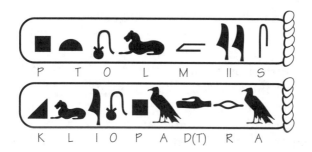

To Bridget and Barnaby's amazement, Babette drew hieroglyphs on a piece of paper and showed it to her two friends.

"The Rosetta Stone turned out to be a decree issued by Ptolemy V. It dates from 196 B.C. As I said, it will take me a little while to figure our scroll out, though." Babette admitted.

"Why not put it in the computer and find out what it tells us?" Barnaby suggested, after he failed to find a way to locate Beauregard to transport him back into the timeship.

Babette placed the scroll in the archy factor. "Egypt" printed out across the computer monitor.

"Hey, it's still Egypt. Why don't we just go there now? We can come back to get Beauregard. If we return that scroll and get the cat, then we can return to the present and hopefully stop Dastardly. It's a plan, anyway," Bridget suggested.

"There's much history in Egypt, we might need to go back thousands of years even from now," Babette pointed out. "Around 3000 B.C., the communities along the Nile River developed into two separate states. Each was ruled by a king. Lower Egypt was the Nile Delta, while Upper Egypt stretched south for about 500 miles (800 km). Then in 3100 B.C., King Menes of Upper Egypt conquered Lower Egypt. The two parts became united. Three Kingdoms followed, each covering a major period of Egyptian History. I learned all this when I was studying hieroglyphics," Babette told them.

"Three Kingdoms? Like in fairy tales?" Bridget asked.

"Not really fairy tales, Bridget," Babette said. "The Kingdoms are the Old Kingdom, Middle Kingdom, and the New Kingdom. The time of the early Egyptians was a time of technological growth and prosperity. People developed irrigation systems to improve farming, and cities grew. Egyptians were very concerned with death and the afterlife. Archaeologists have built up a detailed picture of what Egyptian life was like during the three kingdoms from studying artifacts, the remains of the tombs, and written records."

"Did these people create writing?" Bridget wondered. "I mean, did written histories and language exist before the Egyptians?"

"No, I don't think so," Babette responded. "Though they did prepare the first known textbook on surgery. Among the earliest writings we know of, beyond the cave and rock symbols we learned about, is Sumerian **cuneiform** used in Mesopotamia up to 7,000 years ago. The word came from Latin, *cuneus*, meaning a wedge. Though the first writing was pictographic with each sign representing a small picture of the object, cuneiform was composed of triangular marks made by pressing a wedge-shaped tip into wet clay tablets. It became complex enough so that only the trained scribes could read it. Writing systems for use in accounting developed first, then many separate types of writing evolved. Though the earliest true writings appeared in Mesopotamia, writing quickly showed up in Iran and Egypt. Writing appeared in Egypt around 3000 B.C., but it is thought to have been imported from Mesopotamia. I believe the earliest preserved alphabet dates to about 1400 or 1500 B.C., written on a tablet found at Ugarit in Syria in cuneiform. That alphabet became the ancestor of the **Phoenician script**. The Phoenician script also became the basis for Greek, Roman, Hebrew, Arabic, and Russian alphabets."

"Okay, okay, I'm learning more than I ever wanted to know about writing. Did modern history start with these writings?" Bridget asked.

"Not really, because the early texts are mostly fragments. But after a few centuries, as chronicles and epics appeared, lists of Kings were created, and astronomical information was written down. Recorded history had begun. With the coming of writing, we begin to hear directly from people's own mouths about their lives and learn something of their beliefs and view of the world. However, much of the early writing was on perishable parchments like our scroll and has disintegrated. Archaeologists have much more information about civilizations who used the clay tablets because the information was better preserved. Should we search out the origins of our scroll?" Babette asked.

"I don't know," Barnaby shook his head slowly. The plan looked full of holes to him. What if they never could find Beauregard again? What if they were too late to stop Dastardly? Maybe they should just go back and stop the man, now, and then try to get Beauregard back and forget the scroll?

"This is a dilemma," he commented sadly, putting his face in his hands. As he did, his elbow hit the green button.

"Ee-yikes!" Babette called, falling backwards into the chair as the timeship took off from Alexandria and barreled through time.

"Where are we?" Bridget asked, feeling like she'd been asking this question with almost every episode of time travel. They never knew exactly where they'd end up!

"Let's hurry, wherever we are, to identify this scroll and read it and get back to Beauregard and the future," Barnaby urged, grabbing his backpack and heading for the door.

"Awesome!" Bridget stood at the door of the timeship and looked at the activity bustling all around them. They had landed near a marketplace full of stalls and people bartering. Some people walked along the rooftops of adjoining mud-brick houses of the village. Beyond and across the wide Nile, peasants were working the fields of crops and several canals. Sailors unloaded ships. Other ships of all sizes floated by, some piled high with elephant tusks, timber, clay pots, and other materials.

Babette held the scroll and joined the other two kids outside the timeship.

"Welcome!" A boy their age stood in front of them. He wore a cloth wrapped around his waist and was deeply tanned from the sun. "I'm Besi." He smiled, staring at their clothes, especially Bridget's baseball cap.

"Besi?" Barnaby repeated.

"Yes, I'm training to be a scribe," Besi announced proudly, "and sometimes I dream things that come true. Like your arrival. I live here. I can tell you don't. That's a cool crown you're wearing," he gestured at Bridget's New York Yankees baseball cap. "But you look roasting hot in those layers. Aren't you hot?" He said to Barnaby, pulling on the lab coat. "That mask is also something!" He pointed at Babette's sunglasses. "Did you just arrive on a ship?"

"A scribe? How did you know that's just what we needed? Yes, we did just arrive on a ship, of sorts," Babette cheerfully responded.

"A crown?" Bridget echoed, confused. She pulled her hat down harder on her head, wondering how anyone could mistake that hat for a crown.

"I saw you in a dream. I've always been special. My parents named me after Bes, a comic dwarf god that brings good luck and happiness in the home." Besi told them, grinning mischievously.

"I hope you'll bring us good fortune," Barnaby murmured.

"Besi, we have a scroll. Do you think you can help us understand it?" Babette wondered, handing out the fragile papyrus. Besi took it from her.

"I hope so," Besi said. "I spend a lot of time at school studying the inscriptions to learn to read the language. It isn't much fun. I have to spend most of my days making copies and taking dictations or chanting the texts aloud. I also learn to do sums."

"Hmm, interesting," he said, reading their scroll. "Texts like this help teach me the wisdom of the past to make me a good man."

"Why do you say that? What does it say?"

"You must go to the temple and make an offering to Bastet, the cat goddess, to complete your quest," Besi told them.

'That's it? Just make an offering? We don't have to talk to this god or anything?" Bridget asked suspiciously. It sounded too easy.

"Ordinary people aren't allowed to disturb the god, only the priests can enter the god's presence. You can make offerings in the forecourt. You may also wish to buy a votive tablet. We believe they have ears to hear your prayers. My father works in the temple as a scribe. The temple is where I go to school to learn to be a scribe. I also work in the House of Life, a place of learning where scholars go to copy and consult scrolls. There's another room where my mother practices music for the temple festivals."

"What are we waiting for? Let's go!" Barnaby said.

Besi led them through the marketplace to the side of the village where the huge temple was built. Its outside walls were built of stone. Statues of pharaohs and tall pillars of stones topped with sheets of gold were by the temple's entrance.

"Obelisks," Besi told them, pointing at the pillars. He beckoned at the acres of farmland stretching out to one side of the temple. "Those fields and the people working in them are all for the temple. They store food and grain in silos and a storeroom within the temple walls. That's why all these acres of farmland surround the temple. We bury our dead beyond the farmland. However, we bury the important people and their servants in those pyramids, there across the desert," Besi pointed. Far off in the distance, the kids could see the tops of pyramids.

"Look! It could be Abdul, that Bedouin of the Arabian Desert we met in *Geography Smart Junior* adventures, remember?" Babette said excitedly, pointing at the long-robed and head-geared bedouin tribe parked across the river.

"Maybe, Babette, but I think not! We left him at the Red Sea, and this is the Nile." Barnaby pointed out. "Though he was welcoming and helpful, like Besi here. Of course, bedouins are the masters of trade. The first signs of long distance trade of select materials, such as obsidian, occur in early Neolithic times. Early trade flourished in Mesopotamia and areas of the Red Sea, so Abdul may very well be involved in the trade over time, with his descendants. Those could be his ancestors over there. Trade on a large scale could only be financed by economic surpluses. Those surpluses only became available after the introduction of farming. In simple societies—" Bridget and Babette rolled their eyes, knowing Barnaby was in another lecture-mode. Besi listened, intrigued, especially when Barnaby began pacing and flapping his hands around.

"Simple societies that are based on farming only enough to support the farmers don't go far enough to feed everyone, or to allow economic growth, or to allow them to advance in the social hierarchy," Barnaby continued. "This led to the rise of elites, whose power allowed them to collect fine goods not available to others. The exchange of surpluses led to specialization of crafts to make better things to trade. There was clearly a great deal of local trade, and it was no accident most of the early civilizations were built along rivers. Travel by water lowered the costs of transport and allowed the movement of bulk goods, as there were few good roads or money to maintain them. Pottery and timber could be moved considerable distances. Timber has always been in short supply in Egypt, but with river traffic, it could be brought from Lebanon and other points. Trade became vital to the achievement of prosperity," Barnaby concluded with a flourish.

"Wow! Those lions are cool!" Bridget said, pointing to the sphinx statues lining each side of the forecourt. Men were setting up booths.

"Why can't we just have a priest talk to Bastet, the goddess?" Barnaby complained.

"I can share this scroll with a priest," Besi offered. "They may be able to help you. Priests conduct main temple ceremonies every morning. After shaving and washing on the Sacred Lake within the temple walls, the priest enters the sanctuary and takes the statue of the goddess out of her shrine. He sprinkles water on the statue, changes its clothing, and offers it food and drink. Then he returns it to the shrine and leaves the doors open until evening. When he leaves the sanctuary, he uses a broom to remove his footprints," Besi told them, leading the way to the front of the Pharaoh statues.

"These are statues of the Pharaoh," Besi said. "Here is where you make an offering."

"What do we offer? We don't have anything!" Barnaby said, dismayed.

"Bubble gum!" Bridget announced, pulling out some of her hoard. Besi looked puzzled, obviously not knowing what she was talking about, but he shrugged and showed her how to bow in front of the statue of the Pharaoh and make the offering. She did that.

CRASH! All activity ceased, with people staring and muttering. Behind them, people came pouring out of the temple to stare at the pile of shiny rubble that had landed in the middle of the forecourt.

"Beauregard!" Bridget yelled happily, running and greeting the long-lost cat. He stoically let the three humans pet and cuddle him until he stepped back, having had enough.

"But h-how?" Barnaby wondered, looking at the pile of rubble.

"That's what's left of the *Money Probe*," Beauregard said, examining his claws to make sure they suffered no damage in the landing.

The rubble moved, with pieces clattering everywhere. A head appeared, causing the surrounding crowds of people to stop bowing to Beauregard, who they thought must be a god, and step back in fear. Dastardly walked sheepishly out of the garbage heap, wiping the dust off his clothes.

More rubble moved. Out came a very dusty and embarrassed dog, his tail between his legs.

"Looks like you'll need a ride, huh?" Barnaby said to Dastardly, as the three kids exclaimed about how Beauregard had found them. Dastardly looked humble, hanging his head. His hands were tied securely behind him and a chain led to Sneakers. They couldn't get away and appeared to realize they were finally beaten.

"Where's the Cleopatra bust?" Bridget wondered.

"With Cleopatra where it belongs," Beauregard said. "And," he sighed. "Left with Catra, that royal feline. I must admit it was one of the toughest things I've ever done, to leave her."

"Oh Beauregard, how romantic! But, how *could you!*" Babette admonished him.

The cat looked sheepish. "I knew you young humans were waiting and might get in more trouble requiring my services. Besides, I thought about never, ever cooking with microwaves and convection ovens again."

"Ha! Not to mention the modern felines, eh, Beauregard?" Babette teased him. "Our Casanova!"

Beauregard suddenly slapped himself on the forehead.

"Sorry, almost forgot," he muttered as he dove into the remnants of the timeship. He reappeared, helping Dr. Tempus in his stained lab coat to his feet.

"Dr. Tempus!" The kids said happily, rushing to the man, glad to see he was okay. He looked even happier at seeing them.

"Where's Besi?" Barnaby suddenly asked, looking around and not finding their new friend.

"I saw him slip into the temple. He's probably handing over the scroll to one of the priests," Bridget explained, grabbing Dr. Tempus's arm.

"Well, looks like we'd better get back. It sure will be good to be home. I can't wait! Besides, I'm clear out of bubble gum. The offering, you know," Bridget admitted, laughing, as they all, including Dastardly Looter and Sneakers, walked back to the *Archy Stone*.

"I assume you're now all experienced amateur archaeologists?" Dr. Tempus asked expectantly as they strapped Dastardly and Sneakers into the bunks, since there were no extra chairs to buckle into for the return timetrip home to New York City.

"You betcha!" Bridget responded. The other four and Dr. Tempus slid into the chairs. "Though we didn't visit many places and peoples and civilizations I would have expected we'd see."

"We especially know how much *isn't* known, right?" Bridget agreed.

"Right!" Barnaby said gleefully. "However, if you look at the progression of human knowledge . . .."

Dr. Tempus reached past the young scientist, accurately predicting another Barnaby-lecture was approaching, and pushed the tempometer for home, typing in the location on the computer screen. Before Barnaby could say another word, they were off, the timeship vibrating around them.

✍ ACTIVITIES ✍
Fun With Codes

1. Write a message using English and two other languages or codes. See if a friend can figure out the other languages or codes you developed by comparing them with English.

2. Choose ten examples of modern writing to preserve for future archaeologists to find and study. If these were the only examples any future archaeologists would see, what would you choose? Why did you select each one?

3. Make a clay tablet to write on. Pour soft plaster of Paris into a large cardbox box top or bottom. After it has dried and hardened, peel off the cardboard and carve your message with a large nail, ice pick, or heavy duty needle.

4. Imagine that a new room was discovered within the remains of an Egyptian temple at the village the time travelers visited along the Nile. Draw a picture of the room. Explain the artifacts that were found in it. How will this discovery change the history of Egyptian temples? How will it change our modern ideas about ancient Egyptian culture?

Using the hieroglyphic alphabet, create your own scroll and message.

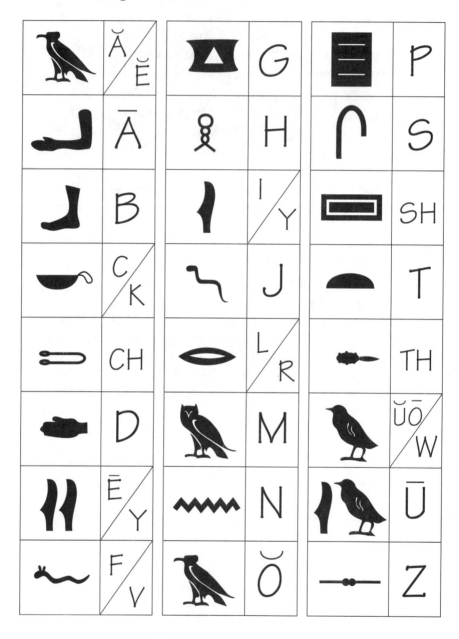

Vocabulary

Cuneiform

Decipher

Phoenician Script

Rosetta Stone

Scribes

Answer Key

QUIZ #1

1. b. archaeology
2. e. paleontology
3. f. artifact
4. g. attribute
5. i. inference
6. l. chronology
7. j. classification
8. h. culture
9. k. data or evidence
10. d. hypothesis
11. a. stratigraphy
12. c. prehistory

QUIZ #2

1. d. cross-dating
2. l. strata
3. h. hypothesis
4. i. inference
5. f. datum point
6. g. grid

7. b. Cartesian Coordi-
nate System
8. e. data
9. a. attribute
10. c. classification
11. j. observation
12. k. sherd

QUIZ #3

1. hunter-gatherers
2. ethnology
3. land bridge
4. petroglyphs
5. Leroi-Gourhan
6. Flint
7. Cores
8. Middens
9. Paleolithic
10. Obsidian

Quiz #4

1. c. magic or religious ceremonies
2. a. dry cave
3. c. culture
4. d. Pleistocene

Quiz #5

1. d
2. c
3. a
4. e
5. b
6. f

Quiz #6

1. A. Old World, New World
   B. Bering Land Bridge
   C. Paleo-Indians
   D. Nenana Complex
   E. Paleo-Arctic
   F. Monte Verde
4. a 2, 3
   b 3
   c 5
   d 1, 4
   e 4, 5

Glossary

ABSOLUTE DATING. Establishing the number of years since an object was made or used.

A.D/B.C... Abbreviations from Latin Anno Domini, meaning in the year of the Lord (Christ). Is also sometimes referred to as the after date and represents dates occurring after the death of Jesus. B.C. is placed after the numerical date (i.e., 89 B.C.), while A.D. is usually placed before (i.e., A.D. 89) Archaeologists and many others often prefer to use B.P., before present, especially for prehistory.

AGATE BASIN. A cultural tradition whose people made or fitted their tools and weapons of agate, a fine-grained chalcedony with striped colors. These people lived on America's Great Plains from around 8,000–7,000 years ago. They may be descendants of Alaska's mesa culture.

ALEXANDER THE GREAT. (356–323 B.C.) One of the greatest military geniuses of all time, Alexander was king of Macedonia, conqueror of the Persian empire, and founded the city of Alexandria in Egypt. Alexandria became one of the intellectual and trading centers of the Greek and Mediterranean world. During his youth, he was tutored by Aristotle. Shortly before he died at age thirty-three from a fever in Babylon, he ordered all Greek cities to worship him as a god.

ANASAZI. One of three desert cultures that shaped life in the American Southwest from around 300 B.C. to A.D. 1300. The Anasazi spread throughout the Southwest, developing the new pueblos and farming on the tops of mesas. They used hand-shaped adobe bricks or stones with adobe to fill in the gaps to build their homes.

ANTIQUITIES/ANTIQUARIAN. Relics, objects, or monuments of prehistoric times. Works of art, furniture, or decorative objects made at an earlier period and according to various customs or laws at least 100 years ago. One who collects or studies antiquities.

ANTONY. Mark Antony (83?–323 B.C.) Roman statesman and general. He defeated Julius Caesar's assassins. With Gaius Octavius and Marcus Aemilius Lepidus, formed the second Triumvirate that ended the Roman Republic when they divided the Roman Empire among themselves. Antony summoned Cleopatra to Cilicia (now Turkey) because of her refusal to aid his triumvirate in the civil war. Instead of punishing her, Antony fell in love with her. Though he married Octavius's sister, he continued to live with Cleopatra. Later defeated and besieged by Octavius, deserted by the Egyptian fleet and Antony's own army, and given a false report of Cleopatra's suicide, Antony killed himself by falling on his sword in 30 B.C.

ARCHAEOLOGY. A science for studying or analyzing material evidence (artifacts and sites) and human cultures. A specialized field within anthropology concerned with the study of humans. Identifying cultures by a set of recurring material remains of features, house types, pottery forms, and burial styles.

ARTIFACT. Object made, used, or transported by humans that can provide information about human behavior in the past.

ATTRIBUTE. A characteristic or recognizable quality of an object, such as size, color, shape, age, how it was made, uses, and so on. Artifact attributes are anything helpful in describing, analyzing, or characterizing it.

AUSTRALOPITHS. Extinct African early humans that evolved possibly 4 million–5 million years ago. They evidently came from an ape ancestor that hasn't yet been identified. Australopiths had little skull behind the hole for the spinal cord, a small brain, a large and dished face, wide midface, and distinctive teeth. They were likely hairy, and though some were not much larger than chimps, others were muscular and nearer to modern humans. Jaws and cheek teeth were large and powerful, suitable for crushing seeds or chewing leaves. Australopiths had lower limbs that were longer than the arms and were designed for walking upright.

B.C.. Placed after the numerical date (i.e., 89 B.C.), while A.D. is usually placed before (i.e., A.D. 89) Archaeologists and many others often prefer to use B.P., before present, especially for prehistory.

BERING LAND BRIDGE/BERINGIA. Land that connected Alaska with eastern Siberia during the Pleistocene. When the last Ice Age ended, the continental ice sheets and other glaciers melted. This caused the sea level to rise, and the water flooded the Bering Land Bridge. Today some of this land is only 50–100 feet (15–30.5 meters) below the Bering Sea. At times the Bering Land Bridge was over 1,500 miles (2,414 km) wide.

BIFACIAL. Having two sharp sides.

BIPEDAL. Movement on two feet.

BLADES. Also called flakes. Sharp edged, thin pieces of stone. Blades were shaped into tools or weapons or left as flintknapping waste.

BLUNDERBUSS. A muzzle-loading firearm with a short barrel and flaring muzzle.

B.P.. Before the present. A unit of time for years before the current one.

CAESAR. Julius Caesar, a Roman aristocrat and soldier, was born around 100 B.C. and elected consul by 60 B.C. He conquered vast new territories for Rome, including Gaul, but he failed to conquer Britain. He schemed until he was made sole ruler of Rome for life. However, he was murdered by two senators in 44 B.C. because they thought he wanted to make himself king and abolish the Roman Republic.

CHRONOLOGY. The arrangement of events; in the order of the time in which they took place.

CLANS. A group of people united by a common interest or a common characteristic. Can also be a group tracing their descent from a common ancestor.

CLEOPATRA. Though there were several queens and princesses named Cleopatra in the generations of the Ptolemies of Egypt, Cleopatra VII (63–30 B.C.) reined as queen and Egypt's last great Pharaoh. Daughter of Ptolemy XII, she became joint ruler with her brother, Ptolemy XIII. However, he drove Cleopatra out and Julius Caesar rushed to her defense. Caesar defeated Ptolemy XII and Cleopatra became Caesar's mistress. Ptolemy XIV, Cleopatra's younger brother and husband, became the new ruler. She returned with Caesar to Rome for two years as his mistress. In 44 B.C., Cleopatra returned to Egypt, and murdered her husband/ brother Ptolemy XIV to make room for her son Cesarion to help her rule the throne. Then she met Mark Antony, won his love and bore him twins. She died in 31 B.C., killing herself after learning the conqueror Octavian intended to exhibit her in his triumphal return to Rome. William Shakespeare memorialized Cleopatra and her tragic loves in a play, *Antony and Cleopatra*.

CLASSIFICATION. To arrange in a category.

CLIFF DWELLINGS. Shelters or villages built along the edges of cliff ledges or alcoves.

COMPUTER TOMOGRAPHY. A technique using X-rays or ultrasound to provide images of layers of the human body or other solid objects. These images are then processed by the computer to present two- and three-dimensional pictures.

CONTEXT. The conditions in which something exists or occurs; the environment and setting. The conditions surrounding an archaeological site that can help throw light on the meaning of the site and its contents. An object's setting in time and place and its general relationship to other objects in the archaeological record.

CORES. A nodule of stone (as flint or obsidian) from which flakes have been struck for making tools, weapons, and implements.

CROSS-DATING. Comparing finds to look for similarities and differences with other finds of known dates. This helps to identify the chronology of the artifacts. If a piece of a basket is found in a site in New York, it can be compared with the types of baskets found at other sites and made by other cultures. This comparison helps to figure out how old the basket is and who made it.

CULTIVATION. To prepare and use for the raising of crops.

CULTURAL TRADITIONS. Characteristic manner, method, or style of a culture or lifeway; cultural continuity in social attitudes, customs, and the production and use of tools, weapons, and implements.

CULTURE. The total way of life of a particular group of people; lifeways; a set of shared attitudes, values, goals, and practices that characterize a group; a group's customs, art, literature, philosophy, religion, and so on. Also defined as patterned, learned, and shared behavior.

CULTURAL DIFFUSION happens when cultures come into contact with one another and exchange goods and ideas.

CUNEIFORM. The earliest writing system. A form of writing on wet clay tablets using a wedge-shaped writing tool called a stylus.

DARWIN, CHARLES. A scientist who first proposed a theory of evolution, publishing Origin of Species and advocating survival of the fittest.

DATING. Figuring out the age of things; determining dates. Many scientific dating techniques are expensive and can only be performed in a laboratory.

DATING METHODS. Nine are listed below:

1. **Radiocarbon (C14, or Carbon 14) dating**. Measures the radioactivity given off by carbon 14 atoms or counts the atoms. Older objects are less radioactive. This method is used on organic remains.

2. **Magnetic dating**. Compares the magnetism in an object with the earth's magnetic field changes from the past. This method is used on baked clay and mud.

3. **Tree ring dating or dendochronology**. Counts the annual tree rings and matches up the ring patterns to make a dating sequence, usually on wooden objects. Oldest form of scientific dating.

4. **Potassium/argon dating**. Measures these two chemical elements in volcanic rocks, with older rocks having more argon and less potassium.

5. **Fission track dating**. Counts the number of tracks made by the breakdown of radioactive elements, with older objects leaving more tracks. This method is used mostly on rocks, pottery, and glass.

6. **Thermoluminescence**. Measures the energy given off from the breakdown of radioactive elements. This energy is trapped in pottery and given off as light. Older objects give off more light.

7. **Fluorine test**. Measures the amount of fluorine, nitrogen, and uranium in bones. Older bones have more fluorine and uranium and less nitrogen, but happens at different speeds in different places, so is not possible to compare bones from a different site. sentence

8. **Cultural dating**. The process of comparing objects archaeologists find with information they already have; comparing cultural attributes.

9. **Obsidian dating**. When obsidian is first exposed by flaking, a physical change begins to take place at a very slow constant rate. Water is taken into the material's structure. This rate varies with temperature, but not with the quantity of water available. Measuring the thickness of the hydration layer on an artifact can help determine age and years.

DECIPHERED. Cracking the code, figuring out the meaning.

DIGS. Archaeological sites, excavations.

ECOFACT. A naturally produced object found on an archaeological site, such as the remains of animals or plants.

ENVIRONMENT. The physical and biological surroundings (plants, animals, climate, inorganic resources) that influence social groups and their cultures.

EOLITHS. Very crudely shaped stones that were first thought to be crude tools, but others thought were natural pieces of stone and not shaped by humans.

ETHNOLOGY. The study of cultures, both modern cultures and past cultures. Ethnography is the description of a culture based on the interactions and observations with living people.

EVIDENCE. Clues or data proving a point or contributing to a solution.

EVOLUTION. The gradual process by which living organisms have developed since the start of life.

EXCAVATE/EXCAVATION. The process of methodically uncovering and searching for remains of the past. Because an excavation removes any deposits, it destroys a site forever. Archaeological evidence is almost always destroyed if it isn't buried, so excavation plays a large part in recovering this evidence. Some excavation methods are grid layout, open excavation, quadrant method, sondage, and rabotage.

FLAKES. Also called blades. Sharp edged, thin pieces of stone. Flakes were shaped into tools or weapons or left as flintknapping waste.

FLINT. A hard but brittle stone found in chalk or limestone. It can be flaked in any direction and easily shaped. It occurs in many locations and often formed the material for human tools until humans learned to work with metals. It was the most common 'stone' of the Stone Age.

FLINTKNAPPING. The process of chipping and shaping flint, a smooth and hard rock, to make sharp edges useful for scraping and cutting.

FOSSILS. The remains or imprints of plants and animals.

GEOLOGIC PERIOD OF TIME. The long period of time occupied by representing the earth's geologic history. Divided into eons, eras, periods/systems, and epoch/series.

HIEROGLYPHICS/HIERATICS. The signs of the earliest Egyptian script, introduced about 3,000 B.C. and used until about A.D. 4. It was used for important inscriptions. It was often painted or written on papyrus rather than carved.

HISTORY. Chronology of people and events since humans kept written records.

HOLOCENE. Period of geologic time from the end of the Pleistocene Ice Age about 8300 B.C. until the present day. Also called Recent or Postglacial Period.

HOMINIDS. Humans, part of the family Hominidae, which includes both extinct and modern forms of humans.

HOMO SAPIENS. Modern humans first appeared in the fossil record during the later part of the Pelistocene, around 35,000 B.C. or a little earlier. Modern humans replaced or evolved out of Neanderthals.

HOMO ERECTUS (PITHECANTHROPUS). Meaning upright man, this Early Stone Age hunter colonized new habitats throughout Africa, Europe, and southern Asia. Bigger and brainier than Homo Habilis or the Australopiths, Homo Erectus had the thickest skull of any member of he human species. Strong muscles at the back of the neck joined the rear skull bump and stopped the front-heavy head from sagging forward. Average height was 5–6 feet (1.5–1.8m), weight 88–160 lbs. (40–72.2kgs). Brain size: 850 cc (homo sapiens' brain size is 1,400 cc).

HOMO HABILIS. Meaning handy man, this was the first known species of our genus, Homo. The homo habilis has a larger brain, but smaller face and jaws and a more rounded head than Australopiths. Nor more than 5 feet (1.5m) tall or about 110 lbs. (50 kg,) with brow ridges, flat nose, and projecting jaws, this species lived about 1.5–2 million years ago, perhaps longer. Hand and foot bones suggest bipedal (upright) walking and a strong yet sensitive grip. Homo habilis brain size: 725 cc (homo sapiens' brain size is 1,400 cc).

HUNTER-GATHERERS. People or societies that are dependent on wild food resources. Hunter-gatherers usually are from technologically simple societies that are small in size and highly mobile. Also sometimes called "foragers."

HYPOTHESIS. Tentative and testable guess or premise.

ICE SHEETS. Ice sheets and glaciers covered much of North America and 30 percent of the world during the Ice Ages.

INFERENCE. A conclusion made from observations. Being able to pass from accepting one statement or truth as fact and changing to accept a new one based on new or evolving evidence and debate. Making a judgment, statement, or conclusion from observations or from what appears to be the results of research.

INTERGLACIAL. A warm period between two glaciers.

INUIT/ESKIMO. Arctic-adapted people, including the Iñupiat and Yupik eskimoes and the Aleuts of the Aleutian Islands, are distinct from all of the other early peoples of the Americas. All human populations in the Arctic have depended on animals for food more than foraging populations anywhere else in the world. Most archaeologists believe the Inuit/Eskimo people were the last to migrate into North America from Asia near the end of the last Ice Age.

KIVA. An underground ceremonial chamber typical of the Anasazi and Hopi. A village may have several kivas. They were used for community gatherings and religious or spiritual purposes.

LAND BRIDGE. Land that was once exposed because of low sea levels during the Pleistocene and Ice Ages, though covered by water in modern times.

LEAKEY, MARY. Her brilliant career, along with that of her husband Louis Leakey and son Richard, was devoted to the recovery and interpretation of the bones and tools of early humans in East Africa.

LIFEWAY. Ways of living. Everyday cultural customs and practices.

MEGALITHIC. Built of large stones. Megaliths include menhir, stonecircules, certain henge monuments, and many kinds of chamber tombs.

MICROBLADES. Small stone blades. They were flaked from stone cores as cutting tools. Usually less than an inch long, they are similar to small, sharp razor blades. Early peoples used microblades alone or set into a handle of wood, bone, or ivory.

MIDDEN. Rubbish or trash heap or remains. At former settlements, often involves broken pots and tools, ashes, food remains, and other discarded items thrown out or left behind.

MIGRATION. To move from one country, region, place, or site to another for feeding or breeding.

MONGOLOID. Also Mongolian, a member or a major racial stock native to Asia with physical features including the presence of an epicanthic fold over the eyes. Includes peoples of northern and eastern Asia, Malaysians, Eskimoes, and often American Indians.

NEANDERTHAL. An extinct form of humans. Normally chinless, with prominent brow ridges and a receding forehead, but the same brain size as modern humans. Neanderthal human flintwork was technically more advanced than any before this time. Existed between 40,000 and 35,000 B.C., but these dates are not confirmed. May have been modern human's ancestors.

NENANA COMPLEX. Some of the earliest people known to have lived in Alaska from around 12,000 years ago. Their artifacts were found in the Nenana and Tanana river valleys of Alaska. Part of the Paleo-Indian Cultural Tradition.

NEOLITHIC. Later part of the Stone Age commonly known as the New Stone Age. When refined polished stone tools and modern plants and animals existed. The period during which food production started in the Old World by cultivation of crops and domestication of animals, but stone was still the material used for tools and weapons. The appearance of food production, sometimes called the Neolithic revolution, began in southwest Asia between 9000 and 6000 B.C. and might be considered the most important single advance ever made by humans because it allowed permanent settlements.

NOMADIC. A way of life where people frequently move from one location to another in search of food.

OBSERVATION. Looking at and critically noting details of a site, artifact, or behavior.

OBSIDIAN. A natural volcanic glass that is usually gray, black or semi-transparent. Very popular for flaking into tools and weapons and for grinding into vessels. Widely traded. Analysis can sometimes pinpoint the source and time period, for trace elements in obsidian help identify trade routes and dating.

OLD WORLD/NEW WORLD. The Old World includes the continents of Europe, Asia, Africa, and Australia and all associated land. The New World includes the continents of North and South America and associated land.

OLDUVAI GORGE. One of the most important sites for understanding of both human evolution and the development of the earliest tools. Human remains of Australopiths including Homo Habilis and Zinjanthropus, Homo Erectus, Neanderthals were recovered here. Tools from the Paleolithic around 1.9 million years ago were found here by the Leakeys and their crew. About 40 miles from the Laetoli archaeological sites in Tanzania.

OMNIVOROUS. Feeding on both animal and vegetables.

PALEOANTHROPOLOGIST. One who studies the emergence of humans through excavating and finding their remains (fossilized skeletons and corpses).

PALEOLITHIC. Beginning with the emergence of humans and the manufacture of the most ancient tools some 2.5 million–3 million years ago. The Paleolithic period lasted through most of the Pleistocene Ice Age until final retreat of the ice sheets about 8300 B.C. It is generally divided into three parts: the Lower Paleolithic with the earliest forms of humans (Australopiths and Homo Erectus) and the dominance of core tools including pebble tools, handaxe, and choppers; the Middle Paleolithic with Neanderthal humans and the predominance of flake-tools over most of Eurasia; and the Upper Paleolithic starting perhaps as early as 38,000 B.C. with Homo Sapiens, blade-and-burin tools and weapons and the cave art of Western Europe. During this stage, humans moved into the New World and Australia.

PALEONTOLOGY/PALEONTOLOGIST. The study of fossils. Human paleontology is the study of human origins.

PALEO-ARCTIC. The Paleo-Arctic Cultural Tradition are the earliest, well-documented human occupations of the North American Arctic, between 7,000-10,000 years ago. These early people are only known from stone artifacts, especially wedge-shaped cores, microblades, and small biface tools.

PALEO-INDIAN. Or Big Game Hunters, the Paleo-Indian Cultural Tradition covers the earliest groups of people in North America, from around 9,000 to possibly 14,000 years ago. Their stone tools are commonly found throughout most of North America. Until 1978 when discovered at the Mesa Site, none of the archaeological sites in Alaska had contained these stone tools.

PAPYRUS. A reed that grew along the banks of the Nile. Writing sheets were made from the pith of its stem.

PECTROGLYPHS. Designs produced on stone by hammering or pecking.

PERMAFROST. Layers of earth that remain permanently frozen year-round, typical of Arctic lands.

PETROGLYPHS. A rock painting or engraving.

PHAROS LIGHTHOUSE. One of the Seven Wonders of the World. The Lighthouse of Alexandria is the only Wonder with a practical use in addition to architectural elegance. It was the tallest building on earth and its mysterious mirror could reflect light more than 35 miles (50 km) off-shore. Archaeologists have recently recovered stones from the sea floor that were part of the lighthouse.

PHOENICIAN SCRIPT. The ancestor of all modern alphabets. Only the consonants were represented with this first alphabet, but the Greeks later added vowels when they adopted the alphabet around 8 B.C.

PICTOGRAMS. a system of writing that uses symbols based on simple pictures of objects instead of letters.

PICTOGRAPHS. A design painted onto a rock surface. A type of writing in which symbols show what they are meant to convey.

PLEISTOCENE. The last Ice Age, from about 1.6 million years ago to about 10,000 years ago (8300 B.C.). An epoch of geologic time. The onset of the Pleistocene began with an increasingly cold climate. The earliest human forms (Australopiths) had evolved by the Early Pleistocene. All of the cultures classed by archaeologists as Paleolithic fell within the Pleistocene. Radiocarbon dating is ineffective for periods older than the Pleistocene.

PLIOCENE. In geologic time, the latest epoch of the Tertiary, from about 5 million years ago until the beginning of the Pleistocene at about 1.6 million years ago.

POTASSIUM-ARGON DATING. The earth's crust contains potassium. Working similarly to radiocarbon dating, the amount of argon in a sample less than about a million years old is too small to measure accurately. Useful, if controversial, results have been found for material of the early Pleistocene where lava flows mixed into deposits containing fossils or artifacts have been dated.

POTTERY. Containers shaped from terracotta, a combination of clay and sand, that can be hardened in the heat of an oven called a kiln. Pottery is one of the commonest finds on any site where it was used or made and is one of the clearest clues to different cultures. It can be modeled, coil-built, or wheel-made. The nature of its fabric, ware, or body; surface paint; and decorations can be identified and compared. Its raw material is common, shaping and baking it are simple, and it can be given an infinite variety of shapes and decorations.

PREHISTORY. The time before the development of written records, to about 3,000 years ago. Prehistory may also deal with a society or culture, not of the individual. It is restricted to the material evidence that has survived and is anonymous. Without records, we can't know the names of people, places, or things, so have invented labels to identify them instead.

PRESERVATION. To keep safe and protect from injury, harm, or destruction. To keep alive, intact, or free from decay, to save from decomposition.

PRIMATES/PRIMATOLOGIST. Any of an order of mammals that includes humans, apes, monkeys, lemurs, and related forms. One who studies primates.

PROJECTILE POINT. Arrowheads, spearheads.

PTOLEMY. Name of fifteen kings of Egypt making up the Ptolemaic or Macedonian dynasty (323-30 B.C.). Ptolemy I founded Alexandria's library and museum, made the city a haven for scholars, and extended boundaries of the kingdom. He also authored a biography of Alexander the Great. Ptolemy II encouraged commerce and trade, developed agriculture, built a canal from the Red Sea to the Nile, encouraged literature and the arts, and made Alexandria the center of Hellenistic culture. He also had the Pharos lighthouse built. Ptolemy III replaced the Macedonian calendar with the Egyptian solar year, restored temple statues, but allowed army to decline. Began temple at Idfu and erected many buildings. Ptolemy V almost lost Egypt to Antioch, but was saved by Rome's intervention. Celebrated his coming of age by having the Egyptian priesthood inscribe a decree on the Rosetta stone.

PUEBLO. A type of dwelling common among Southwest native peoples. Made from stone or adobe bricks, they can be several stories high and contain many apartment-like rooms. Ladders are used to move between different levels.

RADIOCARBON DATING (CARBON 14, OR C14, DATING). Measures the radioactivity given off by carbon 14 atoms or counts the atoms in organic remains. Older objects have less radioactivity. Carbon 14 is a radioactive isotope of carbon 12 produced from nitrogen 14 in the atmosphere by cosmic radiation from the sun. After being taken into the organic compounds of all living matter, C14 acts like C12. The proportions of radioactive and inert carbon are identical throughout the atmosphere and the vegetable/animal kingdoms. When organic matter dies, it ceases to exchange its carbon, as carbon dioxide, with the atmosphere. Its C14 dwindles by decay and isn't replenished. Determination of the radioactivity of carbon from a sample will reveal the proportion of C14 to C12. This identifies the known rate of decay and gives the age or time elapsed since the death of the sample. The given date is never exact and the rate of decay of C14 is based on the half-life of 5568 (plus or minus 30 years), but it is becoming clear the figure is too small.

REPLICA. To reproduce a copy or recreate the original.

ROCK ART. Designs or symbols pecked, painted, or otherwise put onto rock surfaces.

ROSETTA STONE. A basalt slab discovered at Rosetta at the western mouth of the Nile during Napoleon's occupation of Egypt. It is now in the

British Museum. An honorific decree of Ptolemy V (196 B.C.) is carved on this stone in Greek, hieroglyphics, and another form of Egyptian. Champollion was able to decipher the code of the ancient Egyptian hieroglyphics, unlocking a mystery spanning fifteen centuries.

SCRIBES. Egyptians trained to read and write hieroglyphics.

SHERDS. (or shards). Broken fragments of pottery.

STONE AGE. The earliest technological period of human culture when tools were made of stone, wood, bone, or antler. Metals were unknown. The dates vary considerably from one region to another, and some communities were still living a Stone Age life until very recent times. Part of the Paleolithic, Mesolithic, and Neolithic. The Stone Age was followed by the Bronze Age and Iron Age.

STONEHENGE. Near Amesbury, Wiltshire, England. Stonehenge is the finest of the British megalith monuments and is architecturally unique. It stands at the center of Salisbury Plain, surrounded by a complex of cemeteries and ritual sites. Grooved ware pottery with dates of between 275 B.C. and 2780 B. C. suggest Stonehenge was created near the end of the Neolithic period. The function of the monument is thought to be religious, but its arrangement does suggest possible astronomical uses in connection with the calendar.

STRATIFICATION. Layered deposits providing one of the major tools to interpret archaeological sites, stratigraphy. Over time, debris and soils accumulate in layers. Color, textures, and contents may change with each layer. Archaeologists need to explain how each layer came to be added, whether it was natural, deliberate fill, or collapse of structures, and to record it in detailed drawings in a map so others can follow. Follows the law of superposition in that lower, buried deposits would be older than those on top. Adopted from geology, stratification doesn't always work in analysis if there were any major disturbances over time to the layers and their contents.

STRATIGRAPHY. The study of layers of soil and rock where artifacts and fossils are found. One of the major tools of archaeology. The lower layers are thought to be older than the top layers, if there was no disturbance such as an animal burrowing, earthquakes, slipping, erosion, etc. Stratigraphy is vital to the interpretation of an excavation.

STRATUM (PLURAL STRATA). One layer of earth.

SURVEY. To examine the land to locate and record artifacts and sites.

THEORY OF EVOLUTION. Charles Darwin's theory of the origins of species from A.D. 1859.

TRADITIONS. Customs or beliefs passed down from adults to children.

TRAITS. Any element of human culture, material objects, or human practices.

TUFF. Layer of volcanic ash deposits that have formed like a crust over the underlying land.

TUNDRA. Almost treeless plains next to the polar ice. All but the top few inches of soil are permanently frozen.

UNDERWATER ARCHAEOLOGY. Archaeological material covered by fresh or sea water is much more difficult to recover than buried material. With new technologies, underwater archaeology is becoming more possible and more popular. From shipwrecks to uncovering lost civilizations, underwater archaeologists are adapting new techniques and making new finds in this growing science.

VANDALISM. The malicious and intentional destruction or defacing of property.

WONDERS OF THE ANCIENT WORLD. A list made by Greek writers in the 100s B. C.: (1) the Great Pyramid at Giza, (2) the Hanging Gardens of Babylon, (3) the Statue of Zeus at Olympia, (4) the Temple of Diana at Ephesus, (5) the Mausoleum at Halicarnassus, (6) the Colossus of Rhodes, and (7) the Pharos of Alexandria lighthouse. Only the pyramid survives.

Bibliography

BOOKS FOR FURTHER ARCHAEOLOGY QUESTS

Archaeology Smart Junior is an introductory book to the science of archaeology. If you'd like to read more or research any subjects, you may want to try the following books. While writing *Archaeology Smart Junior*, I referred to many reference sources to help with details and obtain the most recent information.

References for Youth

Allan, Tony and Vivienne Henry. *The Time Traveller Book of Pharaohs and Pyramids*, 3rd Edition, Belgium: Usborne Publishing Ltd., 1993. ISBN 0-86020-084-1 (paperback).

Bahn, Paul. *Archaeology: A Very Short Introduction*. New York: Oxford University Press, 1996. ISBN 0-19-285325-2 (paperback).

Blot, Jean-Yves. *Underwater Archaeology: Exploring the World Beneath the Sea*. New York: Harry N. Abrams, Inc., 1996. ISBN 0-8109-2859-0 (paperback).

Cork, Barbara and Struan Reid. *The Usborne Young Scientist: Archaeology*. 2nd Edition. London: Usborne Publishing Ltd., 1991. ISBN 0-86020-865-6 (paperback).

Cox, Reg and Neil Morris. *The Seven Wonders of the Ancient World*. 2nd Edition, New Jersey: Silver Burdett Press, Simon & Schuster, 1996. ISBN 0-382-39267-1 (paperback).

Green, Robert. *Cleopatra: A First Book.* New York: Franklin Watts/Grolier Publishing, 1996. ISBN 0-531-15800-4 (paperback).

Lambert, David and The Diagram Group. *The Field Guide To Early Man.* New York: Facts on File, 1987. ISBN 0-8160-1517-1 (hardcover); 0-8160-1801-4 (paperback).

Laubenstein, Karen Jackson and Robert E. King. *Intrigue of the Past: Discovering Archaeology in Alaska.* U.S. Department of the Interior, Bureau of Land Management: Heritage Education Program, 1996.

Lindsay, William. *Prehistoric Life: Discover the Origins of Life on Earth, From the First Bacteria through the Age of Giant Dinosaurs to the Coming of Humans.* New York: Alfred A. Knopf, 1994. ISBN 0-679-86001-0 (hardcover).

Martell, Hazel Mary. *The Kingfisher Book of The Ancient World: From the Ice Age to the Fall of Rome.* New York: Larousse Kingfisher Chambers, Inc., 1995. ISBN 1-85697-565-7 (hardcover).

Reddy, Francis. *Rand McNally Children's Atlas of Native Americans.* Chicago, New York, San Francisco: Rand McNally & Co., 1992. ISBN 0-428-83494-0 (hardcover).

Schaaf, Gregory. *Ancient Ancestors of the Southwest.* U.S.: Graphic Arts Center Publishing, 1996. ISBN 1-55868-255-4 (paperback).

Sterling, Mary Ellen. *Archaeology: Thematic Unit.* Huntington Beach, Calif.: Teacher Created Materials, Inc., 1995. ISBN 1-55734-296-2 (paperback).

Thomas, David Hurt, Jay Miller, Richard White, Peter Nabokov, Philip J. Deloria. *The Native Americans: An Illustrated History.* Atlanta: Turner Publishing, Inc., 1993. ISBN 1-878685-42-2 (paperback).

Other References:

Bahn, Paul G., Ed. *The Cambridge Illustrated History of Archaeology.* Cambridge, England: Press Syndicate of the University of Cambridge, 1996. ISBN 0-521-45498-0 (hardcover).

Boardman, John, Jasper Griffin, Oswyn Murray, eds. *The Oxford History of the Classical World: Greece and the Hellinistic World.* 2nd Edition, New York: Oxford University Press, 1988. ISBN 0-19-282165-2 (paperback).

Bray, Warwick and David Trump. *The Penguin Dictionary of Archaeology.* 2nd Edition, England: Penguin Books Limited, 1982. ISBN 0-14051-116-4 (paperback).

Canfora, Luciano. *The Vanished Library: A Wonder of the Ancient World.* Berkeley, Los Angeles, Calif.: University of California Press, 1991. ISBN 0-520-07255-3 (paperback).

Chippindale, Christopher. *Stonehenge Complete.* 2nd Edition. New York: Thames and Hudson, Inc., 1994. ISBN 0-500-27750-8 (paperback).

DeGrummond, N., ed. *An Encyclopedia of the History of Classical Archaeology.* 2 vols., Westport, Conn.: Greenwood Publishing Group, 1996. ISBN 0-313-22066-2 (hardcover).

Fagan, Brian et al., eds., *The Oxford Companion to Archaeology.* New York: Oxford University Press, 1996, ISBN 0-19-507618-4 (hardcover).

Gowlett, John A. J. *Ascent to Civilization: The Archaeology of Early Humans.* 2nd Edition, London: McGraw-Hill Publishers and Roxby Archaeology Limited, 1992. ISBN 0-07-3443120 (paperback).

Graves-Brown, P. Et al., *Cultural Identity and Archaeology: The Construction of European Communities.* New York: Routledge, 1996. ISBN 0-415-10676-1 (hardcover).

Green, Kevin. *Archaeology: An Introduction to the History, Principles and Methods of Modern Archaeology.* 3rd Edition, Philadelphia: University of Pennsylvania Press, 1995. ISBN 0-8122-1570-2 (paperback).

Hayden, Brian. *Archaeology: The Science of Once and Future Things.* New York: W. H. Freeman and Company, 1993. ISBN 0-7167-2307-7 (paperback).

Haynes, C. Vance. "The Earliest Americans," *Science* 166: 709-715.

Jennings, Jesse David. *Prehistory of North America.* 3rd Edition, Palo Alto, Calif.: Mayfield Publishers, 1989 and *Ancient North Americans*, San Francisco: W. H. Freeman & Co., 1983. (No ISBN avail.)

Leakey, Richard E. *The Making of Mankind.* New York: E.P. Dutton, 1981. ISBN 0-525-150552 (hardcover)

Leakey, Richard E. *The Origin of Humankind.* New York: BasicBooks-Harper Collins Publishers, Inc., 1994. ISBN 0-465-05313-0 (paperback).

Leakey, Richard E. and Robert Lewin. *Origins Reconsidered: In Search of What Makes Us Human.* New York: Doubleday, Bantam Doubleday Dell Publishing Group, Inc., 1992. ISBN 0-385-41624-9 (hardcover).

Mead, Jim I., and David J. Meltzer, eds. *Environments and Extinctions: Man in Late Glacial North America.* Orono, Maine: Center for the Study of Early Man, University of Maine at Orono, 1985. (No ISBN avail.)

Meltzer, David J. "Why Don't We Know When the First People Came to North America?" in *American Antiquity.* 54 (3): 471-490. (periodical)

Meyers, E., et al., eds., *The Oxford Encyclopedia of Archaeology in the Ancient Near East.* 5 vols., New York: Oxford University Press, 1997. ISBN 0-19-506512-3 (hardcover).

Morell, Virginia. *Ancestral Passions: The Leakey Family and the Quest for Humankind's Beginnings.* New York: Touchstone, Simon & Schuster, 1995. ISBN 0-684-82470-1 (paperback).

Oakeshott, R., *The Archaeology of Weapons.* Mineola, New York: Dover Press, 1996. ISBN 0-486-29288-6.

Renfrew, Colin and Paul Bahn. *Archaeology: Theories, Methods, and Practice.* 2nd Edition. New York: Thames and Hudson, Inc., 1996. ISBN 0-500-05079-1 (hardcover); 0-500-27867-9 (paperback).

Roberts, B. *Landscapes of Settlement: Prehistory to the Present.* New York: Routledge, 1996. ISBN 0-415-11968 (paperback)

Schmidt, P. And R. McIntosh, eds. *Plundering Africa's Past.* Bloomington, Indiana: Indiana University Press, 1996. ISBN 0-253-21054-2 (paperback).

Smith, Shelley J., Jeanne M. Moe, Kelly A. Letts, Danielle M. Paterson. *Intrigue of the Past: A Teacher's Activity Guide for Fourth through Seventh Grades.* United States Department of Interior, Bureau of Land Management: U.S. Government Printing Office: 1993-774-003/8003 (paperback).

Spindler, Konrad. *The Man in the Ice: The Discovery of a 5,000-Year-Old Body Reveals the Secrets of the Stone Age.* New York: Crown Trade Paperbacks, 1994. ISBN 0-517-88613-8 (paperback).

Webster, David L., Susan Toby Evans, William T. Sanders. *Out of the Past: An Introduction to Archaeology.* Mountain View, California: Mayfield Publishing Company, 1992. [Copywright held by The Pennsylvania State University and the Corporation for Public Broadcasting.]. ISBN 1-55934-153-X (hardcover). Also Nancy Gonlin, Susan Toby Evans, David Webster. *Study Guide to Accompany Out of the Past: An Introduction to Archaeology* (paperback).

Williams, Stephen. *Fantastic Archaeology: The Wild Side of North American Prehistory.* Philadelphia: University of Pennsylvania Press, 1991. (No ISBN avail.)

Wolpoff, M. And R. Caspari, *Race and Human Evolution*. New York: Simon and Schuster, 1997. ISBN 0-684-81013-1 (hardcover)

_____, *Natural History* magazine, series of 14 articles on early man in the Americas, beginning in November 1986.

Internet Resources In Archaeology

The World Wide Web (Internet) offers you opportunities never before available. By using your browser and search engines, you can find out more about archaeology than any book could cover! Discover the most recent finds, current theories, and almost anything about anything. Remember the process of scientific inquiry, and question everything. Check and recheck topics from a variety of sources to help sort out fact from fiction, truth for theory, and keep in mind that information constantly changes. Check it out!

AERIAL ARCHAEOLOGY. newsletter featuring history/prehistory of the U.S. Southwest. Photographs (aerial).

AFRICAN ACADEMIC RESOURCES. archaeology in Africa.

AFRICAN-AMERICAN ARCHAEOLOGY NEWSLETTER. online newsletter.

ANCIENT AMERICAN MAGAZINE. online magazine.

ANCIENT ROCK ART INFO. Sources

ANCIENT WORLD WEB. listing of selected web sites.

ANTHROPOLOGY INTERNET RESOURCES. listing from Western Connecticut State University Department of Social Sciences.

ANTIQUITY. online international journal of archaeology from the Oxford University Press.

ARCHAEOLOGICAL INSTITUTE OF AMERICA. publications, journal, news.

ARCHAEOLOGICAL RESOURCE GUIDE FOR EUROPE. organized by country, subject, period, sites, and monuments, but several sites are not in English.

ARCHAEOLOGICAL SITES OF THE SOUTHWEST

ARCHAEOLOGY AND ADVENTURE PAGE. just for kids.

ARCHAEOLOGY IN FICTION. bibliography.

ARCHAEOLOGY INTERNET INFORMATION SERVICE (COUNCIL FOR BRITISH ARCHAEOLOGY). archaeology in Britain.

ARCHAEOLOGY REPOSITORY. Southern Utah University.

ARCHAEOLOGY RESOURCES FOR EDUCATION. what is archaeology, what did our ancestors eat?, glaciers and the ice ages, flints and stones, environmental choices and South Dakota's people from prehistory through the present, middle school archaeology web unit.

ARCHAEOLOGY/ANTHROPOLOGY, HISTORY/SOCIAL STUDIES WEB SITE FOR K-12 TEACHERS. newsgroups, university pages, journals, organizations/museums, digs and site-regional reports, concept and teaching sites, research fields, general.

ARCHAEOLOGY. online journal of the Archaeological Institute of America. Reports latest archaeological discoveries, news briefs, and important links.

ARCHNET. a virtual archaeology library, most sites referenced are located in the United States.

ARCTIC ARCHAEOLOGY. Canadian. The arctic environment, doing fieldwork in the arctic, a Thule culture, books, links.

ARGOS. a search tool listing ancient world web sites.

ASIAN ARCHAEOLOGY INFORMATION PLAZA. Indonesia, Taiwan, Korea, Malaysia, and the Phillipines.

ATHENA REVIEW. online journal.

AUSTRALOPITHECINES OR A. AFARENSIS. both pages discuss early humans.

BRITISH ARCHAEOLOGY GOPHER. includes Young Archaeologist's Club, getting started in archaeology, metal detecting advice for England/Wales, training, education, careers.

CANADIAN ARCHAEOLOGICAL ASSOCIATION. Sites, news, current discoveries, general information for Canada.

CHIMNEY ROCK ARCHAEOLOGICAL AREA

CLASSICS AND MEDITERRANEAN ARCHAEOLOGY. museum exhibits, images, site reports, geographic information, newsgroups, and e-mail lists.

CMC MUSEUM COLLECTIONS. artifact selections representative of archaeology. Library links (Canadian).

CONSTRUCTING A FOLSOM POINT. graphics on how to create this projectile point.

CTICH GUIDE: WELCOME. guide to electronic resources for teachers of history, archaeology, and art history.

EGYPTOLOGY RESOURCES. study of Egyptian archaeology, institutions, museums, and societies.

EXPLORING ANCIENT WORLD CULTURES. an introduction.

FORBIDDEN ARCHAEOLOGY. based on the NBC controversial documentary, includes the Mysterious Origins of Man, Jurassic Art, and the Mystery of the Sphinx. Puts forth ideas such as humans and dinosaurs co-existing. Interesting perspectives.

FOSSIL EVIDENCE FOR HUMAN EVOLUTION IN CHINA. listing of hominid fossil discoveries in China, photographs, timeline, links to articles.

FREQUENTLY ASKED QUESTIONS (FAQ) ABOUT CAREERS IN ARCHAE-OLOGY. describes jobs available to archaeologists and the educational requirements for professional status. Lists colleges and universities with archaeology programs and recommends books.

HISTORICAL AND ARCHAEOLOGICAL CD-ROMS

HISTORY OF EVOLUTIONARY THOUGHT. theory and history, conflicts, FAQs.

HOLLYWOOD ARCHAEOLOGY. is this the latest and newest branch in Archaeology?

HUMAN ORIGINS AND EVOLUTION IN AFRICA. with many related links.

INTERNET ARCHAEOLOGY. online journal.

INTERNET RESOURCES FOR HISTORIC PRESERVATION, CONSERVATION, AND ARCHAEOLOGY. listings.

IRISH ARCHAEOLOGY. sites in Ireland and excavation database.

JOURNAL OF FIELD ARCHAEOLOGY. online journal from Boston University with an author index and abstracts since 1994.

JOURNAL OF WORLD ARCHAEOLOGY. From SUNY, Buffalo.

KINSHIP AND SOCIAL ORGANIZATION. an interactive tutorial.

MESOAMERICAN ARCHAEOLOGY. see the Aztec stone scan.

NEFERTARI: LIGHT OF EGYPT. virtual-reality tour of Nefertari's tomb (requires "Cosmo Player" software, but can download 3-D images of the tomb without it).

OLD WORLD ARCHAEOLOGY. online newsletter.

ORIENTAL INSTITUTE OF THE UNIVERSITY OF CHICAGO. Projects in Mesopotamia, Iran, Syria, Palestine, Anatolia, and Egypt; image archive; current events.

PEOBODY MUSEUM OF ARCHAEOLOGY AND ETHNOLOGY. current displays, such as three generations of women anthropologists or the children of changing woman.

PERSEUS PROJECT. library of study materials on ancient Greece from the end of Mycenaean civilization in 1200 B.C. to the death of Alexander the Great in 323 B.C., with more than 3,000 links to the rest of the Perseus database. Perseus for the Roman world will soon be available.

QUATERNARY ACRONYMS AND ABBREVIATIONS

RADIOCARBON HOME PAGE. Internet journal.

READINGS IN ARCHAEOLOGY. Concept and teaching site.

ROBOTIC TELE-EXCAVATION AT USC. You can actually conduct an excavation on the Internet!

ROCK ART ONLINE. bulletin.

SAA WEB, SOCIETY OF AMERICAN ARCHAEOLOGY. about archaeology, awards, education, meetings, publications.

SCIENCE. journal online with selected articles on new discoveries, theories.

SCROLLS FROM THE DEAD SEA. From the Library of Congress, discovery of the scrolls, map/geography, photographs, artifacts.

SMITHSONIAN FAQS, NATURAL HISTORY FAQS. Answers questions about the origins of Americas native peoples, how to identify artifacts, excavations, and other common questions. Excellent listing of books and references.

SMU GLOSSARY. Glossary of archaeological terms.

THE STONE PAGES. Exciting tours through the Stone Age in Europe.

WORLD CULTURES: ANCIENT AND MODERN. University of Pennsylvania's Museum of Archaeology and Anthropology sites.

WORLD OF THE VIKINGS. runes, sagas, ships, and schools or museums with Viking programs.

About the Author

Karen J. Laubenstein is a writer-editor from Anchorage, Alaska. Karen formerly worked as a writer-editor for the federal Bureau of Land Management's National Heritage Education Program based in Dolores, Colorado, where she assisted various states in preparation of Project Archaeology and cultural heritage education materials.

Karen worked as a speechwriter and public affairs specialist within the Department of Health and Human Services on medical and other topics for former President Bush, the Secretary and Undersecretary for Health, the Surgeon General, and agency directors. She served as the agency photographer for the Health Resources and Services Administration. Her eight years of federal experience also included work on foreign policy and disability topics for U.S. Senator Edward M. Kennedy; as a program analyst reviewing State programs and funding proposals for dislocated worker projects and Job Training Partnership Act programs for the U.S. Employment and Training Administration; and she was instrumental in the establishment of public information activities for the National Institute on Deafness and Other Communication Disorders within the National Institutes of Health.

Karen attended the University of Maine, University of Utah, and University of Rochester. She was in the Peace Corps in Benin, West Africa, in agricultural extension. She has degrees in English (education/humanities) and the behavioral sciences. She also studied anthropology and the biological sciences. She has worked as an adjunct faculty member for the University of Maine and Pueblo Community College, teaching biology, writing, English as a foreign language, and sign language. She was the recipient of the 1990 Public Health Service's Outstanding Handicapped Employee Award, has been listed in several *Who's Who* publications, and served on national boards for committees for the deaf or the disabled. She's a former member of the Society for American Archaeology.

Karen went on her first archaeological digs in Greece in 1972 when she was fourteen and in Italy in 1976. She has always had a fascination for other peoples, other cultures, past and present. She has authored or edited other books on archaeology for grades 3-8, most recently *Intrigue of the Past: Discovering Archaeology in Alaska* (U.S. Bureau of Land Management, 1996).

Karen is profoundly deaf. She loves animals and has a hearing guide dog, Rascal; a cat, Binkee; and an aviary full of zebra finches. She married Ron Laubenstein after meeting him during her first visit to Alaska in 1994. He read about her on the Alaska Mac local computer bulletin board because she fell down a cliff, required reconstructive surgery, and had to remain in Alaska for ten weeks to recover. That break changed her life. Ron wanted to meet her, brought her on a charter salmon fishing expedition (wheelchair and all!) in Seward, AK, and the rest is history. They were married within four months of meeting each other and Karen resigned from her federal employment, packed up her Colorado ranch, and moved to Alaska. Karen could walk again by the time of the wedding.

Karen and Ron love camping and fishing throughout Alaska. Karen also likes reading, photography, wildlife, painting in acrylics or oils, computers and emailing, gardening, and many other hobbies.

Notes:

Notes:

Notes:

Notes:

Notes:

Notes:

Notes:

Notes:

Notes:

More Bestselling Smart Junior Titles from The Princeton Review

A 1995 Parents Choice Gold Medal Award-Winning Series

Join Barnaby, Babette, Bridget, their fat cat friend Beauregard, and all the crazy people they meet as they travel around the world, across time, and through space in search of adventure and knowledge.

"Educational and entertaining describes this series. The Princeton Review has made learning just plain fun."
—*Writing Teacher* magazine

AMERICAN HISTORY SMART JUNIOR
$12.00 • 0-679-77357-6
A time travel adventure through history!

ASTRONOMY SMART JUNIOR
$12.00 • 0-679-76906-4
Blast off to Mars with the Smart Junior gang.

GEOGRAPHY SMART JUNIOR
$12.00 • 0-679-77522-6
The Smart Junior gang has to solve a mystery by finding clues from all over the world.

GRAMMAR SMART JUNIOR
$12.00 • 0-679-76212-4
Good grammar made easy. Selected by *Curriculum Administrator* magazine readers as one of the Top 100 Products of 1995-96.

MATH SMART JUNIOR
$12.00 • 0-679-75935-2
Save a kitten with the Pythagorean theorem and more! "Learning at its giggliest," says the *Chicago Tribune KIDNEWS*.

WORD SMART JUNIOR
$12.00 • 0-679-75936-0
Build a straight A vocabulary with the Smart Junior gang as they have a crazy adventure with over 650 vocabulary words.

WRITING SMART JUNIOR
$12.00 • 0-679-76131-4
Book reports, school papers, letter writing, story writing and even poetry are covered in *Writing Smart Junior*, selected by The New York Public Library for its 1996 Books for the Teen Age List.

THE PRINCETON REVIEW